MULAN'S LEGEND AND LEGACY IN CHINA AND THE UNITED STATES

Mulan's Legend and Legacy in China and the United States

LAN DONG

Temple University Press
PHILADELPHIA

Temple University Press
Philadelphia, Pennsylvania 19122
www.temple.edu/tempress

♾ The paper used in this publication meets the requirements of the American National Standard for Information Sciences—Permanence of Paper for Printed Library Materials, ANSI Z39.48–1992

LIBRARY OF CONGRESS CATALOGING-IN-PUBLICATION DATA

Dong, Lan, 1974–
   Mulan's legend and legacy in China and the United States / Lan Dong.
      p.   cm.
   Includes bibliographical references and index.
   ISBN 978-1-59213-970-5 (cloth : alk. paper)
   ISBN 978-1-59213-971-2 (pbk. : alk. paper)
   ISBN 978-1-59213-972-9 (e-book)
   1. Hua, Mulan (Legendary character)   2. Mulan shi—Influence.   3. Chinese literature—Appreciation—United States.   4. American literature—Chinese influences.   5. Mulan (Motion picture)   6. Animated films—United States—History and criticism.   I. Title.
PL2668.M833D66 2010
398.20951'02—dc22

                                                                    2010019345

      2 4 6 8 9 7 5 3 1

A book in the American Literatures Initiative (ALI), a collaborative publishing project of NYU Press, Fordham University Press, Rutgers University Press, Temple University Press, and the University of Virginia Press. The Initiative is supported by The Andrew W. Mellon Foundation. For more information, please visit www.americanliteratures.org.

For Susanne, with love and tears

Contents

Figures

Acknowledgments

I want to thank all my professors and friends at the University of Massachusetts at Amherst, especially my adviser, Dr. Elizabeth Petroff, for opening many doors in the intellectual world for me to explore. I am deeply grateful for Dr. Catherine Portuges, whose unwavering support and guidance have accompanied me to this day. My greatest debt of gratitude goes to Dr. Paula Varsano, who has spared so much time for me over the years and has given me excellent advice as a mentor and friend. I would not have been able to finish this book without their help.

I owe special thanks to my editor, Janet Francendese, who saw light when I was struggling in the dark and whose encouragement guided me; to the anonymous reviewers whose constructive suggestions helped shape this book; to my friends Fanny Rothschild and Jane Leung Larson, who have been generous with their time in reading parts of the manuscript at different stages and providing invaluable feedback; to Munindra Khaund and media services at the University of Illinois at Springfield for helping me with the illustrations; to my friends and colleagues for sharing my passion and supporting me in various ways; and to my family on both sides of the Pacific, who love me unconditionally.

Early versions of my discussion on Jeanne M. Lee's *The Song of Mu Lan* and Disney's *Mulan* appeared in "Writing Chinese America into Words and Images: Storytelling and Retelling of *The Song of Mu Lan*," published in *The Lion and the Unicorn* 30. 2 (2006): 218–33, and "Mulan: Disney's Hybrid Heroine," published in *Beyond Adaptation: Essays on Radical Transformations of Original Works*, edited by Phyllis Frus and Christy Williams, 156-67. Jefferson, NC: McFarland Publishing, 2010.

Mulan's Legend and Legacy in China and the United States

1 / Prologue

The legend of Mulan—the maiden who performed heroic deeds in battle while dressed as a male soldier—appeared in China some time between the fourth and the sixth centuries and now is well known in North America.[1] This study investigates variations of Mulan's story that feature a cross-dressed character. Certain elements of the story are consistent in its many retellings: a young woman takes the place of her elderly father in war, serves her country valiantly in disguise as a man, and returns home with triumph and honor to resume her womanly life. Mulan's tale, despite its journey across time, geography, and cultures, continues to be about a young woman's successful transgression.[2] The meaning of the story, however, varies in relation to the historical and cultural context in which it is retold and through which its plot and moral import are reshaped.

Beginning as a probably non-Han Chinese folk ballad, Mulan's tale became a part of classic Chinese literature; in the twentieth century the story appeared in Chinese American writing, children's picture books, and even animated films in the United States. This book traces the development of Mulan's image from a Chinese folk heroine in legend to an illustrious icon in local history and literary tradition, to a Chinese American woman warrior, to a range of characters with differing personalities and storylines in children's books, and then to an animated Disney heroine in the global marketplace. In tracing the continuities and discontinuities of Mulan's story, this project poses two main questions: what does the story's evolution reveal about womanhood, heroism, filial piety, and loyalty in premodern China? And what does it reveal about female agency, ethnic identity, and cultural hybridity in Chinese America? The exploration of Mulan's cross-cultural journey ranges from the Northern Dynasties (386–581) until the beginning of the twenty-first century; it considers literary texts in classic Chinese, Mandarin, and English, as well as children's picture books and animated feature films.

The earliest written account of Mulan is commonly acknowledged to be an anonymous folk ballad, entitled "Mulan shi" ("Ballad of Mulan," hereafter "Ballad"). Believed to have been composed during the Northern Dynasties, the tale was collected in an anthology of lyrics, folk songs, and poems titled *Yuefu shiji* (Collection of Yuefu Poems) in the thirteenth century. The three-hundred-odd-word "Ballad" is a narrative poem that portrays Mulan as a courageous daughter. To stand in for her elderly father who has been conscripted by the imperial court, she impersonates a man and fights in the armed forces. After years on the battlefield, Mulan turns down a promotion in the official ranks along with the benefits bestowed on her by the emperor so that she can return home and resume her womanly life. After reuniting with her family and changing back into her feminine dress, she presents herself to her male companions. Her soldier friends are astonished by the fact that Mulan's secret had never been revealed during their many years of service life. They hasten to show their respect and applaud her for her courage and accomplishments. The "Ballad" neither explains Mulan's family background or her military performance, nor does it specify her personal life before departure and after homecoming. As a result, readers and writers enjoy great opportunity to fill in details from their imaginations. Since the formation of the "Ballad," Mulan's story has been adapted, retold, and alluded to in Chinese poetry, prose, drama, stage performance, and folklore. Her tale also has found its way into local histories.

This book argues that, instead of being considered a model character at the first dissemination of her story, Mulan has evolved into an ideal heroine during a lengthy process of storytelling and retelling. The ethical and moral values that her image embodies reflect a collection of the virtues found in a typology of heroines in premodern Chinese culture. The sketchy portrayal in the "Ballad" enables varied interpretations of the ethics implied by the character and her unconventional behavior. One conceptualization takes Mulan as the exemplification of the martial tradition applied to both men and women in the northern literature in premodern China (Hu Shi; Wang Zhong 147–49; Chen Youbing 47–48). Another interpretation underscores the Confucian idea of filial piety to justify her unusual actions (Zhang Rufa). In yet another view, Mulan's story reveals that a female protagonist can be cherished for her talents beyond the domestic sphere (Wang Rubi; Zhang Jing 47). All these readings between the lines have contributed to the character's iconic image; her name has become synonymous with "heroine" in Mandarin, and her story is known in almost every household in China.

By the beginning of the twenty-first century the character Mulan has become familiar to a broad range of English-speaking audiences, owing to three major sources: Maxine Hong Kingston's acclaimed book, *The Woman Warrior: Memoirs of a Girlhood among Ghosts* (1976); a number of picture books for children published since the 1990s in the United States; and Disney Studio's animated films, *Mulan* (1998) and *Mulan II* (2005), together with the commercial products and promotional bundles that accompanied them. Kingston's book reconfigures Mulan as an idealized heroine in a girl's fantasy and transplants her tale into the context of Chinese America. First published as a memoir, her controversial work contains retellings of the folk character Mulan (Fa Mu Lan in Kingston's spelling) and the historical poet Cai Yan (ca. 177–ca. 239; Ts'ai Yen in Kingston's spelling) in its recounting of how the narrator constructs her female ethnic identity as she comes of age. Giving Mulan's tale an autobiographical spin, Kingston writes her work in the style of "talking-stories."[3] Instead of literally translating the Chinese legend of Mulan, Kingston transforms the folk heroine into a Chinese American woman warrior and avenger whose image is enriched through a bicultural legacy and a conscious search for female empowerment.

Mulan probably was introduced to English-speaking readers when the folk "Ballad" was translated in the nineteenth century. In terms of literary renditions of Mulan in English, the stage play *China Marches On* (1938), written by Chinese American actor and playwright, H. T. Tsiang, alluded to this character and predated Kingston's book and Disney Company's films by decades. Moreover, in 1996 William Wu published a short story, "The Ginseng Potion," in which he imagines Mulan's adventure in a military expedition from 398 to 410. Compared to the Kingston and Disney Company's versions, particularly significant in the developing course of Mulan's story as well as for their historical and cultural influences, the more obscure literary renditions such as Tsiang's and Wu's nonetheless add to the multiple layers of Mulan's lore.

Mulan also has emerged as a favorite subject for writers and illustrators of children's literature in the United States. Since the 1990s, a number of picture books have adapted her story with various narrative strategies and artistic styles. These visual materials enrich the Mulan gallery not only by retelling her story, but also by portraying the heroine in feminine dress as well as in masculine armor. Primarily targeting young readers and their parents, they collectively help expand Mulan's fame and influence in a cross-cultural setting. Except for the dissatisfactory reception in the film market in mainland China, the 1998 feature film *Mulan* has achieved such box office success that Disney Company decided to release a sequel, *Mulan II*. These films, together with the picture books, art books, toys, games, as well as the Oriental McRib from McDonald's and other commercial venues, have boosted the character's popularity in the United States and increased her international fame. In North America, the film *Mulan* has provoked differing reactions among film critics and scholars from various fields. Although promoted for its authentic cultural specifics, the film is nonetheless a product of transculturation; embracing a number of profeminist elements in portraying a strong female lead character, the film ultimately represents a false feminist mentality. Whether the film incurs positive or negative responses, the cultural influence of the Disneyfied Mulan is worth exploring.[4]

All these sources contribute significantly to Mulan's expanded popularity, particularly in North America, as well as to her development into an iconic heroine for readers and viewers worldwide. The majority of the English-speaking audience is fascinated by the narratives and visual portrayals of this extraordinary character, but many readers are unaware of the alterations that Mulan's tale has undergone as a result of this multitude of storytelling and retelling. Seldom do these viewers realize the richness and variety of Mulan's story in China before the heroine's journey across the Pacific Ocean. In her earliest incarnation as the leading character of a favorite Chinese folk story, Mulan is neither guided and trained by a magic power to combat social injustice (as is Kingston's character) nor driven by her independent spirit (as is Disney's protagonist). Nor do viewers know that these varied alterations of her tale have targeted audience groups in such diverse social and cultural contexts as the coming-of-age of Asian American identity in the 1970s that informed Kingston's book, the climate to promote bilingual and multicultural education that fostered the publication of the picture books, and the strategy and effort to expand its Asian market that motivated, at least in part, the Disney Studio's production.

Much scholarly attention in North America has been focused on what has happened to Mulan's story after it reached the western hemisphere. But one may ask whether her story was a unified entity before it embarked on its journey to the West. What is Mulan's "authentic" Chinese heritage when it comes to literary texts? When the American versions interpret and reimagine the heroine's tale, on what resources do they rely for the "original" story? What has brought about the differential reception to the reconfiguration presented by a Chinese American writer compared to the image after Disneyfication? These questions, all related to the issue of cultural authenticity and the retelling of Mulan's story, need to be examined through tracing this character's literary voyage across historical and geographical borders.

The retellings of Mulan's story in the United States provide the reader with reinventions of this character embued with new critical agendas. At the same time, these versions all allude, directly or indirectly, to her Chinese heritage. Indeed, some Asian American scholars have noted the multiple layers of Mulan's legend in Chinese culture (Wong, "Kingston's Handling"; Lai; Lan). Nevertheless, no comprehensive study clarifies the evolution of her tale in China and America. In response, this book discusses the narratives and images of Mulan over a long time span and traces the process through which the representation of a model heroine has been built up in her journey from premodern China to contemporary United States. In analyzing an individual character as extraordinary as Mulan, it is important not to remove her evolving image from its cultural environments. In contextualizing Mulan with other Chinese heroines, this study hopes to demonstrate the route on which Mulan develops from a courageous legendary figure to an illustrious historical heroine who embodies a collection of virtues found in heroic women. Through analyzing the variations of Mulan's tale in Chinese culture and highlighting the usually ignored diversity within the "original," this book uncovers the complexities underlying the current discussions on cultural authenticity in Asian American literary studies. By looking at Mulan as a figure claimed by various regions and recorded in their local histories in China, the discussion presented herein deconstructs the monolithic "China" in Chinese America and by extension the "Asia" in Asian America.

In scrutinizing variations of Mulan's story, this study conceptualizes the transmission and transformation of this maiden in the trope of a palimpsest. The term "palimpsest" captures the interplay of continuity and erasure in the evolving process of Mulan's tale. A palimpsest means "a thing likened to such a writing surface, especially in having been reused or altered while still retaining traces of its earlier form; a multilayered record" ("Palimpsest"). Frequently, the trace of the original text can be seen beneath the later writing, showing the process of erasure (that is, the later writing replacing the earlier words) as well as continuity (that is, the new text building on the old). During the long course of evolution, Mulan's story has been written and rewritten into multiple layers that efface and erase the previous versions. The process of preservation and alteration of Mulan's story suggests a layering of literary and visual representations that maintain connections through the cross-cultural journey of Mulan.

Such a transforming process of Mulan's story demonstrates how "literary discourse" and "other discourses" (to use Gérard Genette's words) often find paths into each other. Palimpsest conveys the multiplicity of different versions portraying Mulan in a variety of guises: for example, the ideal embodiment of filial piety, a reflection of young women's awareness and enactment of female agency, and an example of a personal struggle for individuality. This concept also exemplifies Mulan's cross-dressing and re-dressing that have been consistently portrayed in the evolution of her legend. Even the Disney version concludes Mulan's story with the heroine's homecoming and return to womanly life. The resultant transformations therefore share the common standpoints of temporality of cross-dressing as well as reinstallation of femininity in interpretations from historical and cultural circumstances.

One key concept that appears frequently in this book—representation—reflects my priorities in structuring an analytic study of Mulan. The multivalence of the term necessitates clarification of my usage. I use "representation" particularly as it has been shaped by postcolonial and feminist theories to refer to the different versions of Mulan's story that inherit the element of the cross-dressed heroine amidst the combat zone and at the same time reimagine the character and her deeds. During this process, her tale has been built up into a colorful collage of varied aspects that depends on who is telling the story, to whom, and in what context. In "The Other Question: Stereotype, Discrimination and the Discourse of Colonialism," Homi Bhabha observes that the process of stereotyping is "not a simplification because it is a false representation of a given reality. It is a simplification because it is an arrested, fixated form of representation that, in denying the play of difference . . . constitutes a problem for the *representation* of the subject in signification of psychic and social relations" (75). Building on Bhabha's observation, I conceptualize the representation of Mulan within a space contested in terms of ethnicity, gender, and power relations. In this light, the varied faces of Mulan, as they have been created in China and the United States, cannot be judged simply as positive or negative, antistereotypical or stereotypical, or in Frank Chin's words, "real" or "fake." Rather, these representations are dynamic and "mobilized" depending on discursive context (Feng 9).

In terms of combining womanhood and heroism, Mulan's heritage has been and will continue to be contested through feminist readings. Judith Butler argues that representation, like politics, is controversial: "*representation* serves as the operative term within a political process that seeks to extend visibility and legitimacy to women as political subjects"; moreover, "representation is the normative function of a language which is said either to reveal or to distort what is assumed to be true about the category of women" (Butler, *Gender Trouble,* 1). This book emphasizes the negotiation between gender and warrior values as it is reflected in the stories of heroic women among whom Mulan stands out as a model. It also explores how a heroine's boundary-crossing behavior challenges and at the same time is regulated by certain circumstances and for specific purposes to conform to the social norms regarding women and how such balancing compensates for the violation of her gender role, which makes the heroine nonthreatening and hence acceptable and praiseworthy.

To discuss Mulan as a paradigm out of a group image of heroines, chapter 2 starts by identifying a female heroic lineage in premodern China. The moral values and attributes associated with these characters provide a favorable environment for cultivating Mulan as an ideal model. Chapter 3 traces Mulan's "travel" in premodern China, which consists of increased life details and articulated ethical principles. These modifications show an attempt to historicize and localize this heroine. This chapter also analyzes various texts concerning Mulan's biographical information. By dating each source, claim, and assertion as well as sorting all the materials in a chronological sequence, this chapter reveals how different regions have claimed Mulan to be their own folk heroine and how she had become a multifaceted heroine in literature and local history by the nineteenth century. It shows that before an American audience embraced Mulan as a cultural import from China, her story had already experienced a long process of alteration. In this sense, her journey to the West is an extension that adds more layers onto this cross-cultural palimpsest. Chapter 4 discusses Kingston's *The Woman Warrior* and its critical engagement. In Mulan's cross-cultural transformation, Kingston's book attaches new plots and messages to the folk story and establishes a bridge between two cultures that leads to the heroine's popularity in America. In recreating Mulan's lore in a first-person narrative,

Kingston places particular emphasis on female empowerment: Mulan's years of training as preparation for her becoming a military leader, the communal and familial responsibility reinforced by the carved words on her back, and the ultimate accomplishment of a superior model who fulfills both male and female roles in her society. Reading the textual and graphic presentations for a young audience, chapter 5 examines picture books of Mulan on two levels: first, how these works claim cultural roots and aim at introducing Chinese tradition to readers outside China; and second, how the collaboration of written texts and colored illustrations underscore such agendas as female empowerment and cross-dressing, through Judith Butler's theoretical lens of "performative gender." Chapter 6 examines Disney's animated films *Mulan* and *Mulan II*, other animated productions adapting Mulan's story, and Mulan's global fame. Through these and other modifications, Mulan's story and image have evolved for hundreds of years and across cultural boundaries. During the course of erasure, addition, and revision her palimpsestic story serves as a cultural vehicle that carries portable traditions across time and space.

As a result of the Chinese translation of Kingston's *The Woman Warrior* along with the release of Disney Studio's *Mulan* and the publication of picture books adapting the Disneyfied character in China, Mulan has undergone a countermigration back to her cultural homeland.[5] The critical responses that Kingston's work has kindled among Chinese scholars and readers, together with the academic and popular reception of Disney Company's animation, further complicate the question of cultural authenticity in the evolving route of Mulan's tale. A live-action feature film, *Hua Mulan*, released in China in November 2009 and adaptations of Mulan's lore in other performing art forms attest to the heroine's flourishing in the global era ("Tribute" 7) and strong continuation of Mulan's charm.

2 /   Heroic Lineage: Military Women and
Lady Knights-Errant in Premodern China

The footbound Chinese woman who dominates the Western historical
imagination is a product of creative mistaking that has no place in the
family album or storehouse of China's own cultural childhood.
—SUSAN MANN, "PRESIDENTIAL ADDRESS"

In the historical Western imagination patriarchy and patrilineal male
kinship rigidly structure traditional Chinese society to the degree that
women are deprived of fundamental rights and are inferior to men without exception. One missionary has commented that "[t]he condition of
the Chinese woman is most pitiable. . . . Suffering, privation, contempt,
all kinds of misery and degradation, seize on her in the cradle and ac-
company her pitilessly to the tomb" (Huc 1: 248). Abundant examples of
female chastity, footbinding, the indentured servant-wife, and the cult of
widow fidelity have been published in observations of Westerners. Patricia Ebrey has summarized:

> Nineteenth- and early twentieth-century observers described in
> detail the plight of girls who might be killed at birth by parents
> who did not need another daughter, who could be sold at five or six
> as indentured servants, whose feet were bound so small that they
> could hardly walk, who when a little older had to marry whomev-
> er their fathers ordered them to marry, who had to submit to fre-
> quently tyrannical mothers-in-law after marriage, who might not
> be allowed to remarry after their husbands' deaths, who had few le-
> gal rights to property, and who could be divorced easily and denied
> custody of their children. (197)

Before the 1960s a number of scholars in Chinese studies had underdeveloped or misrepresented the role of women in their accounts of Chinese institutions (Wolf and Witke 1). By the 1970s the body of literature

on Chinese women had been growing, including "both the explicitly political and supposedly neutral varieties of feminist-inspired scholarship"
(Stacey 485). Such intellectual interest has continued to propser during
the past few decades and increasingly fosters people's awareness that
"[a]lthough women have been marginalized in Western accounts of Chinese history, China's documentary record on gender relations is rich"
(Mann and Cheng, Introduction, 1). The topic of literary women in
imperial China, for example, has enjoyed repeated scholarly attention.[1]
Within the field of women in traditional China, courageous heroines,
including Mulan as a cultural phenomenon, occur so frequently in premodern Chinese society that a thorough understanding of female stereotypes, literary representations, and social perceptions of such figures
warrants a careful examination.

Citing Mulan as one of the two most prominent female mythic figures
in Chinese culture, Susan Mann's presidential address at the Annual
Meeting of the Association for Asian Studies in 2000 delineates "myths
of Asian womanhood" with a particular focus on Chinese tradition
(835–62).[2] Expanding the term "myth" to include "mythified" histories
and legends as well as historically and culturally overwritten myths,
Mann contends:

> Chinese poets, painters, sculptors, librettists, essayists, commenta-
> tors, philosophers, storytellers, puppeteers, illustrators, and histo-
> rians made a veritable industry of myths of womanhood—an in-
> dustry that . . . far outstrips any of its counterparts elsewhere in
> Asia. . . . Embedded as they are in historical and cultural context,
> though, Chinese myths of womanhood yield unexpected insights
> into historical consciousness *about* women, and *among* women, in
> Chinese history. ("Presidential Address" 835)

Sharing Mann's insight into the significance of deciphering Chinese
women and uncovering the "historical consciousness" through myths,
this chapter maps the cultural landscape of heroic women in premodern
China through analyzing the stories of female combatants found in historical chronicles and literary texts.

An overview of valiant heroines as well as their positions in premodern Chinese society would suggest that even though heroic womanhood
remains an underdeveloped field in scholarly studies until recently, their
stories have enjoyed enduring interest in historical archives and literary
texts and prospered in oral genres such as storytelling and theatre performances in China. Instead of being miserable victims or unusual radicals

these heroic women are agents "who embraced certain aspects of official norms while resisting others" (Ko, Haboush, and Piggott, Introduction, 1). Their existence and popularity challenge any one-dimensional view of Chinese women and any monolithic understanding of premodern Chinese society. Because the "old stereotype construes Asian women as victims of traditional or Confucian patriarchy," a careful study of the interplay between Chinese womanhood and heroic tradition would be helpful to restore "both female subjectivity and historical complexity" (Ko, Haboush, and Piggott, Introduction, 1). Moreover, Susan Mann has pointed out that "these legendary women, through their enduring and continually elaborated myths, become logically constituted elements of what we have been pleased to call China's patriarchal society: integral, if paradoxical and confusing (as befits a good myth), parts of the story of how that proper patriarchy should work. That is, narrating the values of patriarchy in Chinese culture depended on and celebrated powerful women" ("Presidential Address" 842). The female empowerment reflected by heroic characters such as Mulan is ironically an integral part of the patriarchal Chinese society and herein problematizes the common conception of Chinese patriarchy as a "uniform or timeless category" (Ko, Haboush, and Piggott, Introduction, 1). Given the heroines' repeated appearance and lasting popularity in Chinese culture, these women "maintain a much more complex discursive position than one of simple opposition or support of patriarchal society" (Louise Edwards 112). An investigation of the interaction between female identity and cultural heroines brings into light the embedded "historical complexity" of Confucian China. A study of women's expanded social sphere beyond their traditionally assigned domestic space points to the possible space left for women.

One polarity defining gender distinctions in the Confucian ethics is the spatial segregation between male and female.[3] In the Confucian doctrine, men and women are relegated to different domains: in general, the "outer" is for male, and the "inner" is for female. Such gender separation, although not articulated specifically by Confucius (551–479 B.C.) himself, is codified in the classics starting from the *Yijing* (The Book of Changes, ca. tenth to eleventh centuries B.C.) and the *Shijing* (The Book of Odes, conventionally attributed to Confucius) and then reinforced in later periods. For instance, the Neo-Confucian scholar Zhu Xi (1130–1200), in his *Zhuzi yulei* (Quotations of Master Zhu), advocates that the husband's appropriate place is outside the home while conversely the wife's is inside the domestic space (68: 1708).[4] By this token, the varied levels of strictness exclude women from social spheres outside their family space and certainly from the battlefield that has always been the particular territory of "the outer" reserved for men.

While women were required to stay inside the family compound, their influence could nevertheless extend to the outside in various ways. The 1980s have seen scholarly publications that examine the social functions and influences of female life.[5] The "moral instruction" characterized by a wife's support to her husband or a mother's influence on her son, for example, has been viewed as an indirect evasion through which women are able to bypass the conventional morality outlining gendered space (Mann and Cheng, Introduction, 2). Following such scholarly paths, the discussion of Chinese heroines' stories in this chapter continues to explore the possibilities and circumstances of women's involvement in an extended social sphere. The notable assemblage of heroic women in premodern Chinese tradition points to the possible space within an overall patriarchal social structure "for women to negotiate and maneuver toward their perceived interest without outwardly provoking the guardians of the prevailing system" (Hsiung 73). The images of a woman combatant in armor rushing into the combat zone or a swordswoman roaming the road and showcasing her martial skills more overtly challenge the ethical codes of gender segregation. Why then, one may ask, are these gallant women remembered as extraordinary heroines with undying popularity in history and literature rather than rebuked as illbred ladies for their transgressions?

Frederick Brandauer's analysis of the emancipation of women and advocacy of the Confucian ideal of womanhood in the Qing novel *Jinghua yuan* (Destinies of Mirrored Flowers, Li Ruzhen, ca. 1763–ca. 1830) suggests a compromise mode in literary creation where female promotion in social status does not contradict Confucianism-guided social order (647–60). Louise Edwards further describes the complexities and negotiations of gender and power in Confucian China, reflected in the phenomenon of warrior women. In her comparative study of the heroine's domestication in the Qing novels, *Jinghua yuan* and *Honglou meng* (Red Chamber Dreams, Cao Xueqin, ca. 1717–1763 and Gao E, ca. 1738–ca. 1815), Edwards has insightfully discussed the subtle balance exemplified by heroic women in China:

> [T]he woman warrior succinctly embodies the contradictions perceived in the authors' thinking regarding the position of women. . . . She is threatening to the patriarchal power, with its implicit

preference for meek and mild women, and yet primarily instrumental in ensuring its continued existence because the deeds she performs are undeniably consolidating of the existing Confucian social and moral order. The disruptive potential encapsulated within her form makes her an enthralling fictional and dramatic figure and this, combined with her consolidating function, ensures her repeated appearance in fiction and drama at both elite and popular levels. (92)

More often than not, a Chinese heroine's story portrays such subtle balancing between a woman's transgression in breaking the rules and her compliance with the simultaneously prevailing ethical codes. The image of a woman being a warrior on the battlefield or in martial confrontation violates the gender separation that requires women to stay inside the female living quarter. In this sense, whether a historical figure or a literary character, a courageous heroine defies her assigned gender space by marching into a conventionally masculine territory where she either equals or frequently outwits and outperforms her male contemporaries. Such narrative, however, rarely represents the heroine as a feminist revolutionary who takes on armor and swords to battle against the patriarchal social system and to claim female agency. Rather, her valiant behavior is still well defined within the Confucian doctrine because her conduct consistently adheres to such core principles as loyalty or filial piety or both (Lai 78). In this sense, women of extraordinary military or martial skills whose names have been preserved in Chinese history and literature are neither rarities nor anomalies. Their very existence warrants a careful examination of the female heroic lineage and its implications.

Stories of Chinese heroines are of particular value because they illustrate the diversity of ancient Chinese society: complexities exist within the Confucian tradition through which it is possible for a woman to disrupt social norms by crossing the boundaries defining gender roles without incurring severe punishment. Such cultural revision, as represented in the heroine's tales, reflects what Maureen Robertson calls a "mixed process of acceptance and resistance" that articulates "otherness" within the accepted discourse (66). These female combatants' successes on the battlefield or in the martial world are carefully characterized without either challenging or threatening the dominant male-centered rule. Instead, heroic women's achievements are lauded with a particular emphasis on these heroines who are loyal subjects, filial daughters, wise mothers and wives, or lady knights-errant with integrity and virtue.[6] Therefore, their boundary-crossing deeds may take a back seat to their heroic spirit and actions so that these women, among whom Mulan stands out as a prototype, can be appreciated as virtuous heroines rather than being condemned as subversive forces.

My discussion examines, in particular, two legacies that provide the cultural milieu for the growth of Mulan's character in China: in one group are women in armed forces, including generals, officers, soldiers as well as others who were involved in military events; in the other group are female knights-errant who were skillful in martial arts and known for their chivalric spirit.[7] This chapter addresses the first group in relation to the imperial court. Women leaders and assistants in armed service who support its rule have close connection to building up the image of Mulan as a national heroine, while female rebels and bandits who fight against the court to establish a new throne provide a counterimage of Mulan's epitomized embodiment of loyalty. Representing the moral values embodied by heroic women in the military realm, Mulan, as a filial daughter to her father and a dutiful subject of the imperial ruler, ventures into a space traditionally reserved for men. Merits found in other armed women's extraordinary performance in the men's domain, such as loyalty, courage, and wisdom, help enrich the image of Mulan by developing her tale and contributing to her name becoming synonymous with "heroine" in China.

The chivalric heroines belong to the world of knight-errantry that exists beyond and is sometimes connected with the ruling government. This subculture usually abides by its own codes of morality. Similar to their male counterparts, chivalric ladies usually sever their connections with the society and mainstream political power. Tales of lady knights-errant provide colorful details about women as superb martial artists along with captivating particulars regarding fighting scenarios. This aspect has shown significant influence on later variations of Mulan's story, especially plays, performances, and fiction about her in China, Kingston's writing, picture books for children, as well as the Disney Studio's film adaptations. All these sources imagine and display Mulan's martial skills in varied ways and portray exciting action scenes in lively details. Furthermore, the theme of cross-dressing has played a considerable role in literary renditions of Mulan's story as well as in the critical responses to her tale. The chivalrous ladies sometimes resort to disguise mostly for convenience so that they can travel either to redress wrongs or to await the opportunity to take revenge on behalf of their families or friends. Cross-dressed heroines are easily found in Chinese martial fiction and films. Stories of these lady knights-errant help foster the action plots and the portrayal of cross-dressing in later variations of Mulan's tale.

Chinese heroines in military and martial traditions collectively undergird the cultural setting that has nourished the evolution of Mulan's character who becomes an exceptional model of heroic womanhood. To effectively decipher Mulan's developing process from a legendary character to an ideal heroine, the following sections examine the concept of heroic womanhood in premodern China with two questions in mind: What moral values are codified and modified in the stories of heroic women, as they are dispersed in historical and literary documents? And how do female combatants achieve their acceptance in Confucian China, despite their transgression across boundaries that delineate conventionally defined femininity and masculinity?

Heroines Serving the Court: Women in Armed Forces in Dynastic Histories

Despite the fact that war and military service have been primarily masculine territories throughout China's long history, women were never entirely absent from the front lines. Xiaolin Li's article presents a list of military women from predynastic to modern China along with a brief overview of the activities of Chinese women generals and soldiers over the lengthy time span of five thousand years (67–71).[8] My analysis not only acknowledges the heroines' existence in history and literature, as Li does, but also examines what values these military women's stories embody in Confucian China and how their unconventional behavior is represented as heroic and worthy of documenting in historical texts. The first known female leader in the Chinese army who left any written record is Fu Hao (also known as Lady Hao, fl. ca. thirteenth century B.C.). According to inscriptions on the excavated bronze vessels and oracle bones from the Late Shang Dynasty tombs (ca. 1200–1045 B.C.), Fu Hao was one of King Wu Ding's consorts. In the Shang court, the royal ladies' power and status in the ritual system "presumably derived both from the political interest of their kin and from the role they had played as consorts when alive" (Keightley 31). During her lifetime, Fu Hao won the king's trust by leading his army; her military achievements also won the respect of the people. One of the oracle bone inscriptions states: "[c]rack-making on *xinsi* (day 18), Zheng divined: 'In the present season, if the king raises men and calls upon Fu Hao to attack the Tufang, (we) will receive assistance in this case.' (In) the fifth moon" (Keightley 32). This record clearly indicates Fu Hao's participation in military affairs. She was entrusted with a significant position that placed her in charge of considerable ritual ceremonies and bestowed on her the administrative power to manage her own estate.[9] As outstanding as she was as a military leader, Fu Hao was not the only woman who made her way into armed forces in early Chinese history. Although extant predynastic military writings never specifically contemplate the role of women, some passing references indicate their participation in siege defense as well as how they adopt more aggressive roles, such as in spy craft.[10] Brief references to women's participation in military training, strategy, and defense appear in Wei Liao's (fourth century B.C.) *Wei Liao zi* (vol. 5, vol. 6), Shang Yang's (d. 338 B.C.) *Shangjun shu* (vol. 12), and Mo Di's (fl. 400 B.C.) *Mo zi* (vol. 14, vol. 15).[11] In general, all these writings are directed to a male hierarchy and oriented to efficiently cope with ruthless military issues of surviving the Warring States period (475–221 B.C.). None of these early documents provides a portrayal of an individual heroine like Mulan.

Although "the unorthodox deeds and ingenuity of the women warriors have been conventionally reserved for genres like ballads, legends, and dramas" (Lai 81), historical chronicles of female combatants, in comparatively small number as they are, are of particular significance in terms of representing heroic women's *unorthodox* conduct in *orthodox* documents. Compared to the historical accounts, literary renditions of military women have attracted more attention in scholarly research. Sufen Lai, for example, has explored Chinese heroines through studying their stories as "distinct literary types" (78). As a prominent example, the women generals and soldiers of the Yang family in the Song Dynasty have been discussed in detail (Cao Zhengwen, *Nüxing wenxue*, 71–73; Lai 100–02). Among the military women included in histories, local topographies, folklore, fiction, and theatre performances, the female leaders who have entries in the Twenty-Four Dynastic Histories from the *Shiji* (Historical Records, Sima Qian ca. 145–ca. 86 B.C.) to the *Ming shi* (History of the Ming, Zhang Tingyu, 1672–1755, et al.) are of particular importance. These texts, considered official histories of premodern China, are usually compiled under the auspices of the central government. The discussion herein, arranged primarily in a chronological order, investigates how particular cases of heroic womanhood have been accepted and recorded in authoritarian history. The heroines' very existence in official histories with positive commentaries stated or implied is a result of balancing their boundary-crossing behavior; that is, their defiance of gender roles subscribed to women is neglected while their success in service and conformance to such Confucian ethics as loyalty and filial piety is highlighted.[12] Despite the paucity of information about these military women in dynastic histories, the few records that do exist offer a platform to reevaluate Chinese womanhood and reconsider Confucianism.

Xun Guan

Similar to the character Mulan portrayed in the "Ballad," Xun Guan is an unmarried maiden. Her story has been documented in the *Jinshu* (History of the Jin, Fang Xuanling, 578–648, et al.). In the entry under the title "Xun Song xiaonü Guan" (Young Daughter of Xun Song) in the "licnü" (illustrious women) section, Xun Guan is identified as the young daughter of Xun Song (ca. 263–ca. 329), an official of the imperial court. The historical text highlights solely her military achievement with little recognition accorded other details of her life. Xun Guan is remembered as a savior of Xiangcheng. This city was once sieged by enemy troops when Xun Song was in charge of its administration. After being trapped for a while, Xun Song and his people ran out of provisions for survival, and the situation seemed hopeless. Only thirteen years old at the time, Xun Guan volunteered to help when her father, hoping to seek aid from nearby regions, had no suitable person to carry out this crucial yet dangerous task. Xun Guan then "led a group of warriors to break through the barricade and get out of the city at night. The enemy troops chased after them pressingly. Guan directed her soldiers in fighting and making advancement until they reached Mount Luyang where they were exempted from the enemy's pursuit and attack" (Fang Xuanling et al., 96: 2515). Without consideration for their own life and safety, Xun Guan and the soldiers under her lead fought courageously until they accomplished their mission of delivering the request for help to other officials in the nearby areas. Not until Xun Guan brought rescuing forces did the enemy retreat and finally remove Xiangcheng from danger. At the very beginning of his record, the historiographer praises Xun Guan for her "outstanding moral integrity since childhood," and he closes the entry by confirming that the city's release from its siege is "to Guan's merit" (Fang Xuanling et al., 96: 2515).

Later, a fictional account of Xun Guan's achievement appeared in the Ming novel *Dongxi liangjin yanyi* (The Romance of the Eastern and Western Jin, Taihetang zhuren and Yibai zhuren, pseud., date unknown). The chapter mentioning Xun Guan is brief, probably adapted from the historical record without adding many details (Taihe tang zhuren and Yibai zhuren 190–205). The local gazetteers of the Ming and Qing, also including entries under Xun Guan's name, apparently adapted the story from the historical record in the *Jinshu* without providing additional details: "Xun xiaonü" (Young Daughter of Xun) in the *Da Ming yitongzhi* (Gazetteers of the Great Ming, Li Xian, 1408–1466 et al., 27: 32b-33a) and "Xun Song xiaonü Guan" (Guan: Young Daughter of Xun Song) in the *Jiaqing chongxiu yitongzhi* (Gazetteers of the Qing, Jiaqing Edition, Mu Zhang'a, 1782–1856 et al., compiled in 1842, 219: 18b).

The collection of biographies in the *Lienü zhuan* (Biographies of Illustrious Women), conventionally attributed to the Han scholar Liu Xiang (ca. 79–ca. 8 B.C.), initiates a narrative model that was subsequently adopted in later historical works. Starting with the *Hou Hanshu* (History of the Later Han, Fan Ye, 398–445), each dynastic history includes a section titled "lienü" to document brief biographies of filial daughters, wise mothers, faithful widows, women martyrs, talented ladies, and other types of virtuous women. These biographies of exemplary women, in general, emphasize the commonly acknowledged female virtues such as purity, obedience, chastity, and motherhood, despite the transformation of women's roles over China's long history (Raphals 21). Xun Guan's courage and decision to shoulder the responsibility for rescuing the city together with her valor in military combat sets her alone among other illustrious women known for their feminine virtues. To share the liability with her father in protecting the local people can be read as a way to fulfill her obligation of filial piety; to risk her own life to help the city overcome the danger demonstrates her loyalty to the imperial rule. In these ways, this heroic maiden exemplifies traditional female virtures at the same time that her deeds fall outside the range of feminine behavior defined by Confucian ethics.

Zhu Xu's Mother

A mother who assisted her son in guarding a city presents a comparable example in the same dynasty. Mrs. Zhu's historical record appears in the entry for her son Zhu Xu (d. 393) in the "liezhuan" (collected biographies) section in the *Jinshu*. Mrs. Zhu, maiden name Han and personal name unknown, is introduced as a mother at the beginning of this document. Both her husband and son served as officials for the imperial court. Similar to Xun Guan's record, this entry tells of only one moment in Mrs. Zhu's life: her accomplishment in a military defense that was

apparently unfeminine yet won her respect and admiration and therefore a place in the dynastic history. During the Ningkang reign of the Jin
Dynasty (373–375), the position of regional inspector of Liang Prefecture
was conferred on Zhu Xu, and he was stationed in the regional capital,
Xiangyang.[13] Before a foreseeable and severe attack by enemy troops,
Mrs. Zhu mounted the inner wall of the city. After a careful inspection,
she noticed that the northwest corner of the city's defense construction
was vulnerable. To strengthen security, she then "led more than a hundred maids as well as female residents of the city to build a new defense
wall as high as over twenty *zhang* at the corner of the weak point" (Fang
Xuanling et al., 81: 2133). This reinforcement later proved crucial in defending the city. After the enemy retreated with no assault on the city,
the people of Xiangyang renamed their city "Furen cheng" (City of the
Lady) in honor of Mrs. Zhu. In this brief document, Mrs. Zhu appears
as a wise mother who assists her son in fulfilling his duty as administrator. The historical record highlights how she successfully aids her
son in defending his city and does not question her unfeminine actions
of venturing out of the inner chamber of her home—the conventionally
regulated space for women—and participating in the traditionally masculine activity of military defense. Nor does the entry raise any question
about the other women involved in constructing the new defenses under
her lead.

Princess Pingyang

The story of Princess Pingyang also exemplifies the possibility for a woman to participate in military affairs as a family member among her male
kin. Entries for Princess Pingyang appear under her name in the "liezhuan"
section of the *Jiu Tangshu* (History of the Tang, Liu Xu, 887–946, et al.) and
Xin Tangshu (New History of the Tang, Ouyang Xiu, 1007–1072 and Song
Qi, 998–1061). According to these historical accounts, the princess was born
in the Sui Dynasty into the Li family that became, a few years later, the ruling clan of the Tang Dynasty. Her father, Li Yuan (Emperor Tang Gaozu,
566–635, r. 618–626), and her brother, Li Shimin (Emperor Tang Taizong,
599–649, r. 626–649), were the first and second monarchs of the Tang. Princess Pingyang played a significant supporting role in her father's founding
of the new dynasty. Among the nineteen daughters of Li Yuan, she is the
only one who left a written record of her participation in military affairs and
whose exceptional accomplishments in armed forces have won her a place in
the dynastic histories as a martial heroine.

Born as the third daughter of Li Yuan, Princess Pingyang is referred to as the Princess rather than by her personal name in the *Jiu Tangshu* and *Xin Tangshu*. In the year 617, Li Yuan led his troops to rebel against the waning Sui court. When her husband Chai Shao went to Taiyuan to support the rebellion, Princess Pingyang stayed behind in Hu County where she single-handedly recruited an army, distributed her family property to the new force, and sought for collaboration with the bandits around the region. Acknowledged as a wise military leader, the Princess "always stated strict regulations that her soldiers must not encroach. Therefore a huge number of people rushed from far and near to join her troops" (Liu Xu et al., 58: 2315). Her force expanded to as many as seventy thousand soldiers that became known as the "female detachment."[14] To meet up with her father and brothers, she then led more than ten thousand selected troops to march toward the north. Her force contributed in a meaningful way to the capture of the Capital City. After the overthrow of the Sui and the establishment of the Tang, she was honored with the title of "Princess Pingyang" and granted distinguished tributes as rewards for her military accomplishments.

The princess's martial career seems to have terminated when her father ascended the throne in the year 617. From that point on, she probably resumed her female role and retreated from the military realm while her husband and former subordinates continued to serve the court as generals and officials and to build up their military merits. The historical record documents, not the princess's life in the Tang Dynasty, but her funeral. Upon her death, the emperor (her father) issued an imperial edict to attach forty additional persons with drums and trumpets to her funeral parade. The chamberlain for ceremonials protested against such honors because the protocols reserved these honorary rituals for (presumably male) military officials and rejected their use at a woman's funeral. In response, the emperor retorted: "[The use of] drums and trumpets stood for military music. In the past, the Princess rose up in Sizhu to answer the righteous banner. She held the gongs and drums herself and made significant contributions to the foundation of the dynasty. . . . The Princess rendered meritorious services and helped accomplish the mission in which aspect no ordinary woman could rival her. How [could she be buried] without drums and trumpets?" (Liu Xu et al., 58: 2316). In addition to the extraordinary honor accorded at her funeral to validate her military achievements, Princess Pingyang also was granted the posthumous title of *zhao* (brightness, wisdom) to celebrate her keen intelligence and virtue.

Lady Liang

There is probably no better example of a wife serving as a military assistant than Liang Hongyu, whose historical record is included within the entry for her husband Han Shizhong (1089–1151) in the *Songshi* (History of the Song, Tuotuo, 1313–1355, et al.). This account, identifying her as Lady Liang,[15] relates two events in which she rendered significant assistance to her husband: first, she participated in a military confrontation on the battlefield, and second, she played a significant role in administering the troops during peacetime.

In the year 1130, Han Shizhong led his division to ambush the troops of Jin (a regime founded by the Jurchens, 1115–1234) under the command of their prince Wuzhu at Zhenjiang. In an intense battle "fought for about ten rounds, Lady Liang herself got hold of the sticks to beat the war drum. The Jurgen soldiers were eventually not able to cross the Yangzi River" (Tuotuo et al., 364: 11361). The sketchy reference to her in the record shows that Lady Liang participated in the warfare by undertaking the unfeminine activity of pounding a war drum on the battlefield. War drums usually functioned to bolster the soldiers' morale and guide the direction of their attacks. The historiographer of the *Songshi* does not specify the purpose of Lady Liang's drumbeating in the text but confirms its effectiveness by stating the Song army's success in defending their borderline at the Yangzi River. With Lady Liang's assistance, Han Shizhong's troops successfully struck the Jurgens with a smashing blow and for forty-eight days besieged them at a shallow lake named Huangtian.

Lady Liang's role extends from the battlefield to the army's civil life during peaceful periods between battles. In the year 1136, Han Shizhong established a military district in Chu Prefecture. At that time, while Han "worked hard in civil services together with his soldiers," "Lady Liang took part in building cottages out of thatch in person" (Tuotuo et al., 364: 11365). Besides aiding her husband in administrating the troops, Liang's hard work presents a model for others to follow. Their efforts assured that the service men had ample food and clothing under harsh living conditions (see figure 2.1).

Positioned as a wife with scant references to her life within her husband's entry, Lady Liang does not seem to receive any recognition for her heroic deeds or praise for her spirit as a warrior from the imperial court. Instead, in both cases cited above, she is depicted as a helper who supports her husband, although she is a loyal hero with significant

FIGURE 2.1. An illustration by Wu Youru (fl. nineteenth century) portrays Lady Liang beating the drum on a ship. Although she is dressed in armor, her hairdo and earrings indicate femininity. From Wu Youru, *Wu Youru huabao* (Precious Drawings of Wu Youru), Shanghai: Biyuan huishe, ca. 1909.

contributions to fighting the invading Jurgen troops and defending the declining Song court. Yet Lady Liang has enjoyed such enduring popularity as an exemplary heroine in China in literary renditions, theater performances, and folk stories that her husband's name has been overshadowed. Even though the coverage of her participation in combat is no more than twenty words in the *Songshi*, the drumbeat resonates so loudly that her fame has lasted throughout many centuries that followed. Adapted stories and local operas in later periods regarding Lady Liang usually render this battle as a climax of the Song army's defense war against the Jurgen invasion. The battle at the shallow lake Huangtian is dramatized into a chapter in the Qing novel *Shuoyue quanzhuan* (Complete Stories of the Yue Family, Qian Cai, fl. 1729, et al.) in which Lady Liang's drumbeat is depicted as the strategic key in guiding the Song soldiers' moves on the battlefield and thus plays a crucial role in winning the combat (44: 380–87). Moreover, two Ming plays, *Shuanglie ji* (Story of a Heroic Couple, Zhang Siwei, fl. 1567) and *Qilin ji* (Kylin Carpet, Chen Yujiao, 1544–1611) render the stories of Han Shizhong and Liang Hongyu, in which colorful details have been added into Lady Liang's life and military career. Given these adaptations for Chinese-speaking audiences of her story in fiction and drama, Liang Hongyu is widely known as an active heroine instead of simply a dutiful wife to her husband. Her tale has become one of strength and courage. Illustrations of Lady Liang have appeared in many sources. C. C. Low's bilingual children's book, *Liang Hongyu* (1991), published in Singapore as part of a series of "pictorial stories of the great Chinese national heroine," for instance, continues the long-lasting legacy of her story for contemporary young readers.

Xun Guan, Mrs. Zhu, Princess Pingyang, and Lady Liang share the military lineage that enables a daughter, mother, or wife to move into "the outer" realm as a companion to their male kin. If these four military women entered men's territory as assistants to male family members and remained in that position to play a supporting role, the following two heroines—Lady Xian and Qin Liangyu—have ventured even further in their journey into male space; they not only led their armies as commanding officers but also expanded their female presence within the military arena by earning a number of honorary and official titles equal to their male peers.

Lady Xian

Entries for Lady Xian appear under her name in the "lienü" section in the *Beishi* (History of the Northern Dynasties, Li Yanshou, fl. ca. seventh century) and the *Suishu* (History of the Sui, Wei Zheng, 580–643, and Zhangsun Wuji, d. 659). According to both records, Lady Xian was born into the family of a Southern Yue tribe leader. The historiographer introduces her: "Lady was wise and competent at young age. While living in her parents' household, [she] was able to regulate and pacify the troops and direct military operations in coercing other tribes for cooperation. [She] always tried to persuade her clansmen to follow the virtue and collaborated with local people based on faithfulness and good conduct" (Wei Zheng and Zhangsun Wuji, 80: 1800–01). Lady Xian's merits in girlhood earned her such an esteemed reputation that in the year 535 she received a marriage proposal from the inspector of Luo Prefecture, Feng Rong, for his son Feng Bao, the governor of Gaoliang. After their marriage, Lady Xian further demonstrated her outstanding capability in

FIGURE 2.2. An illustration by Wu Youru portrays Lady Xian (identified by her title Lady of Qiaoguo) standing on top of a city wall. From Wu Youru, *Wu Youru huabao* (Precious Drawings of Wu Youru), Shanghai: Biyuan huishe, ca. 1909.

military and civil administration. She helped her husband supervise the region with effective rulings and, at the same time, command their army with a strict hand. Fighting shoulder to shoulder, the couple successfully defeated the rebels in Guangdong (see figure 2.2).

After Feng Bao died several years later, Lady Xian assumed his position and took the charge of civil and military forces in that region. In the year 558, together with her nine-year-old son Feng Pu, she crushed rebels in Guangdong again. To honor her accomplishments, Emperor Chen Gaozu (503–559; r. 557–559) conferred the title of *Gaoliang jun taifuren* (Grand Lady of Gaoliang Commandery) to Lady Xian. She was admired as the "Saintly Mother" by local people. Years later Lady Xian was granted the titles *Songkang jun furen* (Lady of Songkang Commandery) and *Qiaoguo furen* (Lady of Qiaoguo) by Emperor Sui Wendi (541–604; r. 589–604). Upon her death in 601, Lady Xian held

洗夫人高涼人遠高涼太守馮寶佐寶行軍李遷仕反
設計擊敗之寶卒夫人襄集百越子僕以夫人功封信都侯僕卒夫
人率其孫撫循諸部而嶺南悉定後狸獠叛夫人又載詔書稱使者
宣述土意所至皆降自梁大同初至隋仁壽時卒謚為誠敬夫人

譙國夫人洗氏

FIGURE 2.3. Lady Xian by Jin Guliang (fl. seventeenth century) portrays her dressed in armor with a sword and a spear. From Jin Guliang, *Wu shuang pu* (Catalogue of Peerless Figures), Shanghai: Tongwen shuju, 1886.

the posthumous title of *Chengjing furen* (Lady of Honesty and Reverence) (see figure 2.3).

Even though Lady Xian demonstrated her strategic insight and military skills through the direction of her troops in smashing the insurgents in Guangzhou, there is no record of honor or merit bestowed on her in her husband's presence. After she took over her late husband's position as a commander-in-chief, her major military triumphs were followed by honor, merits, and titles issued by the imperial rule. Not only was Lady Xian able to lead her troops in battles against the rebels, defend the local people, and serve the court in times of chaos, but she also was capable of governing effectively in the region during peacetime. As a result, she won respect from local residents as well as the acknowledgment and credit from the ruling government. In this sense, Lady Xian represents an exemplary heroine whose achievements were so distinguished that the imperial court issued several titles to honor her.

Qin Liangyu

If the titles granted to Lady Xian were more honorary than functional, another prominent female leader, Qin Liangyu, went further in thriving within the men's realm: she was listed in official ranks as an equal to her male contemporaries. Successful in military expeditions and skillful at battle strategies, Qin Liangyu led a military command to defend the decaying Ming Dynasty and was responsible for both recapturing cities from the rebels and pacifying revolts over the years. No other woman achieved the high official ranks that she was granted in premodern China—the third and later the second rank.[16]

In the *Mingshi* (History of the Ming, Zhang Tingyu, 1672–1755, et al.) Qin Liangyu's entry under her name in the "liezhuan" section documents her military and administrative accomplishments. In this record, she is introduced as the wife of Ma Qiansheng, the pacification commissioner of Shizhu.[17] In the year 1599, Qin Liangyu led a division of five hundred soldiers and assisted her husband in the defeat of the rebels in Bo Prefecture. Thereafter, the couple's forces gradually took control over southern Sichuan on behalf of the Ming emperor. After her husband's death, Qin Liangyu continued to lead the army in his place as an adept warrior and strategic leader serving the imperial court. The historiographer describes Qin Liangyu: "Liangyu was full of bravery and wisdom. Skillful in horse riding and archery, [she] had literary talent and

FIGURE 2.4. An illustration by Wu Youru portrays Qin Liangyu on top of a city wall and surrounded by her soldiers. Compared to other characters in the picture, Qin is visibly a woman. From Wu Youru, *Wu Youru huabao*, Shanghai: Biyuan huishe, ca. 1909.

presented herself with grace and elegance as well. [She] administered her troops with a firm hand. Every time [she] directed the army or issued orders, the soldiers registered profound respect. The regiment under her command was called the White Rod Force that was feared near and far" (Zhang Tingyu et al., 270: 6944). Such strong leadership demonstrated Qin Liangyu's ability in governing her troops and earning respect in Sichuan and the nearby regions. In fact, it was said that the rebels around the area trembled with fear upon hearing her name (see figure 2.4).

In the year 1620, the imperial court summoned Qin Liangyu's army to pacify insurgent regions. Responding with loyalty and full cooperation, Qin Liangyu sent her brothers, Qin Bangping and Qin Minping, to lead a detachment and serve the government's call. After bringing about order from chaos, she was conferred the badge of the third rank; the government also granted her brothers official titles. In the next year, her brother Qin Bangping was killed in a battle as he was crossing the Hun

River while her other brother Qin Minping rushed out to break through the line of the besiegers. Qin Liangyu herself led three thousand soldiers and succeeded in the rescue. Because of her outstanding contributions the imperial mandate awarded Qin Liangyu the badge of the second rank and the title of commander.

When an antigovernmental uprising flared in the Chongqing region, the chief insurgents, seeking her cooperation, sent a messenger to deliver valuable gifts to Qin Liangyu. She executed the messenger before leading her troops westward to the south of Chongqing to block the rebels' path. In the meantime, she dismantled her forces to reinforce Zhong and Kui prefectures. Later, she directed her force to rescue Chengdu when it was besieged by the dissenters. After having quelled the rebellion, she was granted a series of designations with honor: assistant commissioner-in-chief, regional commander, and pacification commissioner. Furthermore, in the year 1630, the four cities of Yongping fell. The central government ordered Qin Liangyu to use her own finances to recruit a force. After the combat ended with Qin Liangyu's victory, the Ming Emperor Sizong (1610–1644; r. 1627–1644) summoned her to Pingtai and bestowed on her wealth, sacrificial sheep, wine, and poetry to honor and reward her remarkable achievements on the battlefield.

In the year 1644, the large-scale peasant uprising led by Zhang Xianzhong (1606–1646) invaded Kui Prefecture. Without reinforcements Qin Liangyu led her force to defend the area. Because her troops were hopelessly outnumbered, Qin Liangyu lost this battle. When almost all settlements in Sichuan were taken over by Zhang Xianzhong's forces, "Liangyu spoke to her troops passionately: 'both my brothers died for the Emperor. I, a frail woman, have been receiving benevolence from the court for twenty years. Now the situation is so unfortunate. How dare I serve the rebels for the rest of my life'" (Zhang Tingyu et al., 270: 6948)! She then deployed her remaining troops to guard the borders of her home base of Shizhu. This area remained the only region to survive the turmoil without being captured by sweeping insurgents. Qin Liangyu, having survived countless military battles, finally passed away of old age in 1648.

The dynastic history acknowledges Qin Liangyu as a military leader and exceptional heroine. Her loyalty to the Ming government was reflected most strongly in her defeat of the rebels and in her pacification of the Sichuan region. Outstanding achievements in Qin Liangyu's military career of two decades enabled her to gain access to the field of political administration that traditionally excluded women. The strongest theme within the matter-of-fact tone of the historical narrative is Qin Liangyu's unconditional loyalty to the Ming rule, a core principle in the Confucian ethics. Not only does the dynastic history devote a comparatively long entry to her, but it also contains events regarding other attributes of Qin Liangyu besides her military accomplishments. The historiographer includes her insightful plan in strategic deployment predicting severe attacks from the opponents as well as excerpts from her correspondence that reflect her concern about the corruption within the governing system. A letter, dated 1623, to the emperor expressed her disappointment over the timidity of some military officials and her sadness over the slanderous, jealous attack on her. Another letter to Lu Xunzhi, commander of Mian Prefecture, conveyed her concern about the tough situation and her loyalty to the Ming (Zhang Tingyu et al., 270: 6947–49). These accounts show that Qin Liangyu, both courageous and wise, realized the problems within the ruling court and foresaw the imminent danger of a large-scale upheaval.

In historical archives, Qin Liangyu's image is portrayed more in the traditional terms of an "honorary man" than of an extraordinary woman. Her martial excellence and strategic wisdom can be viewed as "male attributes" that were uncommon among her female contemporaries. In terms of historical representation, Qin Liangyu's entry in the dynastic history gives the most complete portrait among all these heroines. Few military women in premodern Chinese history have enjoyed such respect and attention as she did. Perhaps her extraordinary treatment in dynastic history reflects her relation to the ruling power as well as her outstanding achievements. Owing to her longtime military activities and substantial contributions to the court, Qin Liangyu obtained high official ranks that might have assured inclusion of her name and major victories in the lists on official historical documents. She is so exceptional an example for women in armed services that hundreds of entries in historical anecdotes, local topographies, clan pedigrees, family trees, and tablet inscriptions write about various aspects of her life and heroic deeds. Poetry, prose, and drama also celebrate many variation of and allusions to her story.[18]

The acknowledged achievement of this outstanding heroine in dynastic history was of special value during the Ming, a dynasty in which the cult of female chastity and fidelity was particularly prevalent as well as a period that is usually cited as an exemplary era for the blossoming misogynistic Confucian ethics.[19] Qin Liangyu's entry in the *Mingshi* shows that even in a time of rigid rules designed to regulate women's "proper" behavior, it is still possible for a heroine to cross the boundaries drawn between the genders. Qin Liangyu's mettle had been tested over a long period of time during which she was a wife and then a widow. The recognition of her achievements from the imperial government and the respect she won from the local people demonstrate the space left for a woman outside her home in premodern China; such portrayal thus offers a counterimage to the submissive, passive Chinese woman and defies the generalization of the Confucian ethics as utterly misogynistic.

Like their aforementioned heroic sisters, Lady Xian and Qin Liangyu were introduced to their military careers through family connections: their husbands. Yet when they survived their spouses, both showed martial and strategic skills superior to those of their male contemporaries. Besides being an esteemed military leader, Qin Liangyu proceeded to obtain from the imperial court official titles that are conventionally reserved for men. Thus, her achievements and recognition in history extend the negotiation between a heroine's transgression and the ethical codes defining gender roles from the military into the political arena.

Reducing the Tension, Ensuring the Ethics

In examining historical records of women's involvement in warfare, I find that the potential conflict between the heroines' violation of gender roles and their conformity to Confucian doctrines is often neutralized. Their transgression usually is rooted in central values of Confucian ethics, such as filial piety and loyalty, and occurs in exigent circumstances. Whereas some European amazons and military maids dressed as men to pursue power, individual liberty, true love, or happiness (Wheelwright; Dugaw), the Chinese heroine steps out of the family quarter to fulfill her duty as a daughter, wife, or mother in particular situations. As we have seen in these historical documents, the heroine usually acts outside the conventional scope prescribed for women when she follows her father's way as a filial daughter (for example, Xun Guan and Princess Pingyang), marches toward the combat zone accompanying her husband (for instance, Lady Liang), assists her son in defending the region (like Mrs. Zhu), or takes her deceased husband's place to lead the troops (such as Lady Xian and Qin Liangyu). In this sense, these women's participation in military affairs exemplifies Confucian ethics: they were driven either by their loyalty to the emperor and their husbands or by their filial piety to their fathers. Hence, the heroine has a compelling reason to cross the boundaries between gendered domains; she does not intend to defy conventions as such and thus does not activate the alarm of gender revolution or incur penalty. Only under such "extraordinary" circumstances can a Chinese woman bypass some, if not all, restrictions on her gender.

Various reasons might contribute to these women's entries into the authoritative historical documents. First, some of the women provide moral redemption in times of social upheaval, especially at the end of a dynasty when corruption is widespread and social turmoil is prevalent. For instance, both Lady Liang and Qin Liangyu came of age as renowned heroines at the fall of their respective dynasties—the Song and the Ming—when peaceful civilian life was disturbed and the country was torn apart as a result of constant warfare. "The woman warrior is thereby a moral mirror for the degenerating menfolk. When women are more moral than men, a strong condemnation of the depths of depravity into which society has sunk is implied" (Louise Edwards 103). These women serve as role models for the proper behavior that many of their male contemporaries fail to accomplish. They are seen as the last resort; their unconventional behavior can be viewed as an attempt to "create order out of chaos within the limits of notions of order expected by a Confucian society" (Louise Edwards 104). Although the heroine's courage and heroic deeds do not guarantee her role as savior of the decaying courts,[20] her consistent loyalty as an imperial subject and her dauntless actions as a military combatant make her a role model for both men and women to follow.

The second element that is key to the tolerance and recognition of these women's involvement in military and political life is family lineage. All aforementioned heroines embark on their military voyages while standing by the side of their male kin: father, husband, or son. The men's presence brings the women onto the stage. Moreover, the men's absence (departure or death) enables the women to step further to the center and play a leading role. A woman can obtain a primary position in commanding the troops only in the male commanders' absence. In the cases of Xun Guan, Mrs. Zhu, and Lady Liang, because of the continuous presence of their male kin, women never achieve a role other than an aiding hand. Princess Pingyang acts independently after her husband's departure and resigns from the command post once she reunites with her father, brothers, and husband. The stories of Lady Xian and Qin Liangyu show clearly that both women first assisted their husbands in meaningful ways and began to direct their armies as commanders-in-chief only after their spouses' death.

Important prerequisites of such heroic womanhood are military strategy and fighting skills, probably acquired through family connections; however, the training process and girlhood rearing for these heroines are absent from historical records. Undeniably this absence is partly a consequence of the concise writing style of the Chinese historiographers, yet the entries for male heroes often address training or valiance in childhood. The entry for Han Shizhong, for instance, begins with an introduction to the warrior qualities he exhibited in his youth (Tuotuo, 364: 11355). When the record, however, introduces his wife Lady Liang in the same entry, few traces exist about her besides the two brief events: her drumbeating during a battle and her administrative assistance for the military district. Even in the relatively long record of Qin Liangyu, the heroine's history starts with her marriage rather than with her girlhood. Such representations indicate that these women are not trained to be warriors but rather become heroines in time of need. This "blank page" in historical documents leaves space for literary imagination in subsequent literary texts, theater performances, and storytelling in which the female fighters are depicted as either trained by their male kin or gifted by magical powers.[21] Similar elements appear in the development of Mulan's tale: even though absent in the "Ballad," an imagined training process and colorful plots are added in later variations.

The third shared aspect of women's heroic histories concerns female virtues. The heroines' unconventional behavior within the male territory is often attenuated by the Confucian principles of filial piety and loyalty. Furthermore, none of the military heroines in historical records violates commonly acknowledged female virtues, especially a woman's chastity. For instance, none of the historical chronicles mentions remarriage for widowed leaders. Thus, the principles of female marital fidelity and chaste widowhood are strictly followed in heroic women. Moreover, once the social turmoil or regional security emergency is relieved, the heroine returns to her position as a mother, wife, or daughter—a significant sign of a restored social order. The stories of Xun Guan and Mrs. Zhu end soon after the respective cities are out of danger. Princess Pingyang resigns from her military post once the Tang establishes the new throne. This pattern in historical representations—restoration of the heroines' feminine life as denouement—is shared by many a literary text about courageous women, including variations of Mulan's tale in different genres. As a model heroine, Mulan, too, ends her journey in a male territory and returns to her womanhood as soon as her mission is accomplished.

Collectively these records of women's valiant deeds in authoritative histories formulate a female heroic tradition and provide a window through which the reader is able to reconsider women's status as well as the Confucian ethics in premodern China. This discussion offers just a sample of female participation in military affairs during China's long history. Many other heroines' memorable lives are preserved in local gazetteers, operas, folk stories, and literature. Fictional accounts of military women abound in China. This rich tradition is prevalent in the military romances that proliferated during the Ming and Qing dynasties.[22] As a prominent example, the women generals and soldiers of the Yang family appear in many different genres and are known in virtually every Chinese household.[23] These stories were probably conceived from some historical traces but have been revised in keeping with the ideology of storytellers, writers, and audiences. As a result, more plots and aspects about the characters' military life and personalities appear in written and oral genres, giving the heroines colorful lives. In addition, the anonymous women in military service under the lead of Mrs. Zhu, Princess Pingyang, Qin Liangyu, and throughout China's long history reinforce the notion of heroic womanhood as a noteworthy phenomenon, not a rarity in premodern Chinese culture. In such a lineage the essential balance between a woman's transgression and core Confucian moralities is maintained carefully. In this sense, crossing the boundary between gendered spaces makes a woman heroic while respecting the rules makes her acceptable in Confucian China.

Female Rebels and Bandits: The Counterimage of Mulan

Although taking different political stances from those women generals and soldiers who are loyal subjects of the imperial court, female rebels and bandits involved in uprising represent another type of heroic women who also have influenced the development of Mulan's story in meaningful ways. These female revolutionaries were not fighting for gender equality against the patriarchal social system (as Kingston's book envisions the woman warrior Fa Mu Lan would do), but they took advantage of social upheavals to exert more freedom to move outside the domestic sphere and don battle dress. In these very specific situations, the constraints on women "were temporarily absent or at least relaxed" so that "women [could] be inspired, sometimes driven, to strive for excellence or even to take up roles which were traditionally considered masculine" (Lily Lee 3). In history, a number of women generals and soldiers participated in the Taiping Rebellion (also known as the Heavenly Kingdom,

1851–1864). Affiliated to the Boxer Rebellion in 1900, the women's detachments Red, Blue, and Black Lanterns played significant roles, although those women's individual names hardly survive.[24] In the literary field, female bandits in the Ming novel, *Shuihu zhuan* (The Water Margins, Shi Nai'an, ca. fourteenth century) are probably the most famous fictional characters. Although only Hu Sanniang, Gu Dasao, and Sun Erniang were women among the 108 rebel leaders, their miminal descriptions belie their valuable presence among the bandits, their significant role in the story, and their compelling existence in the novel.

They are usually considered historical figures, but female leaders of uprisings are rarely recorded in historical documents. Numerous stories about their lives and deeds appear in literature, drama, and oral genres. Their unorthodox conduct not only trespasses the boundaries between men and women but also reveals political opposition to the ruling power. Dynastic history neglects these transgressive women probably because of the rebellious nature of their deeds rather than their female identity. One exception, Yang Miaozhen (ca. 1193–1250), appears in historical documents that depict her life as "rich in detail, full of drama and color" (Pei-Yi Wu 138) and paint a heroic image of her character. Her failure to conform to the key female virtue of chastity, however, prevents her from reaching the pantheon of the acclaimed Chinese heroines.

Detailed historical documentation of Yang Miaozhen is found in the entry under the name of her husband Li Quan (ca. 1190–1231) in the section of "panchen zhuan" (biographies of rebellious officials) in the *Songshi*. Presenting a counterimage to several Chinese heroines, Yang Miaozhen's story strikes the reader in three particular aspects: her martial prowess and strategic insight as a military leader, her lack of loyalty to any political power, and her violation of the virtue of female chastity as a woman. Important for a woman's participation in uprisings is her familial connection, for political as well as practical reasons. "The participation of whole families enabled men to share their fate with their wives and children and, moreover, strengthened the rebels' military potential through the inclusion of women" (Ono 7). Although Yang Miaozhen is more subversive than Mulan and the other military heroines, she remains defined by her female roles in the historical record: first, she is a sister, and then she is a wife. The historical account in the *Songshi* introduces her as the younger sister of Yang An'er, a chief insurgent. Identified as Si Niangzi (the Fourth Lady), Yang Miaozhen mounted the stage as a successor to her diseased brother because she was deemed "crafty, valiant, and skillful at horse riding and archery" (Tuotuo, 476: 13818). Although her inheritance of leadership broke conventions because she bypassed Yang An'er's uncle and nephew, Yang Miaozhen's career in arms was still affiliated with her male kin. Shortly afterward, Yang Miaozhen married a man of her own choice, Li Quan. Yang became a primary rebel leader and was entrusted with the crucial mission of guarding their home base of Huaian. Overall the historiographer gives a vivid account of Yang Miaozhen, which to some degree detracts from the record of Li Quan, even though her biography was integrated into her husband's entry.

Yang Miaozhen shifted her relationship to the imperial rule as a result of her family loyalties. She started her military journey as a bandit, but, according to historical records in the *Songshi*, she pursued an alliance with the Song court to fulfill her deceased brother's wish (Tuotuo, 476: 13818–19). Together with her husband Li Quan, Yang Miaozhen vowed allegiance to the Song court in exchange for food subsidy. Thereafter the couple led an armed band that was called "Zhongyi Jun" (loyal and righteous army), and Yang Miaozhen was given the title of *lingren* (Lady) in 1219. This alliance was always precarious and ready to collapse in a shifting political wind. When Li Quan switched his allegiance from the Song to the Yuan a few years later, Yang Miaozhen followed the same path. Shortly after Li Quan's defection to the Yuan in Qing Prefecture in 1227, the Song court cut off its food subsidy to his army. In revenge, Yang Miaozhen plotted the death of the Song overseer in Huaian (Tuotuo, 477: 13837). Li Quan and Yang Miaozhen were loyal to neither the Song nor the Yuan government. It is worth noticing that for Yang Miaozhen every shift of political alliance was preceded by that of her male kin, first her brother and then her husband, although she independently commanded her division most of the time.

Disloyalty relegated Li Quan to the legion of rebellious officials in the *Songshi*; violation of female chastity prevented Yang Miaozhen from joining the ensemble of admirable Chinese heroines. In 1226, when Li Quan was besieged by the Mongols in Yidu, the Song government sent armed forces to take over Huaian. Hopelessly outnumbered and without outside aid, Yang Miaozhen sent a peace-seeking messenger to bribe Xia Quan, a former bandit and current general serving the Song court. Later, she came out of the city to welcome Xia Quan and seduced him into her chamber to spend the night (Tuotuo, 477: 13835). The pressing danger on her city and troops was lifted, but safety exacted a high price: Yang Miaozhen's irredeemable sin as a woman. Adultery in history as well as in literature is "absolutely unforgivable, least of all in a woman warrior" (Pei-Yi Wu 167).

Yang Miaozhen's military career suggests a path that demonstrates a woman's valor throughout girlhood, womanhood, and widowhood, but the act of infidelity to her spouse disqualifies her from becoming a heroine held in high esteem. Thus, the character of Yang Miaozhen provides a counterimage of Mulan in the heroic women typology. Her outspoken threatening in imperial rule and her adultery defy Confucian ethics with respect to political order and gender.[25]

Lady Knights-Errant

In her study on the "dangerous women" of the Ming Dynasty, Victoria Cass uses the phrase "female outsiders" to refer to geishas, grannies, warriors, recluses, and demons who comprise the social outcasts of contemporary Chinese society. She contends that an in-depth examination of these women helps the reader look at the Ming China from the other side of the mirror because the woman outsider, "despite her very unofficial and even heterodox life," has survived with a powerful persistence (Cass xi). Sharing Cass's insight, I examine chivalric ladies as "female outsiders" in premodern Chinese tradition, particularly as opposed to military women who compose the "female insiders" and maintain close ties with the governing court. Female knights-errant, like their male counterparts, often act according to their own system of moral values and codes rather than to Confucianism. Chivalric ladies may hold some familial connections or social affiliations, but they usually do not belong to the mainstream society. Even the female avengers who act on behalf of their families eventually resume their independent agency and disappear into the martial world. Although entangled with the Confucian society, the martial world mainly exists as a subculture beyond the mainstream.

Scattered into different sources, chivalrous ladies form a distinctive institution that stretches across a long time span in premodern China. Although Mulan is not a knight-errant, literary variations of her story often draw inspiration from the extraordinary deeds of lady knights-errant and the stimulating plots that their stories encompass. Some renditions of Mulan's legend in premodern Chinese texts, Kingston's book, children's picture books, as well as film adaptations, have added colorful episodes to portray the heroine's outstanding martial skills, which I explore in more detail in the following chapters. In this sense, the palimpsestic image of Mulan combines military heroines and female chivalry.

To sketch a diverse ancient Chinese culture instead of a unified society encoded by Confucianism, James Liu examines the chivalric tradition in his *The Chinese Knight-Errant* (1967), the first and still most important book-length study of the subject in English. Tracking Chinese knights-errant in history, literature, and theater, Liu suggests that "knight-errantry is a manifestation of the spirit of revolt and nonconformity in traditional Chinese society, sometimes lying underground and sometimes erupting to the surface" (193). Following Liu's lead, the analysis herein sheds more light on "certain heroic, romantic, and individualistic qualities which the common reader would not normally associate with the Chinese" (James Liu xi), least of all with Chinese women. In the following section, my focus is on the *nüxia* (lady knights-errant), as I investigate the link between heroism and womanhood in chivalric narratives.

Chinese knight-errantry appeared no later than the Warring States, an era of social and political chaos as well as a time of unprecedented prosperity among intellectual schools of thoughts. While the Confucian, Daoist, Legalist, and Mohist thinkers preoccupied themselves with arguments about how to redeem the prevailing disordered society through ideological and philosophical reform, "the knights-errant simply took justice into their own hands and did what they thought necessary to redress wrongs and help the poor and the distressed" (James Liu 1). Regarding its initiation in written documents, the term "xia" (knight-errant) first appeared in *Han Fei zi* (Han Fei, d. 233 B.C.). In the chapter, "The Five Vermin," Han Fei states "the Confucians with their learning bring confusion to the law; the knights with their military prowess violate the prohibitions" (*Han Fei zi*; translation Watson 105). He condemned the knights-errant as part of the "five vermin" because they were "noted for their daring and strict code of honor, often acted as local 'bosses' in defiance of the government authorities, guaranteeing protection to people who sought their aid or hiring out their services in the conduct of private vendettas" (*Han Fei zi*; translation Watson 105n5). Later in the same chapter, Han Fei explained that knights-errant as swordsmen "gather bands of followers about them and perform deeds of honor, making a fine name for themselves and violating the prohibitions of the five government bureaus"; they formed an element of the customs of a disordered state (*Han Fei zi*; translation Watson 116, 117). In Han Fei's predominantly negative view, knights-errant disregard official rules and regulations but are admired for their martial skills and personal judgment. From Han Fei's Legalist perspective, the motivation behind their individual actions cannot justify the danger and disorder they represent in a stable society regulated by laws and legistlations.

Han Fei however does not provide a clear definition of the *xia*. Not until more than a century later did Sima Qian outline Chinese chivalry in his influential work *Shiji* (Historical Records): "Now, as for the knights-errant, though their actions were not in accordance with the rules of propriety, they always meant what they said, always accomplished what they set out to do, and always fulfilled their promises. They rushed to the aid of other men in distress without giving a thought to their own safety. And when they had saved someone from disaster at the risk of their own lives, they did not boast of their ability and would have been ashamed to brag of their benevolence" (translation James Liu 14–15). These words show that this great historian gave high marks to swordsmen. In Chinese history, Sima Qian was the first person to articulate a characterization of the *xia* and perhaps also the first to write in a positive tone about the values and codes of chivalry.[26]

In probably the first study of lady chivalry, *Nüxia zhuan* (Biographies of Female Knights-Errant),[27] Zou Zhilin applied a broad notion of knight-errantry to include twenty-eight female figures whom he divided into six categories: "haoxia" (knight-errant of gallantry), "yixia" (knight-errant of righteousness), "jiexia" (knight-errant of integrity), "renxia" (knight-errant of chivalry), "youxia" (knight-errant of wandering), and "jianxia" (knight-errant of swords). Within each category, the author first explains the shared traits and lists his commentaries before depicting selected characters. For instance, in summarizing the virtues of knights-errant of chivalry Zou Zhilin states: "A knight-errant of chivalry utterly hastens to aid others in an emergency without any selfish concern. [She] leaves her life and death out of consideration, which cannot be considered anything else but virtuous" (1054). Then he describes Mulan together with three other characters as prime examples of such chivalrous spirit (Zou Zhilin 1054–56).

Compared to their male counterparts, female knights-errant have been studied by few scholars in China or researchers in Chinese studies outside China.[28] Mentioned in passing sentences and paragraphs lady knights-errant occupy an insignificant portion of Chen Shan and Cao Zhengwen's works. Wang Li's *Zhongguo gudai haoxia yishi* (Ancient Chinese Knights-Errant and Righteous Characters, 1996) devotes a chapter to skilled female figures as well as the view of women among knights-errant. At the beginning of this chapter, Wang Li proposes: "Premodern Chinese viewed and talked about chivalric ladies with an extremely subtle mentality. The existence of chivalric ladies together with related narratives affects the view of women among knights-errant" (134). After briefly discussing selected characters in three broad categories, Wang Li concludes, "the view of women among knights-errant is indeed a contradictory combination of tradition and anti-tradition" (160).

Considering textual representations of women's roles in the Chinese knight-errantry, the story of Yuenü (Maid of Yue) is probably the earliest written example that showcases the exceptional martial skills embodied by a female subject. According to the extant record found in the *Wuyue chunqiu* (Annuals of Wu and Yue, Zhao Ye, fl. 40–80), a book including more fiction than history in spite of its title, the minister Fan Li (fl. 497–465 B.C.) recommended a maiden from the southern woods who was well known for her swordsmanship to Goujian, the king of Yue (d. 465, r. 497–465 B.C.). This maiden, personal name unknown, was then summoned by the king. On her way to the palace, her skills were tested by an ape turned old man. Upon meeting the king, she was entrusted with a position to train the army for the kingdom and was granted the honorary title "Maid of Yue" (Zhao Ye 9: 6a-6b). In my research, Maid of Yue is the only female knight-errant before the Qin and Han period who left behind a written record. Her story represents some important features of lady knights-errant that later became prevailing themes in martial literature. Maid of Yue is self-introduced as an independent agent without family ties: "I was born in the depth of the woods and grew up in the wildness without human company" (Zhao Ye 9: 6a). Her exceptional swordsmanship is either magically gifted or self-taught. By accepting a post from the ruling power, she serves the king and therefore obtains certain social affiliations. James Liu regards Zhao Ye's narrative as "a forerunner of the tales about chivalrous ladies with supernatural powers of the T'ang period" (86). Chinese scholars also have viewed her story as an early example of premodern Chinese martial fiction.

A few stories about female chivalry are scattered in collections of narratives and anecdotes before the Tang Dynasty, for example: *Sou shen ji* (Record of Searching for the Spirit, Gan Bao, fl. 317–322). The characters and episodes in these early narratives, which are generally concise and lack development, have proved to be the precursors of the full-fledged short stories that emerged in the late Tang Dynasty, known as Tang *chuanqi* (tales of marvels); the stories show maturity in terms of characterization and plot development that have far-reaching influence on the short stories and novels that followed them in later periods. This literary era is conventionally considered a crucial stage of Chinese fiction because writers started to take on creative writing with full consciousness (Lu Xun 75) and inspired the themes and narrative structures of the short stories from the Song, Ming, and Qing dynasties. In the Tang collection, the tales about independent swordswomen, enchantresses, and female avengers provide a valuable portion of the colorful literary heritage of female chivalry.[29]

Independent Swordswomen

Different from military heroines who are usually introduced into a narrative through their connection with male kin, lady knights-errant often mount the stage on their own. In particular, the heroines who draw their swords at the sight of injustice to help strangers are the ones to display independence, not only by making their personal judgment and decisions, but also by acting as individuals rather than on behalf of their family or any political power.

The Tang story titled "Chezhong nüzi" (The Woman in the Carriage), for example, features such an independent female knight-errant.[30] The tale is narrated from the perspective of a scholar who went to the capital city for his imperial examination. Invited by two young fellows to a small alley, the scholar had his first encounter with a chivalric lady whose name is never revealed. The story portrays the woman as "about seventeen or eighteen years old, having a charming face with her hair decorated by flowery combs" who arrived in a carriage decorated with golded flowers (Li Fang et al., *Taiping guangji*, 193: 1450). Under the woman's direction, the young fellows, who were probably her disciples, demonstrated their outstanding martial skills. After a few days, the two young fellows borrowed the scholar's horse. The next day, it was heard that the royal palace lost some treasure and the officials had captured only the thieves' horse. As the owner of the horse, the scholar mistakenly was detained and imprisoned in a deep ditch. Feeling hopeless and full of agony, he was surprised by food at lunchtime that was sent down via a rope. At midnight, "something flew down [the ditch] like a bird. Only when it came to his side did the scholar realize it was a person [with a mask]" (Li Fang et al., 193: 1451). The person comforted the scholar, carried him out, and set him free. Upon hearing the voice, the scholar recognized the person as the young woman in the carriage. Surprisingly happy and relieved, the scholar hurried back home.

To weigh the story as a whole, a few details directly portray the woman's martial skills, reminiscent of most Tang tales. The martial performance shown by her disciples in the first part of the story foreshadows the woman's marvelous talent. The rescue of the scholar demonstrates this lady knight-errant's exceptional capability to fly, one of the master skills commonly attributed to Chinese martial artists. Not only does she

FIGURE 2.5. Jing shisanniang shows her finger pointing at a flying sword that is assumingly wielded by her magic power. From Wu Youru, *Wu Youru huabao*, Shanghai: Biyuan huishe, ca. 1909.

fly, but she also performs this feat with the scholar attached to her by a silk rope with which she rescues him from both the deep ditch and the heavily guarded palace and protects him until he was safe to travel alone.

Also found in *Taiping guangji* is a story attributed to Sun Guangxian (d. 968). The story of Jing shisanniang (the Thirteenth Daughter of the Jing Family) starts with the heroine's meeting and then marriage to Zhao Zhongxing after the memorial service in honor of her late husband. At the time, Zhao's friend Li was depressed because his beloved was forced by her parents to marry a person in power who had a bad reputation. Upon hearing this news, Jing was angry and promised Li that she would redress the wrong and reunite the couple marked by true love. She arranged the time and place for Li to wait for his beloved. Then Jing arrived with a bag in which Li's lover was hidden. Jing also delivered to Li the heads of the woman's parents. After that, Jing went away with Zhao and her whereabouts were not known (Li Fang et al., 196: 1472) (see figure 2.5).

The anonymous woman in the carriage and Jing shisanniang are two examples of the acts of chivalric ladies who have neither specific family connections nor clear affiliations to the larger society. Their self-governing actions reflect the spirit of the knight-errant: generosity in helping people in need and drawing their sword against injustice. The main plot of the second story—revenge for Li—shows that Jing acts according to her personal judgment and punishes in the name of social injustice. Because the fighting scene is absent in the narrative, the author describes only the result of Jing's rescue through which her extraordinary courage and martial capability are implied.

Enchantresses

Enchantresses utilize magical power to fulfill their promises or to repay debts of gratitude to friends and patrons. These heroines are limited to some social affiliations for a certain period of time. The special talent that they mysteriously achieve makes their stories charming and exciting. Attributed to Yuan Jiao (fl. 889–903), the story of Hongxian (literally meaning "red thread") portrays a heroine who helped Xue Song, a military commissioner of Lu Prefecture, to avoid regional turmoil (Li Fang et al., 195: 1460–62).[31] At the time, an official named Tian Chengsi recruited troops and was about to annex Lu Prefecture while Hongxian was an entertainer in the Xue household. Seeing Xue Song's worries about the upcoming problem caused by Tian Chengsi, Hongxian offered to go to Tian Chengsi's territory several hundred miles away to investigate. Upon her departure, Hongxian "went into her chamber to adjust traveling tools. [She] combed her hair in a high coil with a gold sparrow-shaped hairpin, dressed in a robe with purple embroidery, wore a pair of light shoes in black, and carried a dagger with carvings of a dragon on her chest" (Li Fang et al., 195: 1461). To Xue Song's astonishment, Hongxian was back within a few hours. The next morning, Xue Song sent a messenger to Tian with a letter and a golden box that Hongxian had retrieved from Tian Chengsi's bedside. Upon receiving them, Tian Chengsi was so scared that instead of undertaking a military attack, he sent fine silk, precious horses, and other valuables to Xue Song to show his respect. Thus, an imminent military conflict was prevented and large-scaled bloodshed was avoided (see figure 2.6).

Shortly after this event, Hongxian asked to leave. Upon her departure, Hongxian confessed to Xue Song that she had been a man in her previous life and traveled widely helping others with his knowledge of

FIGURE 2.6. Hongxian flying across city walls and holding the golden box she retrieved from the enemy's bedside in her right hand. From Wu Youru, *Wu Youru huabao*, Shanghai: Biyuan huishe, ca. 1909.

medicine. At one occasion, a pregnant woman died with her twin fetuses after taking a remedy that he prescribed. Because of this fatal mistake, he was reincarnated and demoted as a woman. Fortunately, Hongxian had been living in the Xue residence and adorned with fine cloth and delicate food around her for nineteen years. Her warning of Tian Chengsi was her way to repay Xue Song's kindness. Because of the peaceful solution of the problem, hundreds of lives were saved from a potential bloody disaster. Hongxian atoned for the crime in her former life and therefore was ready to leave. Xue Song thus hosted a feast of farewell to see her off.

Next, the narrative of Nie Yinniang, with the heroine's name as its title, is credited to Pei Xing (fl. 860–873).[32] Born into an official's family, Nie Yinniang was taken away by a mysterious nun at the age of ten and trained in the mountains for years. Nie Yinniang's appearance is not portrayed directly in the story, but the other two disciples of the nun are described as "clever and lovely" (Li Fang et al., 149: 1457). Upon Nie Yinniang's departure to return home as a grownup, the nun hid a dagger into the back of her head for emergency use. After marrying a man of her own choice (instead of being arranged by her parents), Nie Yinniang first lived with her father's support and then served a general before she met Liu Changyi, a military commissioner of the Defense Command Chenxu. Originally sent by the general to assassinate Liu Changyi, Nie Yinniang was grateful for Liu Changyi's hospitable treatment even though he foresaw her mission. Thereafter she served Liu Changyi with loyalty and gratitude, protecting him from danger. Not until Liu Changyi was about to take a position in the capital city did Nie Yinniang decide to leave, and she asked Liu Changyi to support her husband financially. She disappeared for years until Liu Changyi died in his position as commander-general. Nie Yinniang, showing no signs of aging at all, rode a donkey to the capital and wept by Liu Changyi's coffin. A few years later, Liu Changyi's son ran into her on the road, and she gave him a pill that would protect him from danger for one year. From that time, nobody ever saw her again.

The tale of Nie Yinniang differs from its predecesors and contemporaries in various aspects. First, it is longer and more detailed, relating how the nun trained her in martial and magical arts. This is quite unusual since the training process never features in other heroines' stories. For example, women like Hongxian act with extraordinary capability, as if it were a born gift, and enter the stage already as skillful fighters. Nie's story starts with her at a young age and chronicles the process by which she grows into a marvelous enchantress. Her story sets up an example for later fiction writers to follow: a chivalrous lady's tale incorporates a training scene. Second, abundant magical and shamanistic elements besides martial arts enter Nie's story: when Nie begins her training, the nun gives her a pill to help her fly; the nun also uses certain medicine that turns a human head into water; Nie fights against assassins to protect Liu Changyi mainly by employing magic power; and the incredible fact that she never ages once she reaches adulthood suggests magical intervention as well. This pattern of a heroine being a gifted enchantress also finds its way into later transformations of Mulan's tale in which storytellers and writers incorporate magical elements to enrich the plots. For example, in the Qing novel, *Zhong xiao yong lie qinü zhuan* (The Legend of An Extraordinary Girl Who Is Loyal, Filial, Courageous, and Illustrious), the protagonist Mulan inherits the heavenly edict from her grandfather while her supernatural talent is acquired through magical powers displayed in military confrontations.

Female Avengers

As important as it was to apply the code of justice based on their own judgment and to serve friends and patrons, chivalrous women also launched their own missions, sword in hand, to avenge their families. One such example is the story of Cui Shensi's wife that is conventionally attributed to Huangpu Shi (Li Fang et al., 194: 1456).[33] Cui Shensi, a scholar, went to the capital city for the imperial examinations where he married a woman and lived in her household for two years. The woman was a devoted partner who supported the family, took care of the household chores, and gave him a son. Yet she never revealed her name to Cui. One night when Cui woke up, his wife was not by his side. Cui was surprised and suspected that his wife might be having an affair. As he went out to the yard to check, he "suddenly saw the woman leap down from the roof, wearing a robe of white silk, a sharp dagger in her right hand and a human's head in the left" (Li Fang et al., 194: 1456). The woman told Cui that her father was unjustly murdered, and it took her several years before she finally found the opportunity to avenge his death by chopping off his foe's head. Now that she had paid the debt, she had to leave. She would entrust the house, two maids, and other properties to Cui. After these arrangements were made, the woman leapt back up onto the roof and disappeared into the darkness. Before Cui got over his astonishment, the woman came back, saying that she wanted to nurse her baby one last time. After she left again, Cui went inside only to find out that the baby was killed. The ending of the story might look shockingly cruel to modern readers, but the idea of relinquishing one's personal attachments was taken as a virtue in the chivalric codes of that time. At the end of the story, the author added his commentary that praised the woman's actions that hardly were exceeded by those of male knights-errant in the ancient tradition.

A very similar story titled "Guren qi" (Merchant's Wife) and attributed to Xue Yongruo (fl.821–835) also has been collected in *Taiping guangji* (Li Fang et al., 196: 1472–73). Except for the storylines that the husband is an official named Wang Li, the enemy's head is put in a leather bag, and the beautiful woman identifies herself as a widow of a merchant, the core storylines and main plots are identical to the story of Cui Shensi's wife. In both stories, the leading character—an anonymous woman—spends two years living with a partner whom she chooses for herself. Underneath the surface of their happy and peaceful life, she is waiting for the right moment to take revenge for the injustice undertaken against her family. When this mission is accomplished, the swordswoman kills her baby to eliminate any possible connection that might lure her to come back. Even though the fighting scene is omitted in the narrative, the heroine's extraordinary martial skills are left to the readers' imagination, with a hint in the portrayal of her flying across roofs and walls and landing with the foe's head in her hand.

Attributed to Li Gongzuo (fl. ca. 763– ca. 859), another Tang story portrays Xie Xiao'e, who avenged her deceased father and husband (Li Fang et al., 491: 4030–32). Even though Xie was not a martial artist, her story is usually considered a knight-errant tale, given her chivalrous spirit. The story emphasizes her courage and determination to avenge the wrongs to her family and to punish the vermin. Xie started her chivalrous journey after her father and husband, along with other family members and ser-. vants, were murdered in a robbery that she alone survived. After solving the puzzle about the names of the foes (that is, two men who are cousins) from a dream, she traveled in male attire and stayed for years at one enemy's household in disguise, working as a servant. When the proper opportunity finally came, she killed the foes and turned herself in to the court. She was released and later became a Buddhist nun.

The narratives of lady knights-errant taking action on behalf of their kin are often involved in personal vendettas, a favorite theme in martial fiction. An examination of these heroines further supports the validity of such paradigms as filial daughters and loyal wives because they "uphold the ideal of filiality" or "fight for their husbands' causes" (Mou xxi). As we have seen from the examples above, redressing the wrongs done to their families plays a crucial role in the stories of some chivalrous ladies. This type of heroine acts single-handedly and individually, but the heroines by and large take up swords on behalf of their clans. Such motivations indicate the social and familial connections that these women have for a certain period of time before they cut off the bonds entirely and disappear into the martial world.

The swordswomen, who are able to fly over roofs, create a popular image for martial novels in the Ming and Qing dynasties. Their influence has reached as far as modern martial fiction as well as kung fu films. In Ang Lee's Academy Award winning feature film *Crouching Tiger, Hidden Dragon* (2000), for instance, all three heroines (Biyan huli, Yu Xiulian, and Yu Jiaolong, known respectively as Jade-Fox, Yu, and Jen in English subtitles) are endowed with the ability to fly. The new recruits' training sequence and the duel between Mulan and Shanyu in the Forbidden City in Disney's animated feature film *Mulan* show obvious traces from such influence. Chinese American girls like Maxine Hong Kingston growing up in Chinatown in the United States have learned about the heroine who "had to rage across all China . . . [and] got even with anybody who hurt her family" (Kingston, *Woman Warrior*, 19). In the Hong Kong movies at the Confucius Church from noon to midnight on Sundays young Kingston and her siblings saw "swordswomen jump[ing] over houses from a standstill; they didn't even need a running start" (Kingston, *Woman Warrior*, 19). These films, together with her mother's stories night after night, blurred the lines between stories and dreams and inspired the colorful plots in *The Woman Warrior*.

At first glance, female knights-errant seem to be the opposite of women in the military services. The heroines in armed services hold a clear political stance vis-à-vis the ruling power in the form of support (when they are women generals and soldiers of the imperial court) or of revolt (in the case of female bandits and rebels). Moreover, military women's careers are usually closely tied to their male family members and relatives. It is true that valiant women in the martial world, by and large, take up swords by their own initiative and operate as individuals. Yet an inquiry into their motivations suggests another "appropriation of family ethics" (Mou xxiii). These "seemingly unconventional women, who perform most 'unwomanly' actions on battlefields and in revenge cases, paradoxically turn out to promote the most basic literati ethics of loyalty, filiality, integrity, and righteousness (*zhong xiao jie yi*)" (Mou xxiii). For chivalrous ladies like Hongxian, loyalty is shifted from the emperor or a political authority to one's friends or patrons. The revenge stories particularly highlight the extension of family loyalty, in which chivalrous ladies draw their swords on behalf of their clan and take action to redress mostly personal and familial injustices. For such heroines, filial duty remains a guiding principle in their actions, for which they sometimes do not hesitate to sacrifice the happiness of their current lives. In this sense, images of women knights-errant have "become some of the most efficient preachers of literati morality" (Mou xxiii), through filling up the pages of literary texts and lighting up the theatre.

The Myth of Gender: Heroic Women in Confucian China

In these stories of Chinese heroines, conflicting representations of gender identity coexist: one kind of protagonist appears as an "honorary man," and her female identity is neutralized or omitted; the other type is a heroine whose femininity is highlighted and whose image is sexualized. In general, historical records of military women tend to document the heroines' "male talent" without stressing their femininity while chivalric tales usually emphasize the main characters' gender identity and feminine beauty.[34]

In the aforementioned entries found in dynastic histories, military women are recorded mostly as honorary men. The historiographer's narrative by and large focuses on the specific circumstance that validates a woman's involvement in military affairs and the achievements that the heroine acquires. Her female gender is nonetheless downplayed. With the exception of Yang Miaozhen, whose record mentions her "dressing up gorgeously and coming out to meet [Xia Quan]" (Tuotuo, 477: 13835), none of the previously discussed entries emphasizes the gender identity of the female combatants. After the opening lines that introduce the character as a daughter, mother, or wife, in the narrative the historiographer portrays the character as a courageous hero or a dutiful service "man" rather than as an extraordinary woman. The heroine's femininity, an obvious anomaly in the combat zone, is never questioned or brought to the readers' attention.[35] This phenomenon might suggest a common method for historiographers to evade defiance of the social morality regarding gender identity at the time. As we have seen in their stories, military women transgress the boundaries mostly for valid reasons. Once outside, they become honorary men and are therefore judged by criteria usually applied to their male contemporaries. In such historical representations, military heroines' considerable victories in the battleground tend to overshadow their female identity.

The description of the feminine that is omitted in historical records, however, is imagined and emphasized in literary renditions. In both oral genres and literary texts a heroine's feminine beauty is often in the spotlight. Compared to their male counterparts, heroic women's popularity, at least partially, can be attributed to the sexual titillation embedded in her femininity. Chivalrous ladies portrayed in the Tang stories, for instance, never lack femininity. "These heroines, drawn from legends as well as from semihistorical sources, share certain outstanding traits: They are gifted in martial skills, exceptionally valorous, loyal, and endowed with charm and grace" (Hung 161–62). Besides being well versed in swordsmanship and sometimes gifted with magical powers, they are remarkably wise and charming. Being expert fighters does not necessarily make them rough amazons; instead, more often than not these swordswomen "retain their feminine charms" (James Liu 205). There are a few exceptions, but female leaders and swordswomen are commonly portrayed in terms of their outward glamor. Although dynastic histories and local gazetteers seldom provide any indication of the heroines' appearance, their names have become part of the repertoire among the illustrated collections of beauties.

Femininity becomes a crucial point in understanding the heroic womanhood. Such sexualization of warrior women holds great significance in two ways. First, "the notion that the female swordswomen are fantastic and supernatural provides . . . new fictional excitement to an audience already well prepared for the female warriors" (Louise Edwards 109). It explains why their stories continue to find favor with Chinese writers, storytellers, and audiences. Their tales continue to be a delight in fiction and drama, not because they tell of unusual deeds but because they tell of extraordinary women. Second, the emphasis on the protagonists' gender identity ensures the ethical codes of Confucian China. Outstanding as these heroic women might be, the glory of their transgressions, bound with temporality, must be modified and redeemed. The heroine's potential to disrupt the gender order of Chinese society is dismissed when she retreats from the male territory and returns to her womanly life. As a model of upholding filial piety, loyalty, and female chastity, the heroine is thus remembered fondly and praised by her contemporaries as well as by later generations. Historical and literary renditions that document female participation in the military and martial arenas show both resistance and endorsement to the Confucian ethics. Heroines in historical and fictional texts therefore diversify the image of women in Confucian China. Their existence rebukes any simple understanding of Chinese women as exclusively pathetic victims and of the denouncement of Confucianism for its treatment of "the second sex." Indeed, the discussion here shares similar concerns with current analyses of the interplay between feminism and Confucianism in analyzing Chinese women (Chenyang Li; Rosemont; Terry Woo; Tu Wei-ming, "Probing"). I do not intend to defend Confucianism against the accusation that this philosophical tradition has laid the foundation for the ideological and social attitudes and practices that comprise the long oppressive history of Chinese women. Historical and literary representations of heroic women, however, reveal that the complexity within the Confucian ethics has left room for women; moreover, their persistent appearance complicates the social morality regarding gender in premodern China. The stories of female heroism collectively represent what Dorothy Ko calls the "inherent conceptual ambiguity" in Confucian society (*Teacher of the Inner Chambers*, 145).

Through analyzing documents about women fighters in dynastic histories and chivalrous tales, this chapter outlines the cultural history of Chinese heroic womanhood that has fostered the phenomenal palimpsest of Mulan's tale that is now embraced by an international audience and stands as a paradigm. Valiant women in Confucian China who crossed gender boundaries demonstrate that Mulan's enduring growth derives from a rich cultural milieu of heroic women. Her story thus is cultivated out of a heroine tradition and has undergone a process of development in premodern China long before she embarked on a cross-cultural journey to North America.

3 /   From a Courageous Maiden in Legend
to a Virtuous Icon in History

The feet of a male rabbit were leaping.
The eyes of a female rabbit were bleary.
When the two walk side by side,
How can you tell the one from the other!

—"BALLAD OF MULAN"

For folk stories that often first take shape in oral tradition, a tale's transformation into literary form requires careful analysis "not only of the
tale itself, but also of the motives and values of those responsible for its
metamorphosis" (Hallett and Karasek 17). The legend of Mulan is such a
tale. Between the globalized and animated reconfiguration presented by
Disney and its accredited Chinese source, "Ballad of Mulan," stand numerous variations. This chapter investigates what "metamorphosis" the
character Mulan and her story have undergone in China and how these
changes are conditioned by different motives, values, and circumstances. Because some necessary links in the chain of narratives are missing,
the development of Mulan's tale hardly can be laid out on a continuous linear path or be substantiated with solid evidence at every stage.
Despite these limitations, multiple layers of Mulan's story in different
genres are available to the reader; together with literary allusions, commentaries, intellectuals' short essays,[1] and critical explorations, these
variations make it possible to trace this story's inheritance and transformation from one generation to the next until its ultimate recognition as
a distinctive cultural phenomenon. By the nineteenth century, writers
and storytellers idealized Mulan to be a virtuous icon. From the Song
Dynasty until today, different regions in China have claimed her as a
local heroine. Questionable as their historicity and validity may be, the
documents preserved in the local gazetteers and tablet inscriptions suggest the ways in which such a transformation occurred. In the twentieth
century, this character was pressed into national service when China's

anti-Japanese war efforts employed adaptations of Mulan's story in the 1930s. Opera repertoires in various Chinese regions continue to reimagine this character to exemplify women's abilities and equal rights. All of these narratives add more complexity to Mulan's palimpsestic image and indicate that the character's metamorphosis predates her cross-cultural journey, Americanization, and globalization. In my discussion on literary variations, I emphasize two processes: how the literary imagination enriches Mulan's tale by expanding her story from a narrative lyric of three-hundred–odd words to plays, chapters of novels, book-length novels, opera performances, screen plays, and films; and how the heroine comes to embody varied moral values as she is transformed from a courageous legendary maiden to an illustrious historical figure.

Mulan's Possible Non-Han Origin

Mulan's tale has been neither static nor consistent over the long centuries in China. Instead, it has undergone many changes and has been enriched by historical conjecture and literary imagination. Although there has been uncertainty with regards to the inception of Mulan's story, scholars and writers generally refer to the anonymous folk ballad, titled "Mulan shi" ("Ballad of Mulan"), as the source that had crystallized the possible early circulation of the story in oral tradition, the forbearer of all succeeding variations and interpretations, and the foundation of the heroine's fame.

It is believed that the earliest text of the "Ballad" was collected in the *Gujin yuelu* (Musical Collection Ancient and Present, compiled ca. 568). Unfortunately, this anthology has been lost for centuries. Little is known about the editor Zhijiang except that he was a Buddhist monk who lived around the period of the Chen Dynasty (557–588). Verification of the ballad's inclusion and the anthology's existence depends on later sources that refer to both. From the thirteenth to the nineteenth centuries, many scholars mentioned the *Gujin yuelu* in their respective works.[2] If the dating information found in these sources is accurate and the "Ballad" indeed was anthologized in this musical collection, then the "Ballad" should have existed in written form by the sixth century. The exact date of the emergence of the "Ballad" has prompted many studies among Chinese scholars from the premodern period until the present,[3] beginning no later than the early twelfth century when Pan Zimu (fl. 1196, *Ji zuan yuan hai*, vol. 39, in *Siku Quanshu*) dated the "Ballad" to the Jin Dynasty (317–439).[4] This idea later is echoed by a number of scholars.[5]

Another group of authors view the "Ballad" as a work from a later time, around the Liang Dynasty (502–557).[6] Scholars in modern China continue this research, but opinions diverge:[7] most scholars generally agree on the the ballad's inception and recording during the Northern Dynasties (386–581).[8]

This time period associates the "Ballad" with the particular cultural background of the Northern Dynasties and, more important, points to the possibility that the story could have come out of a non-Han Chinese tradition; that is, the character Mulan probably has a foreign origin at the earliest stage of her literary journey. The collapse of the Han Dynasty in the year 220 was followed by three centuries of bitter civil wars, unstable governments, and frequent invasions, which brought tremendous disaster to the Chinese people. In the fourth century, northern China was repeatedly attacked by foreign tribes and experienced almost constant warfare, anarchy, and devastation before the Tuoba clan (also known as Toba) of the Xianbei people (also known as Sienpi) established a unified regime in the year 386. This regime became the Northern Wei (386–534), a dynasty in imperial China whose central government was in the hands of a foreign people instead of the Han nationality. The Xianbei had been a northern nomadic people, and their women were skilled at horse riding and archery. The Northern Wei government conducted several large-scale wars against the Rouran (also known as Ruru), another northern people living around the areas of present-day Mongolia. Representation in the "Ballad" of the masculine spirit as a characteristic of northern women resembles some northern folk songs that portray heroic women as skilled archers and horse riders, for example: *"Li Bo xiaomei ge"* ("Ballad of Li Bo's Younger Sister"). If the "Ballad" came from a similar background, the story of Mulan's excellence in serving the army resonates with the experience of real tribe women. In her study of the "Ballad" published in German, Margaret Barthel calls it "a genuine northern ballad" (462). The style and contents of the "Ballad" indeed reveal its folk origin probably from a non-Han Chinese tribe.

"Ballad of Mulan"

Jiji, sigh! Jiji, sigh![9]
Mulan was weaving facing the door.
The sound of the loom couldn't be heard.
There was only the sigh from her.

What was she thinking of?

What was she recalling?
"I had nothing to think of.
I had nothing to recall.

Last night I saw the military conscription.
Khan was drafting soldiers.
There were twelve military rolls.
My father's name was listed in each of them.

My father had no first-born son.
Mulan had no elder brother.
I would like to purchase horse and saddle
And starting now take my father's place to go on a military
    expedition."

At the eastern market she bought a fine horse,
At the western market she bought a saddle,
At the southern market she bought a bridle,
And at the northern market she bought a long horsewhip.

At daybreak she bid farewell to her parents.
At dawn she camped at the side of the Yellow River.
She couldn't hear her parents' voice calling their daughter.
The only sound in her ears was the water of the Yellow River
    flowing.

At daybreak she left the Yellow River.
At dawn she arrived at the Black Mountain.
She couldn't hear her parents' voice calling their daughter.
The only sound in her ears was the barbarian horse neighing at the
    Yan Mountain.

They ran thousands of miles to cast hundreds into battle.
They crossed mountain passes as if they were flying.
The northern air sent forth the sound of the watchman's metal
    clapper.
The chilly light shone on their metal armor.
The general died after a hundred battles.
And the warriors returned home after ten years.

Mulan was presented in front of the Emperor after coming back
    from the battlefield.
The Emperor sat in the imperial court.

She was honored with a dozen meritorious contributions
And was bestowed riches abundant.

Khan asked for her wishes.
Mulan said: "I have no need for the position of Shangshulang;
And would like to ride the fastest camel
That could take me back to my hometown."

When her parents heard of their daughter's coming back,
They set out along the city walls supporting each other.
When her elder sister heard of the sister's coming back,
She hurriedly tidied her clothes and put on makeup in front of the
    door.
When her younger brother heard of the sister's coming back,
He sharpened a knife quickly, and turned towards their pigs and
    goats.

"I opened the door of my boudoir to the east,
Sat on my bed in the room to the west,
Took off my battle robe,
Put on my old dress,
Facing the window I combed my hair into the cloud hairstyle,
And hanging up my mirror, applied makeup to my face."

Mulan went out to see her fellow soldiers.
They were all astonished.
"We spent twelve years fighting together,
But didn't know that Mulan was a woman."

The feet of a male rabbit were leaping.
The eyes of a female rabbit were bleary.
When the two walk side by side,
How can you tell the one from the other!
(Guo Maoqian 309)

The "Ballad" is composed in the form of *yuefu* (also spelled as *yüeh-fu*),
which comes from folk tradition. "It was during the Han that a distinction began to be made between lyric verse (*shih*) and the ballad (*yüeh-fu*).
The term *yüeh-fu* (music office) was said to have originated as the name
of an official agency, first set up during the Ch'in dynasty, whose duty
was to collect folk-songs to enable the government to gauge the mood of
the people from them" (Frodsham xxxvii). Because these songs are products of people's collective wisdom and talent and usually circulate first in

an oral tradition, the music office attributes anonymity to their author-ship. During the process of collecting, recording, anthologizing, editing, and copying the music office might have altered or polished some songs; however, most works still preserve the spontaneity and closeness to spo-ken language akin to the folk tradition. "These songs became known as *yüeh-fu,* and the same name continued to be used after the abolition of the Music Bureau in 6 B.C. The term *yüeh-fu* was also applied to poems written by men of letters in the style of the anonymous *yüeh-fu* songs" (Frankel, *Flowering Plum,* 216). The earliest extant version of the "Bal-lad" appears in a Song Dynasty collection, *Yuefu shiji* (Collection of Yuefu Poems), compiled by Guo Maoqian (fl. 1264–1269). Under the title *"Mulan shi ershou"* ("Ballad of Mulan: Two Poems") are the anonymous folk "Ballad" and an imitative poem composed by Wei Yuanfu (d. 771), a Tang official. The editor's note to the "Ballad" points to the *Gujin yuelu* as Guo Maoqian's source from which the "Ballad" is anthologized. It also states: "Mulan, name unknown" (Guo Maoqian 309). The poem's pos-sible appearance in a musical collection and its inclusion in Guo Mao-qian's anthology suggest that at the beginning the ballad was probably a non-Han Chinese folk song.

The *Yuefu shiji,* one of the most important collections of *yuefu* poems in Chinese literature, consists of one hundred volumes, including folk songs as well as verses composed by men of letters in the form of *yuefu* from the predynastic period of Yao, Shun, and Yu to the Five Dynasties (907–960). Guo Maoqian's anthology classifies the poems into twelve categories according to their styles, social functions, and places of pro-duction. The "Ballad" in this anthology has been cited repeatedly in vari-ous poetry collections and literary studies after the thirteenth century and has become the best-known version of the poem. In the *Yuefu shiji* the "Ballad" is identified as a *guci* (ancient ballad) and included in the category of *gu jiao hengchuiqu* (songs that are accompanied by drums, horns, and horizontal flutes). The editor Guo Maoqian introduces this particular category as works "used in military services and played on horseback" (259). These songs are believed to have been imports from *xiyu* to imperial China during the reign of Emperor Han Wu (156–87 B.C.; r. 141–87 B.C.).[10] Most music scores were lost after the Han Dynasty; yet, the lyrics were preserved in written words. In Guo Maoqian's an-thology, most songs accompanied by drums, horns, and horizontal flutes originate in the north and depict the northern peoples' nomadic life and portraying warfare. Some of these folk songs first appeared in foreign languages among the northern tribes and then were translated into traditional Chinese; others were composed in Chinese language to depict the northern life and spirit (Yu Guanying 10). It is unclear whether the "Ballad" was originally written in one of the foreign languages and underwent a process of translation in ancient China or was produced in traditional Chinese. However, Guo Maoqian's classification further validates the poem's likely non-Han origin from northern China.

As a masterpiece of the early *yuefu* songs, the "Ballad" is predominantly narrative in nature and represents some typical characteristics of a rhymed folk song. Works coming out of folk tradition *yuefu* songs usually include neither the personal nor the egocentric thrust of the "typical lyric poem"; instead, the narrative tends to focus on one or more key episodes with abrupt changes of time and location. "The oldest *yüeh-fu* were transmitted orally, and throughout its history this poetic form kept some features that are bound up with its musical, illiterate origins. The diction of *yüeh-fu* remained simpler, closer to the spoken idiom, and freer form learned allusions" (Frankel, *Flowering Plum*, 217). The "Ballad" opens in Mulan's family compound, but the setting quickly changes to the market as the heroine purchases equipment and prepares for her enlistment. Then the sound and image of the Yellow River, Yan Mountain, and barbarian horses bring the narrative to the frontiers in a rapid pace before the main character's appearance in the imperial court and homecoming. These abrupt changes of location imply the passing of time. After all, Mulan and her fellow companions cannot run "thousands of miles to cast hundreds into battle" and cross "mountain passes as if they were flying" within days or months. The heroine's changing gender role from a daughter to a soldier as well as the many years of her military career are compressed succinctly within a few stanzas. The key episode is Mulan's successful return: to the imperial court, to her family, and to her womanly life.

As a *yuefu* song that probably has gone through a process of collecting, recording, and editing by persons of letters, the "Ballad" expresses a combination of northern lifestyle and the influence from Han Chinese convention. In history, under the rule of Emperor Xiaowen (467-499; r. 471–499), the Northern Wei government implemented a series of policies that encouraged the nomadic Tuoba clan to assimilate with the Han nationality: for example, the Tuoba people moved the capital city southward to Luoyang, implemented the official ranking system from the Han Chinese court, and adopted Han Chinese clothing. The "Ballad" reflects such a social blending of different ethnic traditions through the heroine's ability to perform feminine duty at home as well as to wield masculine prowess in the frontiers. The "Ballad" opens and closes with the image of Mulan in female garments within the domestic space: as a weaver at the opening and as a daughter at the end. According to Francesca Bray, "womanhood in early imperial China was defined by the making of cloth: with a few rare exceptions, a weaver was by definition a woman, and a woman was by definition a weaver" (115–16). Indeed, Mulan's first appearance in the "Ballad" conforms to the gender division of labor in ancient China—*nan geng nü zhi* (men tilling the farm and women weaving the cloth). As a woman, the heroine is where she is supposed to be (at home) and does what she is supposed to do (weaving cloth) before the plot of the warrior-Mulan unfolds.

The tranquility of the weaving scene that opens the poem's narrative, nonetheless, is quickly disrupted by Mulan's thoughts, expressed by her sigh. The anomaly of that sound—a sigh instead of the sound of the loom—introduces a twist to the storyline. The third stanza explains the problem that worries Mulan: the order of recruitment issued by the ruler. To solve the dilemma represented by the military conscription for her elderly father who has no grown son to stand in on his behalf, Mulan decides to take her father's place and join the army. When the "Ballad" introduces the conflict, it states, in the voice of the main character: "Last night I saw the military conscription. Khan was drafting soldiers." The usage of the Altaic title Khan instead of emperor again suggests the possible non-Han origin of the poem. The "Ballad" uses both "Khan" and "Emperor" when the protagonist ends her military expedition with glory: "The Emperor sat in the imperial court. . . . Khan asked for her wishes." The inconsistency could be either a result of retelling and copying over the years or an indication of a literary person's modification while recording the folk song in written words, perhaps for the purpose of creating a rhyme that makes a smooth reading.

Although the theme of cross-dressing plays a significant role in the enduring popularity of Mulan's story, one might argue that the heroine's femininity is underscored in the "Ballad." As a matter of fact, Mulan's resorting to male attire is neither directly portrayed in the "Ballad," nor is her cross-dressing made explicit before and during her military life. Instead, as Mulan prepares for her adventure, the poem lists a series of objects with regard to horseback riding: "a fine horse," "a saddle," "bridle," and "a long horsewhip." The list of items usually associated with masculinity produces enough ambiguity for later generations to explore. Although the story's subsequent incarnations feature a variety of imaginative subplots around the character's transformation from a weaving maiden to a valiant warrior, the "Ballad" does not deal with this transformation directly until her homecoming.

Once the heroine steps beyond the threshold of her home, the narrative ignores the details of her life in disguise and her martial performance on horseback and focuses instead on sharp contrasts of space (domestic versus the Yellow River, the Yan Mountain, and the Black Mountain), time (daybreak versus dawn), and voice (her parents' voice calling their daughter versus river flowing and barbarian horse neighing) that indicate the passing of time, shifting of location, and Mulan's connection to her parents. The family tie underscores Mulan's position as a child/daughter even when she is far away from home in a harsh military expedition. Repeatedly using the word *nü* (daughter) to refer to Mulan, this stanza reaffirms her female identity in the military camps. Several times the "Ballad" uses *ye* and *niang*, common spoken terms referring to father and mother. In the imitative poem composed by Wei Yuanfu, however, the references to Mulan's parents are the literary and formal *fu* and *mu*. While the "Ballad" does not specify against whom Mulan and her fellow combatants fight, authors from later periods provide a variety of enemy troops. In his play, *Ci Mulan tifu congjun* (Female Mulan Joined the Army Taking Her Father's Place), Xu Wei (1521–1593) imagines the heroine participating in battles to quell a group of insurgents. Chu Renhu (fl. 1675–1695) creates a few chapters in the novel, *Sui Tang yanyi* (Historical Romance of the Sui and Tang Dynasties), in which Mulan is fighting against the invading Turks. In this sense, when Maxine Hong Kingston talks about Mulan's combat against the Mongols in an interview with Bill Moyers for PBS or the Disney's Studio portrays the war between China and the Huns, these contemporary versions add to the already complex palimpsestic collage of Mulan's tale.[11]

The middle stanza of the "Ballad" conveys the hardship the servicemen confronted at the frontiers and addresses the heroine's long military career within a few couplets.[12] In his writing on Chinese literary history, Hu Shi has pointed out that during the Northern Dynasties "the new peoples of the north encouraged a military spirit and were fond of bravery and therefore the folk literature of the north naturally carries such a heroic quality" (67). He further proposes that the "Ballad" is the most magnificent masterpiece of the northern folk literature whose "unique color is the hero, the vehement and fearless hero" (Hu Shi 67, 73). The narrative of the protagonist's experience in the armed forces, condensed into just a few dozen words, reflects such northern spirit. In the lines re-

FIGURE 3.1. Mulan dressed in military attire, holding a bow, and standing by her horse. From Wu Youru, *Wu Youru huabao*, Shanghai: Biyuan huishe, ca. 1909.

counting the heroine's martial career, neither her disguise nor any fierce confrontation on the battlefield is underscored.

Rather, the theme of cross-dressing is expressed explicitly for the first time when the heroine returns home, removes her masculine garments, re-dresses in female attire, and presents herself as a young woman to her dumbfounded companions.[13] Mulan's earlier adoption of male costume unfolds in retrospect through the restoration of her female identity, as it is depicted in the following lines, narrated by the heroine herself:

> "I opened the door of my boudoir to the east,
> Sat on my bed in the room to the west,
> Took off my battle robe,
> Put on my old dress,
> Facing the window I combed my hair into the cloud hairstyle,
> And hanging up my mirror, applied makeup to my face."

Mulan's re-dressing is portrayed in details, particularly through a series of actions—"to open," "to sit," "to take off," "to put on," "to comb," "to hang up," and "to apply" and a list of feminine objects: dress, cloud hairstyle, mirror, and makeup. Even though the "Ballad" provides no indication of the heroine's appearance, Mulan is endowed with feminine beauty in the imaginations of other writers and readers. Similar to the stories of many heroic women discussed in chapter 2, Mulan's beauty becomes another favorite topic for later legacies to expand and to build on (see figure 3.1).[14]

Mulan's decline of the official rank and benefits bestowed on her by the emperor leads directly to her return home and the restoration of her female identity. In fact, it is hard to imagine the heroine's destiny in the official post of Shangshulang (secretarial court gentleman), whether remaining in disguise or revealing her female nature. Chapter 2 discussed two historical cases in which women took official titles from the imperial government. Both Lady Xian and Qin Liangyu served the emperor in warfare and civil administration, but neither of them ever served the ruler in the imperial court standing side by side with their male counterparts. They started their military career as wives and continued as widows. In the case of Mulan, an unmarried maiden, returning to her life as a daughter is essential to balance her transgression of defying the social norms and to assure her future of becoming a wife and mother. Disarming the Amazon is a necessary denouement for the heroine to become an appreciated warrior without activating the alarms of a social revolution.[15]

To sum up, the "Ballad" is probably a legend derived from the tribal life of a northern people, most likely a folk story rather than a historical narrative. It is also possible that people have combined elements from different stories to create the character Mulan—a courageous daughter who once took her father's place in the combat zone or a bold woman who once served in disguise in the armed forces. I concur with Yu Guanying and other scholars that the "Ballad" probably originated as a folk song among a foreign people or a few peoples living in northern China, was later recorded in written words by literate persons, perhaps polished, and then collected in various anthologies. Thus, the "Ballad," as the widely acknowledged origin of Mulan's story, likely has traveled across cultures from a non-Han folk tradition to Chinese literature early in the evolution of this character, hundreds of years before her story embarked on an international journey to the United States and then the global market.

Idealization of Mulan

The first important wave of the influence of the "Ballad" in literature occurred in the Tang Dynasty, a prosperous age of Chinese poetry and prose, as well as a period in which literary persons unpacked the moral values within Mulan's story as they developed her character into an idealized heroine. Several poems modeled on or alluding to the "Ballad" appeared during this era. The most prominent example is the aforementioned imitative poem, written by Wei Yuanfu who served the Tang court in different official posts during his lifetime.[16] In addition to appearing in Guo Maoqian's anthology right after the "Ballad" (310), this poem is also anthologized under the title "Mulan ge" ("Song of Mulan") in the *Quan Tang shi* (Complete Collection of Tang Poems, 3055). It is considered a *nizuo*, a piece modeling the manner or content of a certain author or work, because it primarily imitates the composition form of the "Ballad" and repeats the narrative episodes. The highly polished writing style distinguishes it as a work of literate origin, as opposed to the "Ballad" that derives from folk tradition. Although commentators and scholars in later periods acknowledge the existence of Wei Yuanfu's poem, few people show interest in studying it.[17]

Wei Yuanfu's work contributes to the development of Mulan into a model heroine and the growth of her story by adding details that enhance the drama and underscore her virtues of filial piety and loyalty. The beginning of his poem portrays Mulan's father as not only old but also suffering from a serious illness when the recruitment order arrives. In addition, the couplets portray the extremely harsh environment in the frontier waiting for the enlisted men:

> The sand in the north submerges the horses' hoofs.
> Northern wind cuts open people's skin.
> My aged father is weak with an old illness.
> How could he enlist?
> (Guo Maoqian 310)

The sharp contrast between a weak and aged father at home and the troops in the ruthless environment of the northern border makes the matter exceedingly urgent. Mulan's father cannot possibly fulfill his duty, and to save him Mulan temporarily puts aside her womanhood:

> She changes the elegant dress made of delicate cloth
> And washes off the beautiful makeup.
> She rushes to the military office on horseback

And heroically joins hands with other warriors.
(Guo Maoqian 310)

Different from the matter-of-fact depiction in the "Ballad" of the character's decision to join the army and subsequently depart, Wei Yuanfu portrays Mulan's costume change and then applauds her explicitly by using such words as "heroically" and "warrior."

Next, in describing Mulan's military life Wei Yuanfu makes an effort to describe the heroine's martial expedition, an aspect of her story that the "Ballad" left to readers' imagination:

In the morning they stationed at the foot of the snow mountain.
In the evening they camped by the side of the Green Sea.
At night they made a surprise attack at Lu in Yanzhi.
At dawn they swept over Qiang in Yutian.
The general came back in victory.
The soldiers returned to their hometown.
(Guo Maoqian 310)

The poet specifies whom the troops fought against (Lu and Qiang peoples), where the battles happened (Yanzhi and Yutian), and how Mulan and her colleagues won the battles (waging a surprise attack). Margret Barthel calls Wei Yuanfu's poetic creation "an almost seamless depiction of Mulan's experience" (464). Still concise in its poetic format, Wei Yuanfu's revision leads the way in enriching the heroine's military career with colorful plots for later writers to follow.

Wei Yuanfu ends his poem by concluding that Mulan's achievement is an ideal fulfillment of filial piety as well as loyalty to the imperial rule:

Only if the heart of an imperial subject
Could be as laudable as Mulan's integrity!
Both loyalty and filial piety are constant.
How could her fame be forgotten even after thousands of years!
(Guo Maoqian 310)

This conclusion to Mulan's tale emphasizes ethical values that are only implied in the folk "Ballad." In Wei Yuanfu's poem and thereafter these pivotal moral values of Mulan's character enable her to realize the poet's prophecy of fame that endures for hundreds of years (see figure 3.2).[18]

Several renowned Tang poets also acclaim Mulan and her extraordinary deeds in their works. Du Mu (803–852) dedicated his poem, "Ti

FIGURE 3.2. Mulan bids farewell to her family while mounting her horse. From *Nüzi ershisi xiao tu shuo* (Illustrated Volume of Twenty-Four Filial Women), drawn by Wu Youru, Shanghai: Hongdashan shuju, no publication date, preface for first edition dated 1871, preface for reprinted edition dated 1894.

Mulan miao shi" ("A Poem Dedicated to the Mulan Temple," *Quan tang shi*, 5987) to the Mulan Temple, located at Mount Mulan near present Huanggang in Hubei Province. Du Mu's work is written in the form of *qiyan jueju*, a four-line poem with seven characters to each line, and alludes to Mulan and her heroic actions without copying the style of the "Ballad" or directly referring to its plot. Using only twenty-eight characters, Du Mu emphasizes two aspects of the heroic maiden's story: Mulan's femininity and her patriotism.

> Bending the bow in a campaign, Mulan acted as a man.
> In her dreams, she decorated her eyebrows just like before.
> Several times she thinks about returning home and pouring out the
>   wine.
> She prayed at Fuyundui for the Ming Princess.[19]
> (*Quan tang shi*, 5987)

Imagined by the poet, Mulan's feminine nature is indicated by the hero-ine's yearning for homecoming and a woman's domestic life, even as she serves her country by "bending the bow in a campaign" and "acting as a man." In her dreams, the young protagonist imagines herself decorating her eyebrows the way she used to do as a daughter in her womanly life. The second couplet focuses on lauding the heroine's patriotic spirit par-ticularly expressed by her loyalty and devotion to the imperial govern-ment and her sacrifice of her own welfare; the poetry portrays Mulan's longing to go home and then praises her devotion to the imperial rule at the price of giving up her female life. In this poem, Mulan is juxtaposed with Ming Princess Wang Zhaojun.[20] In these two exceptional exam-ples, women helped the respective political sovereigns with their urgent needs: one served the armed forces in male clothes, and the other acted as a peace emissary who is married off to an ethnic chieftain.

Besides directly dedicating poems to Mulan, Tang poets also use Mulan as a literary allusion and imitate or borrow sentence structures, phrases, idioms, and words from the "Ballad."[21] The large number of imi-tations, allusions, and quotations regarding Mulan and the "Ballad" in the Tang poetry provide strong evidence that her character and story were quite popular, that at least one written version of the "Ballad" was in circulation, and that the "Ballad" was respected as a poetic master-piece at the time. In particular, Bai Juyi's (772–846) poems that extol the flower magnolia—"Xi ti Mulan hua," "Yong Mulan hua," and "Ti Ling-hu jia Mulan hua" ("A Poem Playfully Dedicated to Magnolia," "Ode to Magnolia," and "A Poem Dedicated to Magnolia of the Linghu Fam-ily," in *Siku Quanshu*)—speak for Mulan's popularity. Bai Juyi writes, for example, in "Xi ti Mulanhua," "Mulan once came as a maiden" (in *Siku Quanshu*). He does not mention the heroic deeds or moral values reflected in Mulan's story, but he alludes to the heroine's cross-dressing. In the other two poems, Bai Juyi calls magnolia maiden flower, using the heroine's feminine beauty to describe the flower's loveliness. The poet tries to establish a connection between magnolia and the heroine's name, to encourage people to favor the flower. Celebrated for his simple style and plain language in writing, Bai Juyi usually avoids rarely used words and allusions to ensure his poems' appeal to both refined and popular tastes. He was the leading poet to advocate the "new yuefu" movement, which upheld the style of folk ballads. Mulan appears in his poems with-out additional explanation indicating that the heroine and her story were quite well known among general readership during that time.

After the Tang, Mulan and her tale continued to be a significant poetic theme. For instance, the Yuan poet Yang Weizhen's (1296–1370) work titled "Mulan ci" ("Ballad of Mulan") satirizes the criticism given to the imperial ruler, "implying that if a ruler could advance the loyal and the good while controlling the 'barbarian neighbors,' then Mulan would not have to carry weapons but could remain a domesticated 'mulberry pick-er'" (Lai 86). Another flourishing period of the heroine in poetry came centuries later. During the last two imperial dynasties—the Ming and Qing—numerous (too many to be listed here) poems dedicated to Mulan appeared. They add varied details and some new messages to Mulan's tale; yet most of these works emphasize the core ethical values of filial piety and loyalty.[22] Throughout the years, Mulan's filial piety retains clarity while the matter of loyalty becomes ambiguous. Poets from the Tang and later periods generally applaud her as an extraordinary imperial subject but sidestep the nature of her probable non-Han Chinese ethnicity and the object of her allegiance. As Mulan's image develops generation after generation, her ethnicity seems to become less and less important while her character emerges more and more as a national heroine of China. In the sixteenth century a playwright reimagined Mulan's story as a legacy of the Tuoba clan that nonetheless is enriched significantly by Han Chinese culture.

Xu Wei and His Heroine with (Un)Bound Feet

Among the literary variations of Mulan's story, Xu Wei's sixteenth-century play, *Ci Mulan tifu congjun* (Female Mulan Joins the Army Taking Her Father's Place; *Ci Mulan* hereafter),[23] is probably the earliest dramatization preserved in writing. Known for his eccentric personality and versatility in the arts, Xu Wei's talent encompassed Chinese painting, calligraphy, and literature, including prose, poetry, and drama. His *Nanci xulu* (Criticism on the Southern Drama) is the earliest comprehensive critical treatise on the southern drama. *Ci Mulan* is included in Xu Wei's collection of four plays, under the general title of *Si sheng yuan* (Four Cries of a Gibbon, written ca. 1552–1557).[24] This collection shows a combination of the northern and the southern drama and establishes his fame as a dramatist. The plays not only enjoyed an immediate popularity during the late sixteenth century in Jiangnan China, but they also held a significant place in the history of Chinese drama and became a model for other playwrights to imitate and to follow (Idema 11; Zhou Zhongming 2–3).

Ci Mulan, a short play of two acts, tells Mulan's story in a coherent and complete manner, contributing to the growth of the heroine's image in important ways. It shows the transition from Yuan drama that typically includes four acts and one lead singing role to the Ming drama that varies in the number of acts and has multiple singing roles (Qian Ma ix, 25). Thematically inspired by the "Ballad," Xu Wei's version has developed significant elements of the folk story and at the same time has included remarkable changes that influenced many future writers.

Xu Wei's dramatic rendition gives Mulan the surname of Hua, generates the unique image of a warrior maiden with bound feet from the Tuoba clan, and ends the heroine's military journey with an arranged marriage. As mentioned earlier, the editor Guo Maoqian's note to the "Ballad" states: "Mulan, name unknown" (309). One can interpret this ambiguous statement in several ways: the protagonist's family name is not known; her given name is not known; "Mulan" is not a name but a title to address the heroine; or the author of the "Ballad" is unknown.[25] Although the heroine is widely known as Mulan in later periods, it is not clear whether "Mulan" is a family name, a given name, or a title in the "Ballad," an uncertainty that leads to discrepancies about Mulan's surname for generations, as I will discuss later in this chapter.[26] Xu Wei gives his protagonist the family name of Hua (literally meaning "flower") that became widely known. Variations of her story in modern time unanimously identify the heroine as Hua Mulan, which is pronounced Fa Mulan in Cantonese.

Mulan's self-introduction, which opens Xu Wei's play, sets the story in the reign of Tuoba Khan of the Northern Wei Dynasty:

> My humble name is Hua Mulan. My ancestors were the good people of the six prefectures in the Western Han Dynasty and have lived in the Wei Prefecture of Hebei for generations. My father, Hua Hu, courtesy name Sangzhi, has loved martial arts as well as letters all his life and once served as a famous Battalion Commander. . . . Our Tuoba Khan of the Great Wei has been recruiting soldiers in the prefectures. Twelve military scrolls have come one after another. Each of them has my father's name listed. (Xu Wei 1198)

Although Mulan's father has served the imperial court in an official post, he is now old and frail, without an adult son. As a first-born child, seventeen-year-old Mulan has learned "liberal and martial arts" under her father's guidance since she was young. These opening lines establish a few aspects of Mulan's life that have important influence on later variations of her story. First, Mulan's ethnicity is Tuoba, and the historical context of her activities occurred during the Northern Wei. The clear indication that she is a non-Han Chinese subject resonates with the "Ballad." Furthermore, the playwright creates a military and political lineage for Mulan. Similar to the historical heroines discussed in chapter 2, Mulan's family background and upbringing provide the necessary premise for her heroic deeds and accomplishments.

Although the "Ballad" does not portray the heroine's cross-dressing directly until she returns home and re-dresses in feminine clothes, Xu Wei depicts Mulan's costume change before departure in great detail, adding bound feet that create a provoking image of the character. In the first act Mulan's monologue that introduces her family, herself, and the urgent situation of her father's draft is followed by a series of scenes in which she purchases the necessary supplies, loosens her bound feet, changes into male attire, and then practices her martial skills. Above all, the way in which Mulan readjusts her tiny feet to fit in a pair of soldier's shoes before changing into her newly purchased costume is carefully and strikingly depicted. She sings:

> So hard to tear off the delicate binding cloth, light enough to step
> on ripples.
> It took me many years to achieve these tiny phoenix feet.
> Now I am in a hurry to loosen them, free enough to sail the waves.
> How can they avail to fill up these shoes?(Xu Wei 1199)

Here the significance of a heroine with bound feet is twofold: it enables the reader to reconsider the common view of the footbinding tradition in China as a feudal oppression of women; the protagonist's unbound feet, as a modification of the female body, problematizes the stable notions of body and dress. After Mulan's provocative behavior of abandoning the most important symbol of femininity at the time, the heroine dons a set of male attire before she continues her singing:

> All dressed up—am I not the image of a high officer among the
> troops!
> Perfect for keeping my secret as we march.
> Let me fasten the silk braid and attach the sword hoop to the fine
> pleats.
> The soft hauberk placed underneath
> Could be a double-layered warm blanket.
> When I come back, it will be just right for Yao'er to wear.[27]
> (Xu Wei 1199)

When everything is in order (or out of order), the reader sees a warrior maiden with (un)bound feet who is dressed in male clothes and shoes; she is ready to be enlisted to take her elderly father's place (see figure 3.3).

Probably beginning in the tenth century, footbinding first took shape as an elite fashion before it later became a common practice of the average woman (Ko, *Cinderella's Sisters*, 132). Wives and daughters of Chinese high officials practiced footbinding no later than the early thirteenth century. By Xu Wei's time, the arched foot was recognized as the "marker" of male and female difference and the "substantive difference between male and female footwear" was also established (Ko, *Cinderella's Sisters*, 125). By presenting his protagonist with bound feet in the Northern Wei Dynasty, Xu Wei invites the question of anachronism because footbinding became a social custom during a later period.[28] Instead of attaching bound feet to Mulan by "mistake," as I-Ch'eng Liang has criticized (92), this provoking picture indicates an important message: being heroic does not undermine Mulan's femininity, but it does complicate the heroine's ethnicity because footbinding started among Han Chinese women and later was adopted by some non-Han ethnic minority peoples. Moreover, Xu Wei also stretches the reader's credulity; a woman with deformed feet could hardly be a skillful martial artist in action. Xu Wei's addition of footbinding and unbinding episodes was likewise provocative, given that before the nineteenth century "the subject of footbinding was taboo in such official genres as public history, local gazetteers, and didactic texts" (Ko, *Cinderella's Sisters*, 111).

It is worthwhile noting that a play is an "intended" performance, one that employs role types (male "mo," female "dan," clown "chou," and others), and such identities on stage are always performed. Because segregated dramatic troupes were common (Zeitlin 259n63), cross-dressing in Chinese opera was almost inevitable.[29] If performed, the role of Mulan would be taken by a boy or man who acted the part of the female "dan" character who in turn acted as a man when cross-dressed.[30] Wilt Idema has suggested, concerning sixteenth-century dramatic performance, that the composition of Xu Wei's short play is "a reflection of the growing popularity of private household troupes" at the time: "These troupes mainly performed for the entertainment of their master and his male friends and may well have preferred a repertoire of shorter plays for these private performances, in contrast to the full-length *chuanqi* plays that were performed at community festivals and family rituals for a large and mixed audience. The nature of the audience may also have influenced the contents of these shorter plays and the way in which their action was

木蘭

商丘人父病不能從軍為有
司所苦木蘭代父戍邊十二年人
不知其為女也或云姓花
父名弧北魏時人有妹
曰木難弟曰咬兒

FIGURE 3.3. In this illustration Mulan is dressed as a soldier, holding a bow. The illustrator Jin Guliang portrays her with bound feet. From Jin Guliang, *Wushuang pu*, Shanghai: Tongwen shuju, 1886.

staged" (5). The potential audience of Xu Wei's play would be the male elite class. We thus have to consider the erotic connotations of the bound foot to these upper-class men, particularly the exoticness of having a cross-dressed male performer acting out being a woman who unbinds her bound feet. If the bound foot modifies the female body that has been highly sexualized and associated with eroticism, then re-dressing it in a man's shoe re-modifies her already modified female body.

Furthermore, the image of a heroine with bound feet has nonsensual implications as well. Such a female tradition also indicates that being heroic does not negate Mulan's femininity, and her action of rushing out to war on horseback does not disavow her female role as encoded by social convention. Mulan does not have to give up her bound feet, the most important symbol of femininity at the time; instead, she temporarily covers them with male shoes. Such an act of "covering" points to the inevitable "recovering" as the plot develops. Mulan's changing of footwear is, in fact, accompanied by her serious concern with the danger of losing the tiny size of her feet. She says: "I will still get married after I come back. What should I do [with my feet] then?" (Xu Wei 1199). Upon further reflection, Mulan dispels her misgivings, "I shouldn't worry about this. My family has a prescription for rinsing the 'golden lotuses.' After being washed in the caliche-boiled water, my feet will be even smaller" (Xu Wei 1199). Before leaving home, Mulan already has thought of a way to restore the damage to her "lotus feet." More important, Mulan's concerns are voiced primarily in terms of her role as a daughter, vis-à-vis her family. Her idea of marriage and her concern with large feet are not romantic notions, unrelated to her construction of a subjective identity. Rather, marriage is connected with a maiden's social roles and duties. While much twentieth- and twenty-first-century gender analysis in the West is heavily imbued with notions of individual subjectivity and rights, such focus on the individual seems much less a point for Xu Wei's heroine.

The heroine's concern and solution with regard to her bound feet point to another important aspect: her deviation from traditional womanly life is time-bound. Mulan's vision of the future, after returning from the battlefield, focuses on her marriage. On her way to the military camp, Mulan expresses her wish to end the war victoriously so that she can return to her female self: "After sweeping over the Black Mountain, I could put beautiful makeup on my face just like before" (Xu Wei 1202). She has no desire to remain in the adopted male role any longer than necessary.

The gender reversal in Xu Wei's play does not end with appearance; the second act of the play portrays an event that displays the main character's "masculine" spirit and capacity. Xu Wei creates colorful events for Mulan's camouflaged life. The heroine's outstanding martial skills soon attract the attention of the general, who then entrusts Mulan with the significant mission of capturing the chief rebel, Leopard Skin, who leads the revolt at Black Mountain. A particular aspect of loyalty is emphasized in the play. Instead of defending her country against invasion from another political regime or a foreign people, Mulan fights to quell the insurgents and to restore the imperial rule that has been jeopardized by the uprising. Her success in capturing the rebel commander enables the overall victory of the imperial troops and closes the curtain on Mulan's "male" life in the military. At the beginning of *Ci Mulan*, to save her ailing father from going to war, Mulan "puts aside needles and takes on the bowstring" (Xu Wei 1201). Here the playwright juxtaposes different forms of labor for men and women: archery and needlework. The needle and thread call to mind the arrow and string of the bow. The play indicates that the two are different but mutually implied. After her mission is accomplished, at her triumphant homecoming Mulan "bows to her parents after re-dressing in feminine clothes" (Xu Wei 1205). Thus, to ritually perform the filial task of a daughter (that is, bowing and so on), she must be dressed in female garb appropriate to that role.

Following the "Ballad," the play shows Mulan removing her male garments to dress once again in feminine clothes. Xu Wei highlights this costume change as a symbol of Mulan's return—to her female self and to the social morality defining gender. He adds another element to emphasize the ultimate restoration of the leading character's gender role and social position: Mulan's wedding to a bridegroom chosen by her parents. The groom has successfully completed the imperial examination and has been given an official post. In the closing lines, Mulan sings: "[I] have long heard that you are highly respected in the world of letters. I am embarrassed that I just have returned from weapons and war, not good enough to be a match for you" (Xu Wei 1206). In talking to her husband-to-be her humble words and manner promise that she will become a dutiful wife despite her military accomplishments and her valiant wartime spirit. Qian Ma considers Xu Wei's revision of the ending a requirement as well as an acknowledgment of dramatic and cultural conventions. "The Chinese audience of Xu's time, or perhaps of all times, would not be satisfied until they saw the heroine 'properly' married" (Qian Ma 131). Through her wedding, the heroine returns to her womanly life within the social system.

Appearing along with *Ci Mulan* in Xu Wei's collection of four plays is *Nü zhuangyuan cihuang defeng* (Woman Top Candidate Takes on the Man's Role, five acts; *Nü zhuangyuan* hereafter). It is difficult to determine when the story of the female top candidate was first in circulation. A written account, entitled "Huang Chonggu," appears in *Taiping guangji*, a collection of classical anecdotes and tales edited by a group of scholars under the lead of Li Fang (368: 1404). According to this story, upon reading his poetry and being impressed by his intelligence, Minister Zhou of the Shu Dynasty (907–925) releases an inmate in his thirties by the name of Huang Chonggu. After further testing of Huang's talents, Minister Zhou promotes him to the position of administrator, where Huang soon proves himself to be a capable official. A year later, Minister Zhou proposes that Huang marry his daughter. Only then does Huang reveal "his" female identity through a poem of confession. The poem tells the minister how she, the daughter of a late commissioner, was orphaned at a young age, raised by her nursemaid, and remained unmarried. Upon hearing Huang's extraordinary story, Minister Zhou applauds her chastity, as do the people of Shu. Shortly after that, Huang resigns from the administrative post to return to her hometown in Linqiong. Nothing is heard about her thereafter.[31]

It is believed that after writing the first three plays, including *Ci Mulan*, Xu Wei wanted to add another so that the four could become a collection. Based on the recommendation of one of his students, the story of the woman top candidate came under his consideration (Xu Lun 75). Inspired by sketchy accounts in earlier resources, Xu Wei invented colorful plots and details and rendered a new image of this extraordinary woman scholar in a five-act play. Act One briefly introduces the heroine Huang Chuntao's background and portrays her preparation for the imperial examination in male disguise. Act Two underscores the process whereby Chuntao passes the imperial examination as the top candidate. Her wisdom in dealing with judicial affairs in her post as administrator is described in Act Three, and Act Four centers on the dilemma that Chuntao confronts when Minister Zhou proposes a marriage to his daughter. At this point, she has no choice but to confess her female identity. The play concludes happily, as Chuntao is married into the Zhou household, not as a son-in-law but as a daughter-in-law.

The story of a woman top candidate provides a stimulating revision to the traditional Chinese romance of "caizi jiaren" (talented scholar and beauty). In the conventional Chinese love story, "[p]articipation or success in the imperial examinations was a respected part of the masculine image and signified a desirability and sexual power" (Louie 19). Part

FIGURE 3.4. Huang Chonggu combing her hair in front of a mirror. From Wu Youru, *Wu Youru huabao,* Shanghai: Biyuan huishe, ca. 1909.

of the reward for a talented scholar's success is winning the hand of a beauty. In this sense, Xu Wei's *Nü zhuangyuan* breaks new ground in portraying a woman who is a talented scholar and administrator as well as a beauty. Wilt Idema considers Xu Wei to be the first playwright who portrayed a talented woman scholar beyond the traditional romance.

Like Mulan, changing clothes is a prerequisite for Huang Chuntao before she embarks on her journey to take the imperial examination. "While not all warrior women have to hide their female identities like Hua Mulan, every story about the woman scholar features her disguised as a man" (Qian Ma 35). Orphaned since age twelve, Chuntao lives in reclusion with her nursemaid for eight years while she learns needlework and studies the classics. Financial difficulty motivates her excursion into the male territory of imperial examination and civil administration. Once Chuntao passes the examination and is granted an official post, the two women will be able to live comfortably on her salary, save money for the future, and avoid being overtaken by poverty after they return home. As demonstrated by the dialogue between the heroine and her nursemaid in Act One, the modification of Chuntao's female identity through resorting to male attire is a means to solve the contradiction between her ability to pass the imperial examination and the disfranchisement caused by her biological sex. "The 'Dragon Gate,' literally the gate of entrance to the imperial examination hall and symbolically the pass through which a man could change his status from that of a commoner to that of a government official, was never open to a woman in the entire history of China, not even in fiction" (Qian Ma 35). Upon hearing Chuntao's proposal to solve their financial problem, her nursemaid asks: "If you go to attend the imperial examination, you would definitely pass. But how could you change the fact that you are a girl" (Xu Wei 1208)? Chuntao responds: "How hard is this? Let me put on my father's old clothes, shoes, and hat, and put aside my skirt, blouse, and hair coil. How could others tell that I am a woman not a man by looking at me" (Xu Wei 1208)? In the social realm of civil examination and administration, dress defines one's gender and affects one's perception by others (see figure 3.4).

Nü zhuangyuan, however, portrays the heroine's costume change with less detail than is found in *Ci Mulan*. The plot detail of unbinding the feet is not included here; instead, the author criticizes the imperial examination system through the clown role of Hu Yan, another participant in the examination. In Act Two when the minister tells Hu Yan that his composition does not rhyme properly, Hu responds: "Rhyme is not really a serious matter. Rhyme for a poem is like destiny for a person. If Master says the rhyme is good, bad rhyme becomes good. If Master says the rhyme is bad, good rhyme becomes bad. The destiny is in the hands of Master, not Hu Yan" (Xu Wei 1211). Taking into account Xu Wei's frustrating personal experience in the imperial examination, Hu Yan's comments convey the playwright's criticism of the examination system as well as Xu Wei's lament of his own unrecognized talents. Furthermore, the fact that a cross-dressed woman becomes the top candidate also points to the failure of male scholars at the time.

Dressed in her late father's clothes and adopting the name of Huang Chonggu, Chuntao not only achieves success in the imperial examination but also proves her ability as an administrator. Her intelligence impresses Minister Zhou Xiang so much that he proposes to take Chuntao as his son-in-law, which compels Chuntao to reveal her secret in a poem. After reading the poem of confession, Minister Zhou praises Chuntao's purity and decides instead to marry his son to this extraordinary woman. When it comes to costume and stage performance, Xu Wei treats the issue of gender in a daring way. In Act Four Chuntao's old nurse-maid goes as far as to "rip off [her clothes] and expose her breasts" (Xu Wei 1228) to prove that she is a woman before the nursemaid testifies to Chuntao's purity, despite her intrusion into a male territory surrounded by men.

At the play's end, Minister Zhou asks his daughter to bring over a new dress and hair decorations for Chuntao so that she can get ready for the wedding ceremony. In the meantime, Chuntao's rank of administrator is taken over by her husband-to-be, the new top candidate. "The final scene of the play is a playful spoof on the *tuanyuan* convention of Southern drama: the tale may allow Huang Chonggu to disappear again without a trace into the community from which she emerged, but a Southern play preferably has to end in a wedding as long as it has one unmarried female in its cast" (Idema 9–10). In the finale, Chuntao resumes her womanly role, a transformation emphasized by her changed manner of address-ing her father-in-law: she kneels shyly when talking to Minister Zhou, a sharp contrast to her demeanor when performing as a man. Now female, both biologically and culturally, Chuntao forfeits the right to speak to Minister Zhou as a male subordinate.

The idea that the gender displacement in *Ci Mulan* reflects Xu Wei's implied critique of the male-dominated society is provocative, especially if we read it together with *Nü zhuangyuan*. Read together these two plays seem to suggest a critique of gender hierarchy. The two heroines excel in traditional male spheres—the battlefield and civil service. These heroines demonstrate their excellence in different male arenas, but nei-ther transgresses so far as to threaten patriarchal culture. Despite their extraordinary capabilities, both end their journeys into the male realm with marriage and presumably traditional deference to their husbands. Once her mission is accomplished, the heroine resumes her conventional female role.[32]

The plays *Ci Mulan* and *Nü zhuangyuan* provide vivid examples of the complexity and ambivalence of the Confucian gender system, in which "there was a space for women to negotiate and maneuver toward their perceived interests" without provoking the prevailing order (Hsiung 73). In Mulan and Chuntao's stories, such a "space" is created through cross-dressing. In this play the costume change both violates and conforms to the dress code that delineates the division between men and women. Similar to the female transvestites in literary and historical documents in Europe, Xu Wei's Chinese heroines "conform to androcentric models by assimilating maleness" (Hotchkiss 3). The heroines succeed in their adventure of stepping out of the boundary defining gender without pos-ing a threat to the social morality because they resort to male clothes. Conforming to the convention that martial combat and civil service are fields reserved for men, they perform and look like men in that realm. Thus, to respect the rules of the game Mulan and Chuntao become "men," and their behavior is thus judged by criteria usually applied to their male contemporaries.

Xu Wei's play not only allows the reader to examine how Mulan's story has been readjusted in a somewhat altered social climate but also explains why such a transgressive woman could be well accepted and acclaimed throughout Chinese history. As Mulan herself explains to her companions after returning home and exposing her female identity, her disguised enlistment was a matter of expediency to meet an urgent need. It was analogous to a brother-in-law giving a hand to his drowning sis-ter-in-law despite the prohibition against physical touch between them (Xu Wei 1205).[33] The references to Qin Xiu and Ti Ying, two well-known exemplary daughters, in Mulan's opening remarks indicate that the heroine's unconventional behavior is a way of enacting filial piety,[34] an improvised measure in time of emergency for a noble cause. Similar to Wei Yuanfu's poem, Xu Wei's revision of the Mulan story explicates the two significant ethical values in Confucian ethics, beginning with filial piety and climaxing with her triumph in loyalty. In this sense, Mulan becomes a two-sided heroine: a filial daughter as well as a loyal "man." The story of a disguised daughter in military service and its conclusion with her arranged marriage feature prominently in Xu Wei's play and profoundly influence later treatments of Mulan.[35]

Furthermore, the heroine's strong self-discipline in keeping her femi-ninity a secret and in maintaining her virginity conforms to the Confu-cian definition of female virtue in *Ci Mulan*. Upon her departure from home, Mulan makes a promise to her mother who is worried that the all-male environment would prevent her daughter from coming back intact (Xu Wei 1201). At her return, the warrior maiden's purity is con-firmed, again through the dialogue between mother and daughter right before the closing scene of the wedding. To her mother Mulan sings: "Return you a bud in the spring breeze. How can I humiliate my father and mother" (Xu Wei 1205)? Xu Wei's play clearly expresses the signifi-cance of maintaining Mulan's virginity to allow her full appreciation and admiration. His Ming contemporaries also underscore the theme of the heroine being an illustrious woman and praise her purity. Lü Kun (1536–1618), for instance, applauds Mulan's "fair conduct being as pure

FIGURE 3.5. The illustration included in Lü Kun's *Gui fan* (Behavioral Rules for Women) shows Mulan, dressed in military attire, greeting her parents at the door. The characters in the background (Mulan's sister making up her face and her brother preparing a sheep for the feast) indicate this is Mulan's homecoming.

as ice and jade" (245). In his writing, he highlights in Mulan's military career neither her victory in combat nor her fulfillment of filial or loyal obligation; rather, he commends her ability to maintain her virginity during many years of living in an all-male community. In his writing on this extraordinary warrior maiden, Lü Kun gasps with admiration at the fact that people have never doubted Mulan's purity despite her many years of military life among men (248) (see figure 3.5).

Although, as a writer of the sixteenth-century, Xu Wei was probably not advocating for women's equal rights, the image of confident, intelligent, and strong women juxtaposed with the implied critique of women's social status in his plays reveals the complexity within the patriarchal Chinese society and challenges any monolithic view of the Chinese woman as a victim in Confucian China. Furthermore, as an author well known for using literary sources in unconventional and provocative ways, Xu Wei communicates both his social criticism and his personal grievance for his own unrecognized talents through these able-minded and able-bodied heroines and their unusual adventures.

A native of Shaoxing, Xu Wei revealed his literary talent at a young age, yet he was stranded in his official career. After three attempts, he passed the county-level imperial examination and earned the title of *xiucai* in 1540. During the next years, Xu Wei failed the provincial imperial examination several times and never earned the title of *juren*. While serving on the staff of Provincial Governor Hu Zongxian (1511–1565), Xu Wei demonstrated his literary talent, knowledge of military strategy, as well as "a strong resentment against regulations of any kind" (Leung 16). He served as an insightful military strategist and commander in defending the eastern regions of China against the Japanese invasion from 1553 to 1555 (Xu Lun 39–58). After Hu Zongxian's political downfall, Xu Wei experienced a period of depression. At the age of forty-five, he wrote his own tomb epigraph. After several failed suicide attempts, Xu Wei killed his third wife out of jealousy in 1566 and was jailed. A friend arranged for his release in 1572; he spent the next two decades traveling, drinking, painting, and writing.[36] In assessing his own work, Xu Wei ranked his calligraphy first, poetry second, prose third, and painting fourth. This list does not even mention playwriting, perhaps because drama in traditional China was generally perceived as a low entertainment. Nevertheless, Xu Wei's drama has been much more influential than he probably expected. Wilt Idema has pointed out:

Xu Wei probably wrote *Ci Mulan* and *Nü zhuangyuan* first of all as social criticism venting his frustration over the general condition of society and his own lack of success. His choice of subject matter enticed him to consider matters of sex and gender, which he treated in a remarkably explicit manner. His dramatization of sources placed the change of costume on stage, in full view of a select (male?) audience and featured the conspicuous enactment of male behavior by a heroine in male attire. More than any literary qualities the texts may have, these aspects of the performance may well have ensured the early reputation of these plays. (15)

Xu Wei's drama with sartorial conventions, male-female boundaries, and cross-dressing is more a male literati's concern with being unrecognized for his talents rather than serious concerns with actual women. The idea that Chinese male authors, for example, employed female voices in poetry to express their loneliness and their hope for recognition has been well analyzed. Similarly, Xu Wei probably projected his own concerns and frustrations onto his female protagonists through "male ventriloquism."[37] His cross-dressed heroines, gifted with "an unyielding spirit and superior 'masculine' abilities" (Hsiung 78), thus may be self-referential for the playwright. The gender displacement then may reflect Xu Wei's personal frustrations and grievance more than his critique on a male-dominated society. Later adaptations of their stories, especially those of Mulan, have taken more of a feminist turn and portrayed the heroines' actions as a challenge to cultural notions of feminine fragility, physical weakness, and lack of intellectual ability.

Literary Variations after Xu Wei

The emphasis on female sexual purity continued throughout the Ming and reached its height in the Qing Dynasty. Although filial piety remained an important virtue for both male and female, the celebration of female chastity and of suicide to protect chastity flourished on an unprecedented level in the Qing era (Du and Mann 227). *Jie* (purity) that refers "not simply to sexual purity but to absolute fidelity to one husband, expressed in a refusal to remarry and lifelong devotion to the parents and heirs of the deceased spouse" and *lie* (illustriousness, martyrdom) that "a woman's absolute commitment to fidelity and sexual purity might require self-sacrifice ending in death or suicide" became the two highest virtues for women (Du and Mann 220). Both were incorporated into the variations of Mulan's story that were produced during this period.

In the Qing Dynasty Mulan's legend found its way into fiction in the form of book chapters and full-length novels. These works not only reveal cultural inheritance from the "Ballad," Tang poetry, and Xu Wei's play but also reflect a new emphasis on the heroine's female chastity. Chapters 56 to 60 in the *Sui Tang yanyi* (*Historical Romance of the Sui and Tang Dynasties*, Chu Renhu, fl. 1675–1695) retell the heroine's story in some colorful episodes of a long historical romance that is set during the transition period between the declining Sui and the founding of the Tang Dynasty (1: 426–70). This fictional account shows the direct influence from Xu Wei's play, yet it also imagines new aspects of Mulan's story. The protagonist, born into the Hua family, was named after the magnolia tree planted in the garden by the Hua couple because the tree blossomed at their daughter's birth. Her parents raised Mulan, their first-born child as both a daughter and a son. Although her feet were bound, she learned martial skills from childhood under the guidance of her father. Shortly after Mulan's departure for battle, her father died, and her mother married a man of the Wei family to raise Mulan's younger sister and brother. After the heroine returned home, the ruler, Hesuona Khan of the Western Tujue, summoned her to become a consort in his palace. To defend her purity without disobeying the value of loyalty, Mulan committed suicide at the site of her father's tomb. These chapters mark a transitional stage of Mulan's story between Xu Wei's play and the full-length novels written in the nineteenth century as well as an important stage in her development into an idealized heroine (see figure 3.6).

Beiwei qishi gui xiao lie zhuan (The Legend of A Filial and Illustrious Girl in the Unusual History of the Northern Wei) develops Mulan's story into a book-length novel. The novel is attributed to Zhang Shaoxian, but little is known about him. The existing version is a woodblock-printed edition with twelve illustrations. In the introduction, dated 1850, one Meidaoren (pseud.) introduces the novel as an elaboration of the "Ballad" aimed at encouraging the reader's sense of loyalty and filial piety. Even though this rendition takes the themes from the "Ballad" as its inspiration, its main storyline, the names of the protagonist and some other characters, and most locations indicate a debt to Xu Wei's play. The martial expedition has been greatly expanded with lengthy passages dedicated to military strategies and confrontations in the battlefield. Colorful events in Mulan's military life, such as the pacifying of rebellion, are featured in careful narrative and vivid description. Similar to Xu Wei's dramatization, *Beiwei qishi gui xiao lie zhuan* closes with Mulan's reunion with her family and her marriage. The bridegroom, Wang

花木蘭

FIGURE 3.6. A portrait of Mulan included in one of the editions of the *Sui tang yanyi* (Historical Romance of the Sui and Tang Dynasties) by Chu Renhu (fl. 1675–1695). Shanghai: Shangwu yinshuguan, ca. 1911, preface dated 1695.

木蘭　朱夫人　朱若虛

FIGURE 3.7. An illustration from one of the reprinted editions of *Zhong xiao yong lie qinü zhuan* (The Legend of An Extraordinary Girl Who Is Loyal, Filial, Courageous and Illustrious) under a different title portrays Mulan (on the left) in military uniform and holding a spear. From *Nüxia xiashuo Mulan congjun* (A Novel of Female Chivalry: Mulan Joins the Army), Taipei: Fenghuang chubanshe, 1974.

Qingyun, is also a warrior. The novel particularly emphasizes the female virtue—*lie*—by underscoring the heroine's sexual purity and adding it to the collection of moral values that Mulan's character represents.

Another surviving Qing novel featuring Mulan's story is *Zhong xiao yong lie qinü zhuan* (The Legend of An Extraordinary Girl Who Is Loyal, Filial, Courageous and Illustrious). One of its extant versions is a woodblock-printed edition in which the "Introduction" is dated 1878 and the "Afterword" is dated 1827.[38] After the introduction and before the table of contents, this edition cites and annotates the "Ballad" as its literary source. This novel gives Mulan a different family name, Zhu, and suggests that she is a native of Han Chinese origin, living during the transition period from late Sui to early Tang (see figure 3.7).

The storyline starts with the life of her grandfather Zhu Ruoxu in the midst of the uprising that overthrew the rule of the Sui Dynasty and founded the new imperial dynasty of the Tang. Growing up under the guidance of her grandfather, the young Mulan shows exceptional gifts in both liberal and martial arts. During the reign of Emperor Tang Taizong, the Tang army recruited soldiers for an expedition against the Tujue people in the north. In this context Mulan took the conscription of her ailing father, Zhu Tianlu, and served the emperor in disguise. Receiving instructions from the gods, Mulan's outstanding accomplishments played a crucial role in the imperial army's defeat of their opponents. Owing to her military achievements, Mulan was granted the title of General Wuzhao. After returning home and revealing her gender identity, Mulan was given the title of Princess Wuzhao and the honorary surname of Li, the ruling family's name. After listening to slanderous talk, however, Emperor Tang Taizong suspected Mulan's loyalty and considered her a potential threat to his rule. He thus summoned Mulan to the capital city three times. In response, Mulan submitted three letters to state her loyalty. In the end, she slit her chest with a sword and lay open her heart in the presence of the messenger to prove her pure loyalty to the Tang rule. After her death, she was buried at the foot of Mount Mulan and granted the epitaph of Princess Zhenlie. Mulan's suicide in this Qing novel is "the tidiest way" to resolve the contradiction between "the expectations of an audience who has become attached to the characters as Amazons" and "the ideological requirements of a patriarchal discourse that perceives that women can only be men during temporary periods of social disorder" (Louise Edwards 106). The symbolic meaning of her death confers upon females another Confucian virtue—illustriousness; her martyrdom erases the potential threat in the form of an unleashed Amazon.

After Mulan's illustrious suicide, the emperor inscribed a memorial archway in her honor with the words *zhong xiao yong lie* (loyal, filial, courageous, and illustrious). The introduction to the novel, written by one Xiuqing shi (pseudo. fl. 1878), praises Mulan as a model of morality: the writer refers to her replacing her father in the army as filial, to her exceptional service at the frontier as loyal, to her twelve outstanding exploits in the desert as courageous, and to her letters to the throne and baring of her heart as faithfulness (*Zhong xiao yong lie qinü zhuan*, 3a-4a). Similarly, in the Afterword, Zhou Huizong (fl. 1827) praises General Mulan's outstanding character and conduct. Mulan's character explains her longevity in Chinese culture, and she remains a vivid example even a thousand years later. According to Zhou Huizong, the heroine inspires not only women but also men to rise up against their oppressors with force and spirit (*Zhong xiao yong lie qinü zhuan*, 4: 64).

After the nineteenth century, Mulan's story continues to flourish and transform in China. During the time of anti-Japanese war in the 1930s her image was promoted as the embodiment of patriotism. Indeed, in war-torn China, no better example than Mulan symbolized "the spirit of patriotism and resistance" (Hung 72). Adaptations of her story, together with historical plays of other heroic figures at the time, strive to fulfill two main goals: "cultivating political symbols in the fight against the Japanese invasion and spreading patriotic messages to a wider audience in the interiors as well as in occupied cities like Shanghai" (Hung 64). The Peking opera play by Ma Shaobo, *Mulan congjun* (Mulan Joins the Army, 1949), and the film by Ouyang Yuqian, *Mulan congjun* (Mulan Joins the Army, 1939), both portray the legendary maiden as a patriotic heroine who is fighting against the Japanese invasion. "For Chinese dramatists, Hua Mulan best personified the spirit they sought to instill in their audience. As a symbol of loyalty, filial piety, youth, courage, sacrifice, and integrity, she surpassed all others" (Hung 77). During the Cultural Revolution (1966–1976), "female Red Guards donned male military uniforms," which evoked the legend of Mulan for political and ideological purposes (Perry and Dillon 282). In twentieth-century propaganda for gender equality Mulan was lauded as the model woman who "holds up half of the sky." The well-known Yu opera of Henan Province retells Mulan's story as "Shui shuo nüzi buru nan" ("Who Says Women Are Not as Good as Men"), a well-known performance that advocates gender equality in China. Well into the twenty-first century Mulan's character remains in the repertoire of local operas in a number of regions of China.[39] Mulan's legend has inspired folktales, stories, stage plays,

FIGURE 3.8. In *Lidai mingyuan tu shuo* (Illustrated Records of Famous Women in all Dynasties), the entry entitled "Mulan nü" (Girl Mulan) cites the "Ballad" in full and identifies the protagonist to be its author, expressing the same opinion as Zou Zhilin did in *Nüxia zhuan* (Biographies of Female Knights-Errant), and more specifically identifies her as a historical figure who lived during the Liang Dynasty. The illustration, by Qiu Shizhou shows Mulan bids farewell to her parents while getting ready to join her fellow companies for her military adventure. From *Lidai mingyuan tu shuo*, drawn by Qiu Shizhou, Shanghai: Dianshi zhai, 1879. Volume 2: 5a-b.

opera, films, and television series that, in turn, help further popularize this heroine. Mulan remains the most commonly cited model image of heroines in China to this day.

Naturalization of Mulan

Although dynastic histories never mention her, numerous accounts found in intellectuals' essays and notes, tablet inscriptions, and gazetteer entries have attributed a variety of hometowns, family names, and other biographical details to her; all claim that she existed as a historical figure. Before the thirteenth century, brief records relating to Mulan's biographical information appeared in the notes and essays of the literati.[40]

Dated before the well-known edition of the "Ballad" that appeared in Guo Maoqian's thirteenth-century *Yuefu shiji*, these early records include no documentation. In their informal style of writing, the authors do not provide an argument either to establish Mulan's historicity or to show how they deduced the details of her biography. Rather, they matter-of-factly write about the heroine as a person living in a certain period or a native to a certain region.

In the Song Dynasty, attempts to naturalize the heroine began to thrive; Mulan and her heroic deeds started to appear in local histories. Since then various writers wrote about Mulan and provided biographical details linking her to a particular area to claim her as a native daughter. Over time, this character is cherished as a local treasure more and more often and insistently. These attempts peak in the Ming and Qing dynasties. At the same time as interest in this distinguished character continued among intellectuals, various regions established memorial shrines, temples, or similar constructions in Mulan's honor and preserved her "life story" in local historical archives. Since the Ming Dynasty, besides literary persons' essays and notes, local histories with accounts of Mulan's biography have appeared, mostly in local gazetteers, and generally associated her with a number of regions.

Considering Mulan to be one of the outstanding lady knights-errant of ancient China, Zou Zhilin tracks her hometown to Shaan in his *Nüxia zhuan* (Biographies of Female Knights-Errant, ca. 1610). Considering the "Ballad" a poem composed by the heroine herself to describe her experiences in the defensive war at the frontiers, Zou Zhilin particularly praises Mulan for her "bravery and honesty" (1054–55). Viewing Mulan as the author as well as the first-person narrator of the "Ballad" is an idea original to Zou. His writing cites the "Ballad" and Du Mu's poem but provides no other evidence to support his statement of Mulan's place of origin and her authorship. In modern times, the Huayuantou village in Yan'an, Shaanxi Province became one of the alleged hometowns of Mulan, where local people, proud of their native daughter, constructed a grave for Mulan and circulated folk stories about her (Huang and Li 8, 159–62) (see figure 3.8).

Wang Yun (1277–1304) introduces Wanzhou (modern Wan County in Hebei Province) as Mulan's hometown based on the temple built in her name and the dedications inscribed in it (*Qiujian ji*, vol. 28, in *Siku Quanshu*). This region is also identified as Bo Prefecture and Wan County in other local records.[41] Da Shi'an's essay collected in *Wan xian zhi* (Gazetteer of Wan County, Zhu Maode and Tian Yuan, comp.) used the word goddess to address Mulan. It is believed that her blessing has protected the region by securing its safety and prosperity over the years. The annual sacrificial ceremony held by the local people to show their gratitude to the goddess usually attracted many devotees (Zhu Maode and Tian Yuan 9: 390–93). Another entry in the *Wan xian zhi*, written after the temple's renovation in 1522 and signed by one Shi Lin, prefect of Baoding, attempts to reiterate the historicity of the character Mulan and to clarify why her name and heroic conduct have never been includ-ed previously in dynastic histories. Shi Lin explains that the goddess's achievements are so great that they would not die out as time passes by; hence there was no need to write them down in official history. He further justifies his statement by pointing to the fact that Mulan's fame has been carried on since the Han Dynasty until his time—the sixteenth century—and the heroine-turned-goddess still enjoys being sacrificed to and worshipped by the natives (Zhu Maode and Tian Yuan 9: 393–96). These records collectively try to portray Mulan as a native of Wan and offer evidence that indicates the enduring interest in Mulan among writ-ers while enriching the literary rendition of this heroine.

Another shrine in honor of Mulan—the Memorial Shrine of General Filial Piety and Illustriousness—is found in Yucheng County in Shangq-iu, Henan Province. At this shrine, two tablets with inscription survived: "Memorial Shrine of General Filial Piety and Illustriousness: Correction and Rectification" by Hou Youzao (cited in *Gujin tushu jicheng*, Collecta-nea of Books Ancient and Present, comp. Chen Menglei 1651–1741, Jiang Tingxi 1669–1732, et al., 398: 12b-13a) and "Memorial Shrine of General Filial Piety and Illustriousness: Correction and Rectification" signed by one Meng Yuqian in 1806.[42] In addition, the *Shangqiu xian zhi* (Gazetteer of Shangqiu County, Liu Dechang and Ye Yun, comp., ca. 1665, reprinted edition 1969) and Zhang Zhidong's (1837–1909) *Bai xiao tu* (Hundred Illustrated Stories of Filial Piety, 18–19) also credit Shangqiu as Mulan's hometown (see figure 3.9).

In the Ming Dynasty (1368–1644), several local histories and essays record Mulan as a native of Huangzhou (modern Huanggang region in Hubei Province). Jiao Hong's (1540–1620) *Jiaoshi bi sheng* (Notes by Jiao) took the existence of the memorial constructions as persuasive evidence of Mulan's historicity to support the claim that she is a native daughter of Huangpi County in Huangzhou, even though these memorials might have been built during a later period than the "Ballad" appeared and might have come into being as a result of literary influence (3: 86). His conclusion is obviously questionable.[43] The biographical information

FIGURE 3.9. *Bai xiao tu* (Hundred Illustrated Stories of Filial Piety) records Mulan as daughter of Hua Hu from Shangqiu who lives during the Sui Dynasty. The illustration included with the story shows that upon leaving home, Mulan is dressed as a man and bids farewell to her parents and younger brother. Guangzhou: no publisher indicated, ca. 19th century.

about Mulan included in this and other records points to noticeable similarities with the Qing novel *Zhong xiao yong lie qinü zhuan*. In particular both works agree on Mulan's family name (Zhu) and her hometown (Huangzhou). It is impossible to find out who started this branch of her chronicle, yet these scattered documents in local histories and the Qing novel suggest the possibility of Mulan's story traveling between literature and history.

Zhu Guozhen's (1557–1637) essay "Woman General" similarly notes that Mulan was a daughter of the Wei family living in the Qiao region of Bo (21: 6b). Other records, found in the Ming collectanea *Gujin tushu jicheng*, the *Jiangnan tongzhi* (*Gazetteer of Jiangnan*, Zhao Hong'en, Huang Zhijun 1668–1748, et al., vol. 181, in *Siku Quanshu*), the *Bozhou zhi* (Gazetteer of Bozhou, comp. ca. 1825, reprinted edition 1985, 1678–79), the *Da Qing yitongzhi* (*Gazetteers of the Grand Qing*, also known as *Jiaqing chongxiu yitongzhi*, Mu Zhang'a et al., comp. ca. 1842, 34: 12b), share many details about the heroine with the aforementioned seventeenth-century novel, *Sui Tang yanyi*. Dated between the late sixteenth and the nineteenth centuries, these local history entries and literary persons' notes assign Mulan to Bo probably following the historical romance. It is possible that such plots as Mulan's suicide and the title conferred to her of "Filial Piety and Illustriousness" were in circulation at the time and made their way from fiction to local histories.

In the Qing Dynasty, Yao Ying (1785–1853) wrote a short essay titled "Investigation of the Birth Place, Time Period, and Events of Mulan" in which he accepts the view that Mulan was a person living around the Northern Wei period. Yao further specifies that the heroine's enlistment occurred in the last years of the fifth century, during the reigns of Emperor Xiao Wendi (467–499; r. 471–499) and Emperor Xuan Wudi (483–515; r. 499–515). Moreover, Yao Ying proposes Mulan's hometown to be Liang Prefecture (Wuwei city in Gansu Province), which was called Wuwei during Mulan's lifetime (4730). Yao Ying's piece is probably the first critical essay that attempts to structure an argument that historicizes and localizes Mulan as well as the events, places, and time about her and her deeds. In contrast to the casual literary notes discussed above, Yao no longer takes for granted that Mulan is a real person documented in history. Instead, he draws his conclusions about the heroine's biography based on a textual analysis of the "Ballad." Nonetheless, drawing on literature to substantiate the heroine's historicity is obviously problematic.

These efforts to naturalize Mulan have been questioned as her story evolves over the years.[44] The desire to locate Mulan in history was so persistent, however, that some writers attempted to reconcile inconsistencies between various accounts. During the Qing Dynasty, for example, Yu Zhengxie (1775–1840) proposed that "Mulan probably was a native of Bo and was buried in Wan" (reprint of the 1848 edition, 13: 314a). Such attempts connect two alleged hometowns for the heroine. Even though efforts as such are no more valid than other biographical accounts of Mulan, they show another direction in telling the heroine's story. A similar tendency also appears in fiction. In the aforementioned Ming novel *Sui Tang yanyi*, Mulan was born a daughter of the Hua family. During the course of her military expedition, her father passes away, and her mother is remarried to a Wei person (Chu Renhu 430). In this case, the writer similarly tries to make sense of two family names alleged to Mulan.

The existence of these memorial constructions is more a result of people's admiration for the courageous maiden and of their efforts to claim Mulan as their local heroine than evidence to substantiate Mulan's historicity. "Literary travelers passing by the sites, following a long established practice, often wrote poems recalling the memorable past, tapping the wellspring of history and reinforcing the continuity of myth" (Pei-Yi Wu 164). These materials came into being much later than Mulan's appearance in literature, probably as an outcome of her popularity in both literati and folk traditions. In some instances, an element taken from a nonhistorical text has been imaginatively expanded in detail. There is evidence that a false account, once released, remained in circulation and gained further credibility as it was passed on, for example: accounts alleging Mulan's tomb to be in Wan County, Hebei Province. A record in the *Wan xian zhi* states "Mulan defended this region taking her father's place and won acclaim. Therefore the natives offered sacrifice to her honor. Later she passed away and [her body] was returned to Bozhou. . . . Since Mulan Temple was destroyed, natives buried the old statute underneath and called it Mulan's tomb playfully" (Zhu Maode and Tian Yuan 27: 178). Later a local official of the Qing Dynasty had Mulan's cemetery rebuilt and the tomb tablet constructed to preserve the so-called "historical relic" (Zhu Maode and Tian Yuan 27: 178). Interestingly, this site was perceived thereafter as the "genuine" burial site of the heroine. Other would-be sites of Mulan's grave are possibly results of similar inaccuracies. The same thing might have happened in the hearsay of the heroine's birthday on the eighth day in the fourth month in the lunar calendar, which is also the birth date of the historical Buddha Siddhartha (563–483 B.C.). Hence the extant tablet inscriptions and memorial constructions provide additional layers to the palimpsest of Mulan, which demonstrate the expanded popularity of her legend rather than being actual relics or physical evidence to prove Mulan's life in history.

In tracking the evolution of Mulan's story, it becomes clear how fiction and history have become blended at times. Intertextual references to the title—General Filial Piety and Illustriousness—are found in local histories starting from the fourteenth century and in fiction dating from the seventeenth century. Such references probably were drawn from contemporary folk stories. Obscure as her origin is, the character has been endowed with many invented biographical details. Memorial constructions are usually based on certain accounts at the time, such as the casual writing of literati, local history, or folk stories, all of which emerged later than the "Ballad." Through all these accounts, we can see that Mulan's endearing and long-lasting popularity is related to the theme of a young woman's transgression. She breaks the rules by acting in defiance against the definition of gender of her time, thus making her story particularly exciting and exceptionally attractive. The frequent adjustment in representing a positive image of the heroine secures her acceptance in various social climates. Such balancing recurs in many literary variations and historical records. Furthermore, one might argue that the deification of Mulan is a way to decrease the subversion that a woman's transgression might incur. Because the heroine is "extraordinary" due to the magical power bestowed on her or the supernatural influence that aided her, she can bypass some regulations. In the process of multiple revisions, the image of Mulan therefore has been enriched layer upon layer—in the realms of literature, history, and deity worship—into a palimpsest.

In its varied incarnations, Mulan's story had such vitality that people in various parts of China wanted to claim her and attempted to locate her in their regional histories. These attempts functioned in enhancements to her story that demonstrate its flexibility and further augment its vitality. Through the centuries Mulan heeded the people's imagination, and, as I demonstrated in this chapter, her story while growing and changing, embodies the moral values of its time and constructs, challenges the norms, and reconstructs gender identity in China. Mulan has been, in Susan Mann's vivid words, "stashed, and repeatedly unpacked, in China's cultural house" ("Presidential Address," 846).

4 / The White Tiger Mythology: A Woman Warrior's Autobiography

Is it autobiography if parts of it are not true? Is it fiction if parts of it are?
—LYNDA BARRY, ONE HUNDRED DEMONS

Memoir is memory. And memory is mythic. Memory is the thing that stands between the self and the absence of self. In looking in this uncompromising mirror, memoir is the setting down in stone the stuff of ordinary lives. It is also the taking of an extraordinary life and showing how courage is born from ordinariness.
JANET MASON, AGAINST ASSIMILATION. THE ROOTS OF MEMOIR

Just as the precise origin of Mulan's legend in China eludes cultural historians, so does the period when her story and cultural influence began to migrate to other lands. By the twelfth century, for example, her story was known in neighboring Korea. In a study of female characters included in *History of the Three Kingdoms*, the twelfth-century Korean historiography, Hai-soon Lee observes that the history's editor Kim Pusik briefly compared the Korean filial daughter Sŏlssinyŏ with Mulan. Sŏlssinyŏ accepted a marriage proposal so that her husband could take her elderly father's place in the army, in effect offering herself to ensure his safety (79).[1] Mulan did not appear in the English-speaking West until the 1881 publication of W.A.P. Martin's "Mulan, the Maiden Chief" by Harper & Brothers in New York, apparently the earliest English translation of the "Ballad."[2] In terms of adaptation Mulan seems to turn up for the first time in the United States in 1922 when a group of Chinese students at Columbia University in New York City staged a performance based on her legend (Yao Darong, "Mulan . . . biaowei," 96).[3] In the 1930s, the Chinese American actor, poet, and novelist H. T. Tsiang wrote, published, produced, and acted in *China Marches On* (1938), a play designed to educate working-class American audiences about Japanese imperialism and to inspire them to support their fellow workers struggling in China. Tsiang spins Mulan's tale into a melodrama in which her loyalty is directed toward the working-class defenders of China and social class solidarity. Tsiang's play was staged in New York City and Los Angeles from 1939 to 1944.[4] Although Mulan's story circulated in the United

States in the first half of the twentieth century, it was not widely known among English speakers until the 1976 publication of Maxine Hong Kingston's *The Woman Warrior: Memoirs of a Girlhood among Ghosts.*

Breaking new ground in several dimensions, *The Woman Warrior* generated mixed responses from early reviewers and a vast amount of criticism in the ensuing years. Kingston herself once stated: "I expected *The Woman Warrior* to be read from the women's lib angle and the Third World angles, the *Roots* angle" ("Cultural Mis-Readings," 55). Kingston did not, however, expect her book to be read, interpreted, and discussed from many other vantage points as well. *The Woman Warrior* has become a canonical work in Asian American literary studies and remains a staple on classroom reading lists across a variety of disciplines and interdisciplinary studies; the number of scholarly publications on Kingston and *The Woman Warrior* continues to grow steadily.[5] Particularly pertinent to my discussion of the continuities and discontinuities in Mulan's story over the centuries and across geographical locations is the cultural complexity within which Kingston's work has transformed Mulan's tale and the far-reaching influence of the unique woman warrior character she created. The second chapter of *The Woman Warrior*, "White Tigers," inspired by the mother character's story yet departing from the "Ballad" in significant ways, marks Mulan's development from a Chinese folk heroine to an extraordinary Chinese American woman warrior and significantly influences later versions of her story. In presenting Mulan's tale as an autobiography that incorporates other generic elements, *The Woman Warrior* successfully relays the heroine's story in her own voice and represents female subjectivity, sensibility, and feelings. Her book also inserts a new literary voice to the pantheon of American literature, a voice that rejects any single generic categorization.[6] Kingston's work reconfigures Mulan's image into a gifted and trained warrior who seeks revenge on behalf of her family and community, participates in a peasant uprising, helps overthrow imperial rule, establishes a new regime, and beheads the misogynistic baron. Situating the book in terms of feminism, roots, and Third World activism, Kingston points to the ways in which *The Woman Warrior* represents the historical moment in which she wrote it. She reinvented Mulan's character and story. Using a first-person narrative, Kingston imbues her book with an ambiguity that is essential to both embodying the narrator's childhood confusion about the images of Chinese women being warriors, avengers, wives, and slaves and representing the Chinese American experience (Kim, *Asian American Literature*, xvii). *The Woman Warrior* modifies the theme of cross-dressing in the

"Ballad" and emphasizes the coexistence of womanhood and militance in Fa Mu Lan's character: she embarks on her journey as a maiden combatant, becomes a wife and mother during the military campaign, and returns home to be a daughter-in-law. Furthermore, in contrast to previous as well as subsequent versions, Kingston does not conclude the story with the heroine's re-dressing and return to her womanly life; instead, she conflates the characters of Mulan and the historical poet Cai Yan to constitute an evolving image of the woman warrior who surrenders her sword and takes up words as her chosen weapons.

Kingston/"I"/ Fa Mu Lan: Story of a Warrior Avenger

In *The Woman Warrior* Kingston retells Mulan's story as autobiography and develops her character as a warrior avenger. As an adult, the narrator recalls the images of women that her mother and Chinatown immigrants seared into her girlhood memory. The opening chapter, "No Name Woman," presents the story of the narrator's paternal aunt. As the narrator learns from her mother's talk-stories, this no name aunt dishonored her family by having an extramarital affair and an illegitimate baby after her husband had sailed to America with a group of village men. The punishment for the aunt's infidelity and disloyalty extends from being treated as an outcast and abandoned by her kin during her lifetime to profound silence that turns her existence into a family taboo after she kills herself along with her newborn. It is quite understandable that many readers as well as the young narrator of *The Woman Warrior* see the no name aunt as a victim of the patriarchal early twentieth-century Chinese society, an exemplification of the woman-as-wife-and-slave image. She was cruelly punished for committing adultery, even though her sexual "extravagance" might have been forced on her. As the narrator imagines, perhaps "[s]ome man had commanded her to lie with him and be his secret evil. . . . His demand must have surprised, then terrified her. She obeyed him; she always did as she was told" (Kingston, *Woman Warrior*, 6; unless otherwise noted, all in-text references in this chapter refer to Kingston's *Woman Warrior*). As a subjugated wife and slave, the aunt silently endures childbirth and humiliation from her family and other villagers. The man's name is never disclosed; she bears the punishment alone.

Nevertheless, the narrator reminds the reader that the no name aunt is also an avenger. By jumping into the family well, she poisons the drinking water; she becomes a drowned one whose weeping ghost in the well waits to pull down a substitute for herself. The drowned are objects of fear in Chinese culture (16). No name aunt exacts her revenge by becoming a fearful presence; the family secret surrounding her lived among the younger generation through female talk-stories, traveled across the Pacific Ocean to arrive in America, and haunted the narrator fifty years later. The maternal warning that opens the book: "You must not tell anyone . . . what I am about to tell you" ironically points to the indelible imprint the no name aunt has left in the family history and memory (3). Its vividness is restored by the mother's and daughter's oral and written talking-stories. Facilitated by the narrator's remembering and retelling, the no name aunt's story becomes one of the articulated silences—"textual ellipses, nonverbal gestures, authorial hesitations" (King-kok Cheung, *Articulate Silences,* 4). Introduced early in the book as distant memory and ghost, the image of the female avenger develops further in the newly minted, fierce character Fa Mu Lan.

At the beginning of the second chapter, "White Tigers," Kingston's series of predictions in the future perfect tense signals both the transition from the narrator's Chinese American life to daydream-like sequences and the shift of narrative voice from the narrator's to that of her imaginary persona Fa Mu Lan.

> She [Brave Orchid, the narrator's mother] said I would grow up a wife and a slave, but she taught me the song of the warrior woman, Fa Mu Lan. I would have to grow up a warrior woman.
> The call would come from a bird that flew over our roof. . . . I would be a little girl of seven the day I followed the bird away into the mountains. . . . I would break clear into a yellow, warm world. New trees would lean toward me at mountain angles, but when I looked for the village, it would have vanished under the clouds. (20)

Then the chapter adopts past tense to narrate Fa Mu Lan's story in her own voice. Such a beginning works in concert with the chapter's ending that brings the reader back to the narrator's confusing and at times frustrating Chinese American life. The narrator's and Fa Mu Lan's dual first-person narratives reconfigure the Chinese folk story of Mulan and reflect the narrator's wishful fantasy as compensation for her bewildered girlhood and disappointing Chinese American reality. Kingston's use of mixed genre exemplifies the idea that "memory is as much the product of articulation as it is the result of remembering; memory is created as well as recalled" (Mejia-LaPerle 118). In discussing *The Woman Warrior's* critical role in the development of autobiographical writing by ethnic women writers, Rocío G. Davis proposes that Kingston initiates a challenge to the "pervasive notion of the individual as the prime subject of autobiography;" in Kingston's writing the subject views and inscribes her story from "the prism of intersecting lives" (*Begin Here*, 149). By so doing she revitalizes Mulan's tale in a new context and presents a refreshing generic experiment for autobiographical works.

Within the context of the cross-cultural evolution of Mulan's tale Kingston's rewriting creates a unique image of this character that is more than just a warrior. Enriched by different resources and rendered in a first-person narrative, the character and story of Fa Mu Lan exemplify the complex image of a woman being warrior, avenger, wife, and slave. "When we Chinese girls listened to the adults talk-story, we learned that we failed if we grew up to be but wives or slaves. We could be heroines, swordswomen. Even if she had to rage across all China, a swordswoman got even with anybody who hurt her family" (19). To the narrator of *The Woman Warrior*, Fa Mu Lan is an avenger as much as a warrior. Her mission is not only to save her ailing father from going to war but, more important, she also needs to fight against social injustice on behalf of her family, her village, and other women. Fa Mu Lan's narrative in the "White Tigers" chapter makes it clear that her decision to stay with the old couple in the high mountains and endure fifteen years of intensive training comes from a revengeful motivation. If Fa Mu Lan takes on this apprenticeship, then not only will she learn how to fight so that she can avenge her village and recapture the harvests from the thieves, but the Han people will also remember her dutifulness (22–23).[7] In the account of her physical and mental training under the instruction of an old man and an old woman, the theme of revenge appears repeatedly. On New Year's mornings, the old man permits Fa Mu Lan a look into his water gourd to see her family and the villains she will have to execute once she completes her martial schooling: powerful men counting their money, bandits raiding households, thieves stealing from their neighbors, and the baron looking down upon girls and taking away her younger brother by forceful conscription (30–31). The trainee Fa Mu Lan watches, studies, and remembers those faces so that she can identify the foes worthy of her steel on her future mission as an avenger.

As the narrator articulates in the "White Tigers" chapter, Fa Mu Lan's character and story come from a conflation of various sources. Besides the chant that her mother taught her to sing when she was a little girl, her mother's stories of swordswomen in woods and palaces, Sunday kung fu movies in Chinatown (a modern media genre related to the Chinese chivalric tradition), the letters and hearsay about communist China from relatives and immigrants, as well as her dreams all make their way into the woman warrior's autobiographical narrative. As I have addressed in the first three chapters, neither the "Ballad" nor historical records mention Chinese heroines' precombat training. Kingston's literary reconfiguration uses colorful sequences and details to portray the process in which Fa Mu Lan is transformed from a village girl into an extraordinary fighter. These elements inevitably call to mind the Chinese lady knights-errant discussed in chapter 2, some of whom are guided by magic power and undergo special training before becoming strong-willed and able-bodied swordswomen. Like the enchantress Nie Yinniang, Fa Mu Lan is gifted and guided by magic power in Kingston's recreation. Fa Mu Lan's parents knew from her birth that she is different and "would be taken" some day (22). Her training program in high mountains removes her from social life so that she can acquire the concealment and combat skills used by various creatures, learn how to merge into nature, and immerse herself in dragon ways to make her mind large enough to wield a sword. In this sense, the warrior avenger Kingston portrays is "a combination of the cross-dressing, filial Mulan and the mysterious lady knight-errant" (Lai 78). Although the conflation of the heroine's tale and martial arts plot is not unique to Kingston's writing in the long developing course of Mulan's legend, the seamless fusion of bedtime stories, dreams, kung fu films, and communist China as an imaginary territory with an autobiographical spin in the "White Tigers" chapter is distinctive in the development of Mulan's stories.[8] Kingston's book breaks down the delineation between fiction and nonfiction by creating a "transgeneric mode" that embraces elements from autobiography, biography, myth, history, talk-stories, fantasy, and memory in order to encompass the multiple dimensions of the narrator's life (Blinde 60). The fragmentation of the narrative sequence in Fa Mu Lan's autobiography is partly a result of the narrator's multiple roles as the interpreter, audience, agent, and participant in piecing together her mother's talk-stories and making sense of her own life experience (Lim, "Twelve Asian American Writers," 69). Such a narrative mode works effectively in rendering the complexity and ambiguity embedded in *The Woman Warrior* and illuminates the possibility for a new literary genre and a new reading of literature.[9]

When revisiting Kingston's use of multiple narrative discourses, Silvia Schultermandl argues that Kingston's intervention of cross-over genres and "her attention to local (Chinese American) and global political and social issues" raise issues about how we read and classify literature in

general ("Writing Agaist the Grain," 111). Kingston's generically crossing over pronounces Chinese American women's experience against the
label of "outsiders twice over" (Dearborn 5). Adopting a complex generic format to retell Mulan's tale, *The Woman Warrior* is the first text
to critically interrogate the notion of being a Chinese American woman growing up in between 1950 and 1980. In her seminal work, *Asian
American Literature: An Introduction to the Writings and Their Social
Context* (1982), Elaine H. Kim has pointed out that in the 1970s, while
a number of Asian American male writers were busy at defining their
ethnic minority manhood, Maxine Hong Kingston attempted to delineate a Chinese American woman's point of view (197–98). *The Woman
Warrior* leads the way in portraying fully developed female characters in
Chinese American literature and calls for "a new feminist reading and
writing strategy which would not only respond to the transnational condition of women . . . but also consider the specific historical and cultural
contexts of minority and third-world women's experiences" (Shu 219).
Centering on women's storytelling, the family history of female members, and coming out of an age when feminist awareness was on the rise,
The Woman Warrior lends itself readily to a reading from a gendered
perspective.[10] This is not to say, however, that feminist and gender studies
scholars agree on a definitive reading of the book; the ambiguous nature
of *The Woman Warrior* as represented through the complex image of a
woman as warrior, avenger, wife, and slave does not lend itself to a single
interpretation.[11]

Born and raised in an enclosed community of Chinese immigrants
and their American-born children, the young narrator in *The Woman
Warrior* tries to make sense of the inconsistent images of women that she
perceived from both her mother's talk-stories and her own life experience filled with the contradictory cultural values encountered at home
and at school: women as passive and victimized wives and slaves, as
strong-willed avengers, and as independent heroines. Sexist comments
from her parents, relatives, and immigrant villagers abound: "Feeding
girls is feeding cowbirds"; "There's no profit in raising girls"; "Better to
raise geese than girls." These proverbial phrases enraged the narrator
when she was young (46). She feels trapped in a devastating and helpless
position simply because she was born a girl. Her Chinese heritage seems
hostile toward girls. "There is a Chinese word for the female *I*—which is
'slave.' Break the women with their own tongues" (47)! Her experiences
in American life, however, are also unsatisfactory. Even after she gets
straight As, she receives no praise or encouragement from her parents.

Throughout adolescence, the narrator struggles to reconcile the demands placed on her to be "Chinese-feminine" in the Chinatown community and "American-feminine" among the Caucasian, Negro, Chinese, and Japanese American teenagers at school (11–12). Her confusion and struggle lead to her dismal situation of having no dates at school and being a bad girl at home. Drawing analogy from Alvina E. Quintana's study on Chicana literature, Silvia Schultermandl has called Kingston's narrator a "home girl" without a clearly defined cultural home ("What am I," 4, 14n8). Her difficulties in determining who she is point to the imperative to seek her own unique Chinese American female identity.

Apart from its cultural status in helping establish a Chinese American consciousness, the particularly complex and important genre question of *The Woman Warrior* intertwines ethnicity and gender identity with the narrator's personal experience and struggle over bicultural heritage.[12] In exploring the narrator's fragmented identity and autobiography's intertexuality, *The Woman Warrior* challenges the conventional understanding of the genre and provides a case study of feminist revision of autobiographical studies. Indeed, enmeshed in the feminist movement, Kingston's struggle to match her mother's storytelling skills in *The Woman Warrior* is "both a familial rite of passage and a feminist struggle for self-articulation" (Janette 144). Growing out of the milieu of the civil rights and women's liberation movements of the 1960s and 1970s *The Woman Warrior* embeds the political agenda within the personal narrative. Despite their seeming disconnection, the chapters of Kingston's book are actually structured and organized to develop the themes of women as both victims and victors (Ling, *Between Worlds*, 125) and to articulate the young narrator's confusion about the ambiguous images of Chinese and Chinese American women.

When *The Woman Warrior* was published in the 1970s, the Chinese heroines whom the previous chapters examined were popular topics among neither scholars of Chinese studies nor English-speaking audiences in general.[13] The narrator's struggle in forming a female identity is exacerbated by Orientalist perceptions of Chinese and Chinese American women that have portrayed them primarily in two types of images: that of meekness, docility, and obedience and that of exoticism and entertainment (Ghymn 153). The mixture of different generic elements enables Kingston to tease out the multiple threads of identity—of gender, ethnicity, class, culture, and history. In this sense, Kingston's writing occupies a seminal place in the recent history of feminist thought (Grice, *Negotiating Identities*, 19). By way of rewriting Mulan's story and achieving impressive success in American literature, Kingston has inserted a new and complex image of Chinese and Chinese American women into American culture.

The Woman Warrior's multifaceted narrative reconstructs the Chinese American identity that is closely related to but distinct from Chinese tradition. In Kingston's work, China as a geographical location is transliterated into a semiotic space of recollection; China as personal experience is translated into a cultural repository for reproduction; and China as a text is "reconfigured into a variety of discourses: myth, legend, history, fantasy, films, and talk-stories" (Yuan 292). Thus "China" as well as "Chinese tradition" are invented and imagined through Kingston's literary representation of Fa Mu Lan. "Despite the stress laid on attending to historical or textual materials, Kingston's goal is not to disseminate tradition in its 'original' form but rather to keep cultural myths alive by drawing their relevance to the present" (Deborah Woo 185). In her writing, strands of Chinese folk tales, Chinatown communal narrative, her mother's talk-stories, and her girlhood experience are intertwined and disentangled through the bewilderment of a Chinese American girl. The story combines fantasy and reality, transforming rather than displacing or distorting Chinese tradition; it presents a literary reflection of Chinese America that draws Chinese tradition into self-invention and cultural amalgamation.

In rewriting the Chinese folk story as an autobiographical, postmodern, feminist, and avant-garde text, Kingston established a crucial turning point in Mulan's transformation; equally significant is her opening of the way for writers to engage the complexities of ethnicity and signaled "a narrative boldness and maturity regarding the appropriation and subversion of traditional genres" (Davis and Ludwig 9). The figure of Fa Mu Lan portrayed by Kingston with female sensitivity has become an influential image in Chinese American literary tradition and has inspired other writers. Chinese American playwright David Henry Hwang, for instance, credits the roots of his debut play *FOB* to be the Chinese American (instead of Chinese) literary character of Fa Mu Lan in Kingston's *The Woman Warrior* (*FOB and Other Plays*, 3). Writing this play is Hwang's attempt to "validate the existence of a previous Asian American literary tradition, through an exploration of two mythological characters: Fa Mu Lan . . . [and] Kwan Gung" (Hwang, "Evolving a Multicultural Tradition," 16). Staged at the Public Theatre in New York in 1980, Hwang's play depicts the tension and conflict between American-born Chinese and immigrant newcomers from China. It won an Obie

Award for best play for 1980–1981. Hwang's surrealist drama dismantles "the realist character paradigm in favor of more theatricalized representations" of Chinese American identity (Jew 190). In drawing on tradition as a "reference point," Hwang traces the origin of his character Fa Mu Lan to *The Woman Warrior* and uses Kingston's Chinese American mythology to present his own agenda on racism, sexism, and imperialism.

Cross-dressing, Womanhood, and Loyalty of another Kind

The heroine's cross-dressing occurs earlier and under a different circumstance in *The Woman Warrior*, thus presenting another important departure from the "Ballad." The old couple gives Fa Mu Lan men's clothes and armor upon her completion of the fifteen-year training. As a result, when twenty-two-year-old Fa Mu Lan returns home from the mountains, she is welcomed as a "son." Different from a secret kept between Mulan and her family until her victorious homecoming, as implied in the "Ballad" and depicted in many Chinese versions, Fa Mu Lan's cross-dressing is portrayed as a communal knowledge shared by the villagers before she rides to war in Kingston's book. Collectively they witness her return from the training as well as her departure to combat in cross-dressing. When Fa Mu Lan puts on men's clothes and armor and ties her hair accordingly upon leaving, the villagers come to bid farewell, bringing gifts and praising her to be "beautiful," as if attending a wedding or a ritual sacrifice. Once she is on the battlefield, her husband, a representative of the community, functions as an informed viewer about her female identity. Kingston's rewriting also dramatizes the consequence of women's cross-dressing by stating that "Chinese executed women who disguised themselves as soldiers or students, no matter how bravely they fought or how high they scored on the examinations" (39). This thread, bearing no trace in the "Ballad," is developed further in the Disney Studio's film *Mulan* to create theatrical suspense.

Before her departure to the combat zone Fa Mu Lan's female body is doubly modified: not only is it covered by male clothing but it is also marked by an oath of revenge. Kingston portrays Fa Mu Lan's transformation from a newly graduated apprentice to a warrior avenger representing her family and community in vivid details:

My mother put a pillow on the floor before the ancestors. 'Kneel here,' she said. 'Now take off your shirt.' I kneeled with my back to my parents so none of us felt embarrassed. My mother washed my back as if I had left for only a day and were her baby yet. 'We are go-ing to carve revenge on your back,' my father said. 'We'll write out oaths and names.'

'Wherever you go, whatever happens to you, people will know our sacrifice,' my mother said. 'And you'll never forget either.' She meant that even if I got killed, the people could use my dead body for a weapon, but we do not like to talk out loud about dying.

My father first brushed the words in ink, and they fluttered down my back row after row. Then he began cutting; to make fine lines and points he used thin blades, for the stems, large blades.

My mother caught the blood and wiped the cuts with a cold tow-el soaked in wine. It hurt terribly—the cuts sharp; the air burning; the alcohol cold, then hot—pain so various. . . . The list of griev-ances went on and on. If an enemy should flay me, the light would shine through my skin like lace.

At the end of the last word, I fell forward. Together my parents sang what they had written, then let me rest. . . .

When I could sit up again, my mother brought two mirrors, and I saw my back covered entirely with words in red and black files, like an army, like my army. (34–35)

The metallic iron smell of blood described at the carving scene helps es-tablish connections with menstruation (of both the narrator and Fa Mu Lan), childbirth (of the no name aunt and Fa Mu Lan), and death related to sacrifice and battles. Half way through her apprenticeship in the high mountains Fa Mu Lan starts menstruation and is asked to put off hav-ing children. She tells the reader that during menstrual days "I bled and thought about the people to be killed; I bled and thought about the people to be born" (33). These words refer back to the story of the no name aunt whose childbirth and suicide are used as warnings when the narrator enters puberty; likewise, they foreshadow Fa Mu Lan's forthcoming mili-tary campaign during which she sheds blood and gives birth to a male heir. When the warrior avenger rushes onto the battlefield, the carvings on her back serve as a reminder of her responsibility to take retribu-tion for her family and village and to rescue her fellow men and women. These inscriptions legitimize the woman warrior avenger's violence (Gil 237). They also record her communal history and individual identity. Fa Mu Lan becomes "the embodiment of a communal moral imperative—on her back are written the grievances of the people; her moment of re-vealing herself as a woman is coextensive with her articulation of those wrongs" (Palumbo-Liu, *Asian/American*, 403). In this sense, Fa Mu Lan is as much a warrior as an agent.

The image of a tattooed female body dressed in men's attire is Kingston's unique contribution to the Mulan gallery and has invited critiques from many. The probably most continuous and aggressive criticism on this image comes from another Chinese American writer and critic, Frank Chin, who considers Kingston's rewriting of Mulan a distortion of the "real" Chinese folk tale, particularly in its affirmation of the female body's materiality as a bearer of both history and identity.[14] According to Chin, the carvings are used to dramatize cruelty to women in Kingston's book; her version of Mulan is a "white racist fabrication" ("On Amy Tan," 26) and is rewritten "to the specs of the stereotype of the Chinese woman as a pathological white supremacist victimized and trapped in a hideous Chinese civilization" ("Come All Ye," 3). Chin's virulent position and language in the field of Chinese American literary criticism are "signs of a deeper crisis than simply the recuperation of Chinese masculinity against a traitorous femininity" (Viet Thanh Nguyen 149). His discomfort with an encoded female body exposes his anxiety surrounding the emasculation of Chinese American men, particularly as felt in response to the deprivation of their patriarchal power in America.

As Chin and many other readers and critics have noted, the inspiration of Kingston's carved-words-as-motto scene comes from the story of a Chinese hero, Yue Fei (1103–1142; Ngak Fei in Kingston's spelling). A historical figure, Yue Fei was a military officer, serving the Southern Song court, who commanded his troops victoriously in combats and was executed because of a fabricated charge. According to the entry for Yue Fei in the biographies section of the *Songshi* (History of the Song, Tuotuo et al.), when a messenger arrived at the frontline to arrest him on a false charge of disloyalty, Yue Fei "ripped off his clothes to show the carving on his back, which says 'to serve one's country with complete loyalty.' These words were engraved deeply into his skin" (Tuotuo et al., 365: 11393). His record in the dynastic history does not specify who carved these words on his back. Later his patriotism is rendered even more clearly in the Qing Dynasty story that his mother carved on his back the phrase "to serve one's country with utmost loyalty," a phrase that would become an enduring motto throughout his life. In the Qing novel *Shuoyue quanzhuan* (Complete Stories of the Yue Family, Qian Cai, fl. 1729, et al.), Yue Fei's mother decided to carve words on his back after he declined the recruitment offer from a rebellious chief. Lady Yue said:

I fear that after my death, there may be some unworthy creature who will come and entice you. And if you should momentarily lose your principles and do something disloyal, will you not have destroyed in one day your fragrant reputation gained in half a lifetime? For this reason, I have prayed to Heaven and Earth and to our ancestors, because I want to tattoo on your back the four characters 'Utmost', 'Loyalty', 'Serve' and 'Nation'. I only hope you will be a loyal official, so that after your mother's death, people going to and fro will say, 'What a good lady, she has trained her son to achieve fame by serving his nation with the utmost loyalty, and so his reputation will continue its fragrance for a hundred generations'. I shall then smile even in my grave under the nine springs. (T. L. Yang's translation 248)

In literary renditions, folk stories, and theater performances, Yue Fei's character is portrayed with particular emphasis on his unconditional loyalty to the imperial rule. Even when he is wrongly charged, Yue Fei accepts imprisonment and execution without resistance. In China, his name has long been synonymous with "national hero." The mother's instruction to Yue Fei in the form of engraved words on his back has become a symbol of heroic patriotism, cited repeatedly to encourage others to follow his path.

Indeed, in *The Woman Warrior* it matters that Fa Mu Lan is tattooed and that the carved words are changed from "utmost loyalty" to "revenge." Kingston's writing emphasizes the importance of a female body with history and identity carved onto it. Kingston herself has explained: "The myths I write are new, American. That's why they often appear as cartoons and kung fu movies. I take the power I need from whatever myth. Thus Fa Mu Lan has the words cut into her back; in the traditional story, it is the man, Ngak Fei the Patriot, whose parents cut vows on his back. I mean to take his power for women" ("Personal Statement," 24). In *The Woman Warrior* the engraved words become Fa Mu Lan's secret "army" and empower the woman warrior avenger before she launches the battle. As an individual, the carvings mark Fa Mu Lan as a carrier of the communal and familial history; she literally carries the historical traces ("names") on her back. As a member of her community, a woman with "oaths and names" tattooed on her body becomes recognizable. Thus, her personal life, interlaced with history, will not be forgotten. Wherever she goes, whatever happens to her, "people will know." Here the woman warrior avenger's unforgettable body exemplifies female empowerment.

Different from the "Ballad" that portrays the heroine as a loyal subject who answers the enlistment call from the imperial court, Kingston's book directs Fa Mu Lan's loyalty toward her family and village and depicts her military adventure as part of a peasant uprising. This revision connects Mulan's image with the female rebels and bandits that we have addressed before and changes her social role in the story. Fa Mu Lan leads the rebellious army to take over the capital city, behead the emperor, clean out the palace, and inaugurate a peasant to set out a new order in China (42). For the warrior avenger the misogynistic oppressing baron is as responsible as the imperial court for what has happened to her, to her family, and to her community. After the establishment of a new political rule, Fa Mu Lan dismisses her troops and attacks the baron's stronghold alone and executes him with her sword. The public trials and corporal punishment for the baron's family and servants and the confiscation and redistribution of their property are political allusions to the social reform in China after the Communist Party seized power and established the new republic in 1949. These allusions are important in *The Woman Warrior* not only because they refer to contemporary Chinese history, particularly the socialist reform that aimed at helping the poor and affected Kingston's relatives living in China at the time, but because it also reinforces the blurry boundaries between reality and imagination in the autobiographical narrative of Kingston/Fa Mu Lan/"I." Through the letters from relatives and conversations between her parents the narrator acquires episodic pieces regarding the social changes in China and their impact. These portions, together with other hearsay from immigrant villagers in Chinatown, provide sources for the narrator to construct an imaginary homeland that has a root in China as well as Chinese America.

The intimate connection between the narrator and Fa Mu Lan has as much to do with gender as with cultural heritage. The Chinese "Ballad" does not allow the woman and the warrior to appear at the same time. When taking on the role of a warrior, Mulan appears as a man; her female identity is suspended, a secret to be revealed only when her mission is accomplished. Her female identity is exposed only at the moment when she resumes her womanly life. Kingston's recreation, however, emphasizes the coexistence of Fa Mu Lan's womanhood and warrior's life. Although her biological sex remains a secret on the battlefield (with the exception of her husband, an informed viewer), Fa Mu Lan's disguise neither forfeits nor disrupts her womanhood. In contrast to the girlhood portrayed in the "Ballad," Kingston's work imagines Fa Mu Lan's life as an adult woman. This warrior avenger is not a maiden like Joan of Arc:

she does women's work and is strengthened by marriage and childbirth (48). As I discussed in chapter 3, Xu Wei's play, *Ci Mulan*, ends with Mulan's wedding to a man chosen by her parents; she still stands at the edge of becoming a wife. Kingston's rewriting realizes the character's womanhood at the same time as her heroic identity. Fa Mu Lan emerges as a warrior avenger as well as wife and mother.

In *The Woman Warrior*, while the army under her command is storming over the land, smashing the corrupt ruling power, defeating varied opponents, and beheading vicious enemies, Fa Mu Lan fulfills her dual roles: a warrior leader in public domain and a wife-mother in private life. Her childhood-friend-turned husband rides side by side with her as a fellow soldier on the battlefield and shares intimate moments with her as a partner in her tent. During her military expedition Fa Mu Lan is portrayed in both masculine and feminine characters. When she is a cross-dressing, horse-riding, and sword-yielding warrior, her body appears masculine in public and feminine in private.[15] Her husband is presented as a privileged viewer who witnesses this combination and realizes her femininity. The power of this provoking image is further strengthened when Fa Mu Lan becomes pregnant. Her female body is thus triply marked: by male disguise, by the words carved on her back, and by "the baby large in front" (47). At this moment, the character of Fa Mu Lan is highlighted as both a warrior and a woman who "performs the climactic action of her tale" while carrying out the task of revenge (Eakin 261).

The birth scene in "White Tigers" presents a sharp contrast to that described in "No Name Woman," the first chapter of Kingston's book. After the watchful villagers attack her house, the no name aunt gives birth in a pigsty in silence without a partner. She is punished for violating the role of a loyal wife and family member as well as for having a private life apart from the communal living. Her infant who is denied descent and purpose remains genderless in the story. In contrast, Fa Mu Lan is temporarily exempted from her social obligation (that is, she hides from battle once) to give birth, and she is accompanied by her husband. The newborn, a male heir, is ritually celebrated by the entire army when the couple ties the umbilical cord to the pole and lets it fly with the red flag. When Fa Mu Lan rides back to combat, the baby boy is cradled in a sling inside her armor. He remains by his mother's side for a month and returns home with his father after the full-month celebration.

In the final duel, the baron is not even a foe worthy of Fa Mu Lan's steel. When she finally faces the baron alone, Fa Mu Lan identifies herself as a female avenger, rips off her shirt to reveal her womanly body, and declares: "I want your life in payment for your crimes against the villagers" before she slashes him across the face and cuts off his head (43, 44). Empowered by imagination and recreation Kingston depicts a character "who is perhaps the most fulfilled woman ever, historical or imaginary" (Joseph Lau 51). The "White Tigers" chapter does not close with the woman warrior avenger's glory in the combat zone; rather, it ends with the restoration of Fa Mu Lan's womanly position in family life after she successfully completes her mission. The heroine is, after all, a woman with female duties to fulfill. Upon returning to her village, Fa Mu Lan re-dresses in feminine clothes and goes to her in-laws' house. "Wearing my black embroidered wedding coat, I knelt at my parents-in-law's feet, as I would have done as a bride. 'Now my public duties are finished' I said, 'I will stay with you, doing farm work and housework, and giving you more sons'" (45). Kingston presents a triumphant role model for both male and female at the finale: an invincible warrior and exultant leader as well as a dutiful daughter, daughter-in-law, wife and mother. Fa Mu Lan's return to her womanly life in its domestic sphere as the denouement, however, again points to the complex image of a woman being warrior, avenger, wife, and slave who once married belongs to her in-laws' family and whose prime responsibility is to serve her in-laws devotedly, to honor her husband's ancestors, and to extend the family line by bearing male heirs. Upon her arrival at home, Fa Mu Lan gives her helmet and swords to her son, a symbolic gesture for her return to womanly life as well as for the heroic heritage to be carried on by the family heir.

Kingston's character Fa Mu Lan undoubtedly and pointedly differs from the heroine Mulan in the Chinese folk "Ballad."[16] Yet it is never the writer's intention to present a point-for-point identification or a word-for-word translation of the Chinese story. As I have discussed, even in Chinese culture a "real," "popular," and "universally known" Mulan (to use Frank Chin's words) can hardly be found in a single text. In the long developing course of Mulan's story, Chinese writers and storytellers have envisioned this heroine in a variety of ways. Therefore the emphasis on "how Kingston's version deviates from a 'definitive' one that alone chronicles the life of a 'real' Fa Mu Lan" misses the point of *The Woman Warrior* (Sau-ling Wong, "Kingston's Handling," 29). Rather, Kingston's use of Chinese narrative transcends its original context and is re-rooted in her Chinese American actuality. Key to Kingston's reconfiguration of the woman warrior avenger is not only the character

Mulan's transformation but also how her story is told and retold through communal and maternal storytelling. As the young narrator tells the reader, her acquaintance with Mulan's legend comes from her mother's chant that accompanied her childhood, a significant reflection of Chinese American folk tradition. Speaking as an adult, the narrator reflects:

> At last I saw that I too had been in the presence of great power, my mother talking-story. After I grew up, I heard the chant of Fa Mu Lan, the girl who took her father's place in battle. Instantly I remembered that as a child I had followed my mother about the house, the two of us singing about how Fa Mu Lan fought gloriously and returned alive from war to settle in the village. I had forgotten this chant that was once mine, given me by my mother, who may not have known its power to remind. (19–20)

The narrator also reminds the reader that, whenever her mother needs to warn her American-born children about life, she talks stories that are for the younger generation to grow up on (5). The mother alters and codifies stories originating from Chinese tradition in order to discipline her children as well as to preserve the cultural legacy that she has brought with her across the Pacific Ocean.

The narrator unfolds her identity pursuit as she tries to piece together what she has heard about the past, the cultural legacy inherited from her family and community, and her American life in the present. The image of the woman warrior avenger Fa Mu Lan is "a hybrid product, situated in a non-place, between Chinese mythology and American modernity" (Gil 236). Kingston has transformed Mulan from a filial daughter who enters combat to protect her father to a warrior avenger who fights against social injustice. The young narrator in *The Woman Warrior* uses fantasy to reshape her life that has been filled with confusion and disappointment. In claiming the power of legend Kingston simultaneously claims "her own personal strength and her ability to act in a social context" (Frye 297). By this token, the writer's translocation of the Chinese folk story signifies a cultural repositioning that helps Kingston construct a distinctive identity of her own. Kingston shares her belief that "myths have to change, be useful or be forgotten. Like the people who carry them across oceans, the myths become American" (Kingston, "Personal Statement," 24); she also creates her own mythology that draws from the past of elder generations to recollect the childhood memory among Chinese immigrants in America from her mother's talk-stories and her own imagination. She is telling the reader a story her mother told her. The beginning is her mother's, but the ending is her own (206). Kingston's story of Fa Mu Lan is a Chinese American tale that strides across national and cultural boundaries.

With her perfect fulfillment of filial piety and social duty, Fa Mu Lan achieves recognition in her life as well as an enduring name. The young narrator longs for such appreciation that is missing in her real life. In this respect, imagination plays a compensatory role in the made-up "gun and knife" fantasies, through which the reader can hear the voice of the girl narrator who wants to be loved, recognized, and valued. In addition, through the woman warrior avenger, the narrator expresses her eagerness to fight against social injustice. David Palumbo-Liu calls Fa Mu Lan's carving scene "the most striking illustration of the sublimation of the political into the personal" that presents a "symbolic parallel drawn between the act of narrative vengeance of the woman warrior and that of the narrator" (*Asian/American*, 403). The narrator's body, while not physically tattooed, is nonetheless branded with demeaning words that diminish and occlude her. As she claims, she and the swordswoman are not so dissimilar. They share the words at their backs (53), but the words carved on Fa Mu Lan's back are "oaths and names," while "chink," "gook," and "no good" affix themselves to the narrator. "From the fairy tales, I've learned exactly who the enemy are. I easily recognize them—business-suited in their modern American executive guise, each boss two feet taller than I am and impossible to meet eye to eye" (48, 49). The narrator's subsequent actions, such as declining to study hard at school, refusing to cook at home, breaking dishes on purpose, and rejecting the duties imposed on her by Chinatown sayings and stories are her ways of objection and rebellion. Facing her discriminatory bosses in the American business world, the narrator uses a rebellious voice that may come from a small person—whispered and squeaking—but it is insistent. Self-affirmed the narrator also takes on the role of a female avenger. In her fantasy, she imagines herself as a fighter with a sword storming across China and the United States to take back family properties from the Communists as well as the Americans.

In a 1989 radio interview with Frank Abe on Seattle's radio station KIRO, Kingston stated her idea of writing life stories: "I think to write true biography means you have to tell people's dreams. You have to tell what they imagine. You have to tell their vision. And, in that sense, I think I have developed a new way of telling a life story" (qtd. in Chin, "Come All Ye," 29). In creating the character and story of Fa Mu Lan in *The Woman Warrior*, Kingston appropriates Mulan's tale autobiographically

THE WHITE TIGER MYTHOLOGY / 111

in a cross-cultural context and uses the power of her familial and communal mythology to reinforce her Chinese American identity. Her transfiguration invents a way of telling the stories of Chinese American women's lives and hopes. The combination of wife, slave, and avenger in the no name aunt reflects such a dilemma and reveals both acceptance and disavowal of Orientalism (Su-lin Yu 69). In imagining Fa Mu Lan as a woman warrior, avenger, wife, and mother, the narrator "transforms what could be seen as a handicap into an advantage, integrating limitations and restrictions into her own enterprise for liberty" (Storhoff 89). In portraying women being both forceful and submissive, Kingston not only represents a bewildered girlhood truthfully but also challenges the common social misconception of Chinese and Chinese American women. As an apprentice following the old couple's instructions in the high mountains Fa Mu Lan says, "I learned to make my mind large, as the universe is large, so that there is room for paradoxes" (29). As readers, we might have to expand our minds as well so that we can embrace the provoking image of Kingston's woman warrior avenger.

A Warrior with (S)words: Personal is Political

As widely noted, Fa Mu Lan's story appears in the first half of *The Woman Warrior*. Kingston has explained, "Readers tell me ['White Tigers'] ought to have been the climax. But I put it at the beginning to show that the childish myth is past, not the climax we reach for" ("Cultural Mis-Readings," 57). In *The Woman Warrior* Kingston gives the image of woman warrior in different shapes: she begins with Fa Mu Lan who not only wields a sword but also sings glorious songs coming out of the sky into her head at night to inspire her army, and then Kingston turns to the mother character, Brave Orchid, whose life in China and America is portrayed mainly in the third and fourth chapters, "Shaman" and "At the Western Palace." Brave Orchid's talk-stories enrich the young narrator's girlhood and imagination; her character and experience as a pioneer woman in her family set an example of tenacity and courage. In the fifth and final chapter, "A Song for a Barbarian Reed Pipe," Kingston introduces Cai Yan, a poet whose power is realigned through words. Cai Yan's story brings the book to a climax and opens a path for the narrator. In this structure, Kingston's book presents an image of the woman warrior who moves from wielding swords to employing words.

Kingston reimagines the story of the Chinese poet Cai Yan, telling it through an intricate structure of mother-daughter conversations that stem from reality, memory, talk-story, and imagination. The historical Cai Yan, though tragic, is not regarded as heroic. Daughter of an influential scholar and statesman Cai Yong (133–192), Cai Yan (commonly know by her courtesy name Wenji) married three men, but none was her choice. According to historical records, Cai Yan was "quite knowledgeable and eloquent, and was also a master of music. [She] was first married to Wei Zhongdao, a native of Hedong. After her husband passed away and left no child, [she] returned to her maternal family" (Fan Ye, 84: 2800). Around the years 194 and 195, Cai Yan was abducted by the Southern Xiongnu people (Hsiung-nu in Kingston's spelling). She lived among them for years and became a consort of a chieftain, by whom she bore two children. After being ransomed by Cao Cao (155–220), a friend of her late father, she had to leave her children behind and returned to the Han court. Later, Cao Cao married her to Dong Si. The historical record in the *Hou hanshu* (History of the Latter Han, Fan Ye, 398–445) identified her as Dong Si's wife. Cai Yan is remembered in Chinese literature for three sorrow-stricken poems conventionally attributed to her: two poems under the same title of "Beifen shi" (Poem of Affliction) and another titled "Hujia shiba pai" (Eighteen Stanzas of the Barbarian Reed Pipe) (see figure 4.1).[17]

In Kingston's retelling, Cai Yan becomes a woman of heroic spirit and strong mind who adjusts to her captivity among the Xiongnu people. In Kingston's imagination, Cai Yan "fought desultorily when the fighting was at a distance, and she cut down anyone in her path during the madness of close combat. The tribe fought from horseback, charging en masse into villages and encampments. She gave birth on the sand." She spent years in exile, lonely and unable to communicate with her captors, "until one night she heard music tremble and rise like desert wind" whose sharpness and cold made her ache (208). Cai Yan sang about China and her family through Chinese lyrics, high and clear, accompanied by barbarian music. She understood their yearning as expressed in the high, sharp notes produced by reed pipes, and they understood her sadness and anger, even though she sang in a language that they did not speak (208). At this moment, the poet's voice functions as "both a subject and an icon for cultural change" (Crafton 52). When Cai Yan was ransomed and returned to her homeland and life among the Han people, she was forced to leave her children behind, but she brought the songs with her. "[O]ne of the three that has been passed down to us is 'Eighteen Stanzas for a Barbarian Reed Pipe,' a song that Chinese sing to their own instruments. It translated well" (209). Cai Yan's personal affliction and tragedy

FIGURE 4.1. In this illustration drawn by Wang Hui (1736–1795), Cai Yan (identified by her courtesy name Cai Wenji) holds a string instrument. From *Baimei xinyong tuzhuan* (Illustrated Hundred Beauties with Dedication Poems), edited by Yan Xiyuan (fl. 1787–1804) and Yuan Mei (1716–1798), China: Ji ye xuan, 1804.

embedded in the "translated" poetic form, like the high-pitched notes in the barbarian music, touch the reader deeply to the heart.

Kingston portrays Cai Yan as a heroine empowered by words. Responding to readers who regard Fa Mu Lan, the swordswoman and military commander, as the archetypal woman warrior, Kingston, a pacifist, would rather "we use the powers of Cai Yan, the woman warrior who made words of the formations of birds in the sky, V for 'human'" (Kingston, *Through the Black Curtain*, 8).[18] In closing her book with a revised tale of the poet, the narrator reviews her bewildered girlhood from the distance of a mature point of view so that the pen replaces the sword, hope replaces hatred, and anticipation replaces agony (Yan Gao 42). The ending of *The Woman Warrior* hints that the narrator, like Cai Yan, has survived the ordeal of "obviating cultural barriers through mutual understanding and emotional empathy" (Yan Gao 45). The mutual understanding applies to Cai Yan vis-à-vis her captors as well as the narrator vis-à-vis her reader. Mulan and Cai Yan share their adaptability in a completely new environment: nature in high mountains for the former and a foreign tribe for the latter. Re-imagining the poet's story, Kingston further transforms the woman warrior's image from the character of Fa Mu Lan, sanctioned by the sword in the narrator's girlhood fantasy, to the figure of Cai Yan, empowered by words. After all, the narrator lives in present-tense America; she admits, "no bird called me, no wise old people tutored me. I have no magic beads, no water gourd sight, no rabbit that will jump in the fire when I'm hungry. I dislike armies" (49). Yet, the narrator confronts an even more difficult mission and faces multiple enemies: "To avenge my family, I'd have to storm across China to take back our farm from the Communists; I'd have to rage across the United States to take back the laundry in New York and the one in California. Nobody in history has conquered and united both North America and Asia" (49). Being neither able nor wanting to wield a sword like Fa Mu Lan, the narrator chooses the path of Cai Yan: to resort to words for female empowerment in writing *The Woman Warrior* into a Chinese American tale. Her writing is "dizzying, elemental, a poem turned into a sword" (Leonard 77). For Kingston, writing becomes a powerful act of self-definition, just like swordsmanship for Fa Mu Lan and singing for Cai Yan.

In an interview, Kingston discloses that her publisher chose the book's title *The Woman Warrior*. "I don't really like warriors. I wish I had not had a metaphor of a warrior, a person who uses weapons and goes to war. I guess I always have in my style a doubt about wars as a way of solving things" (qtd. in King-kok Cheung, "The Woman Warrior versus The Chinaman Pacific," 124). In retrospect, Kingston regretted the title and that she had not ended "the feminist war" in the book with a story of a female war veteran who becomes a peacemaker (Bonetti 40; Seshachari 193; Sabine 8). In *The Fifth Book of Peace* (2003), Kingston writes the "strange and sexy" story of another woman warrior, Ming Hong, whom her mother said was "better than Fa Mook Lan" (58). In this version of a woman top graduate, a cross-dressed woman outwits her male contemporaries in the imperial examination and civil administration, a tale connecting and extending the power of words displayed in Cai Yan's story.

Susan Evangelista calls Kingston's story of the Chinese American woman warrior avenger the "most sensitive, most authentic, and certainly most compelling voice" to articulate the narrator's struggles, defeats, and triumphs (244, 252). In particular, her provoking translocation of Chinese mythology of Mulan and the story of Cai Yan empowers the characters in the process of identity formation (Yuan 301). Thus, *The Woman Warrior* lends itself to a complex investigation of Chinese American identity politics during the past few decades. Through the autobiographical narrative of Fa Mu Lan, *The Woman Warrior* addresses the narrator's personal dilemma together with the political situation of Chinese America. It provides an example from Chinese American literature of the "problematic of ethnic and diasporic identification within and outside social space and historical time" (Palumbo-Liu, *Asian/ American*, 348).[19] As a personal narrative set in Stockton, California, in the 1940s and 1950s, *The Woman Warrior* provides a useful case study for discussing "how one conceives of Chinese American literature, and, by extension, ethnic literature in America" (Sau-ling Wong, "Necessity and Extravagance," 3), particularly the issue of self-definition and identity politics. In recreating Mulan's tale *The Woman Warrior* conflates two sources of cultural legacy and is essentially about a Chinese American's attempt to "come to terms with the paradoxes that shape and often enrich her life and to find a uniquely Chinese American voice to serve as a weapon for her life" (Kim, *Asian American Literature*, 207). Through Fa Mu Lan's autobiographical narrative, Kingston explores female heroism in the mythic past as well as possibilities for Chinese American women's empowerment in the present.[20] A large number of book reviews, reader responses, and criticism of *The Woman Warrior* address the "White Tigers" chapter and its revision of Mulan's story with particular emphasis. Many scholars have explored the historical and cultural information that contextualizes Kingston's writing. Also examining Kingston's text from the "roots angle," another group of critics have addressed her misrepresentation of Chinese and Chinese American culture.[21]

As representatives of the cultural nationalists in Chinese American literary studies, the editors of the anthology *Aiiieeeee! An Anthology of Asian American Writers* (1974) declare their stance with a strong denial of "the goofy concept of the dual personality" of Chinese Americans; their rejection of "both Asia and white America" is meant to prove that "we were neither one nor the other. Nor were we half or more one than the other" (Chin et al., xii). In 1991, the *Aiiieeeee* editors published a sequel, *The Big Aiiieeeee! An Anthology of Chinese American and Japanese American Literature*, which principally reiterates their perception of Chinese and Asian American literature. Frank Chin's ninety-two-page introduction to this collection, "Come All Ye Asian American Writers of the Real and the Fake," has become a representative piece in the contest over identity politics in Chinese as well as Asian American literature. For Asian Americans, whose history in North America is marked (although Chinese were the only group excluded by immigration laws) by exclusion, discrimination, and isolation, choosing "both/and" in the 1960s and 1970s ran the risk of seeming un-American, inassimilable, and hence being forever foreign and "Oriental." Elaine Kim explains the rationale: "In the late 1970s . . . I sought delimitations, boundaries, and parameters because I felt they were needed to establish the fact that there was such a thing as Asian American literature. . . . That is why cultural nationalism has been so crucial. . . . Insisting on a unitary identity seemed the only effective means of opposing and defending oneself against marginalization. . . . Yet Asian American identities have never been exclusively racial" (Foreword, xi-xii). Kim talks about Asian American cultural nationalism as a pan-ethnic perspective rather than group-centered consciousness. They coexist without canceling each other. Cultural nationalism was crucial at that time for the purpose of establishing the legitimacy of Chinese American literature, a freshly established field in academia. At the time the urge to claim America and to establish the Chinese American presence in U.S. history and reality seemed to be oppositional to the affirmation of one's Asian origins. However, the "fixed, closed, and narrowly defined" Chinese American identity inevitably produced conflicts and problematics (Kim, "Beyond Railroads and Internment," 12). The enduring critical debate, a historical milestone in Chinese American literature, led by Frank Chin on one side and Kingston on the other, centers on cultural authenticity.[22] This war of words, provoked particularly by Kingston's retelling of Mulan's story, "has enlivened university conferences and inspired academic papers, doctoral dissertations, and college lectures. Entire papers have been devoted to what Kingston got 'right' and 'wrong' in *The Woman Warrior*" (Solovitch) and is a microcosm of the critical issues that help shape Chinese American literary studies.[23]

Upon reading *The Woman Warrior* as a text of the "Chinese American discourse," David Leiwei Li points out that its multiple narrations invite the reader to be a participant of the talk-story community and help empower narratives ("Production of Chinese American Tradition," 329). The process of questioning the notions of tradition and the gendered ethnicity in the Chin-Kingston conflict pertains to "the urgency and prevalence of the politics of identification" (Rey Chow, "A Phantom Discipline," 1386). The questions raised in Chinese American writers' creative as well as critical writings encourage the reader both to think about Chinese American identity in a way that differs from the Orientalist imagination and to engage critically with female agency in the context of Chinese America.

Opposing both American Orientalist discourse and conservative notions of a single correct representation of Chinese America are representations of "invented tradition" that create, change, and repeat tales in the light of history and contemporary circumstances. Divergent as the themes and forms may be in their writing, generations of immigrant and American-born writers, to claim their Chinese Americanness, take part in constructing the "Chinese American discursive." Their literary efforts mark the opening of possibilities for a renewed and multivalent movement in Chinese America. In my opinion, the appropriate way will neither build a temple to Chinese Americanness nor deliver a uniform monologue about the "tradition." Rather, Chinese Americans need to invent a collective identity through a constant dialogue among themselves and to theorize the emergent minority culture with its dynamic fluctuation and heterogeneity. Hence, Kingston's self-evaluation—"my role in Chinese American literature is that I write in such a way that it helps our work to be taken seriously as literature, not merely as anthropology, entertainment, exotics" (cited in Yin 229)—not only summarizes her own contribution but also underscores that of other Chinese American writers.

For American women writers of Chinese heritage who are daughters and granddaughters born in the United States, Chinese culture inevitably is linked to their familial and communal connections, especially to the maternal stories.[24] For the young narrator in *The Woman Warrior*, the smell of China usually flies out from her mother's suitcases, full of memories. China, in the daughter's mind, is an image of the past, a remote and larger Chinatown. Deborah Woo differentiates two versions of authenticity in her discussion of Kingston's writing—the historical and the experiential—that are revealed respectively in the writer's concern for "recovering or preserving some aspect of the historical past" and for "articulating some experiential reality about the present" (184). Kingston's reinvention of Mulan is therefore a result as well as a literary reflection of such "dual authenticity." The familial and communal tradition in *The Woman Warrior* reflects a fused version of her mother's "talk-stories," a shared cultural memory of her immigrant family and community, along with her own confusion and imagination while growing up. The complex stories of past and present, of factual and imaginative, are embedded in the narrator's personal recollection.

Taking into account Kingston's experience of growing up a Chinese American daughter in Stockton's small Chinatown, Sau-ling Wong defends *The Woman Warrior* against the charge of its "confirmation of notorious Oriental inscrutability" because "Kingston's chief artistic enterprise . . . is to establish the legitimacy of a unique Chinese American (as opposed to 'Chinese Chinese') experience and sensibility" ("Kingston's Handling," 26–27). Kingston's writing complicates, rather than distorts, the "authentic" by drawing on different strands that help shape the cultural tradition for the American-born children of Chinese heritage. Chinese Americans' bi- and multicultural identity is shaped by Chinese tradition, by the memories and experiences of their immigrant parents going abroad, as well as by American culture. Such varied resources connect the second and later generations with their ancestors' past and place of origin, which are remembered and passed on mainly through storytelling, as portrayed in *The Woman Warrior*. For the young narrator, the cultural environment around her is comprised of her mother's accounts of her Chinese life in the village, of her mother's talk-stories as recalled by the daughter, of the Chinatown subculture that is constructed by Chinese immigrants and influenced by their birthplace and host society, and of her own American life. "*The Woman Warrior* ends with the narrator negotiating the translation of Chinese myth to Chinese American solidity, reconciling herself to the absolute distance between the mystified past of China and the concreteness of American life by way of an adjustment of expectations and values, identities and potential" (Palumbo-Liu, *Asian/American*, 404). In *The Woman Warrior* the narrator's fantasies and imagining in her girlhood serve as vehicles for her to seek a place of her own while growing up a Chinese American woman.

Chinese American literary production as "an active engagement" (David Li, "Production of Chinese American Tradition," 321) has gained significant visibility during the past few decades or so. David Leiwei Li considers Kingston's works significant landmarks in constructing the "Chinese American discourse" in order to displace the "American Orientalist discourse" and to change its status in American literary tradition from that of "a near absence" to that of a presence.[25] Instead of taking a confrontational and combative posture, Kingston has chosen a subtle and complicated path. In *The Woman Warrior* the past (China) is represented through the explicit review and revision of the "American Orientalist discourse" and of her mother's talk-stories while the present (Chinese America) is reconfigured. *The Woman Warrior* has nourished "the inscription of a female tradition in a Chinese American sense" (Arfaoui 45). In *The Woman Warrior*, the folk story of Mulan has been given a feminist spin to empower Chinese as well as Chinese American women (Sheng-mei Ma, *Immigrant Subjectivities*, 17). This self-empowering, self-affirming process is imbued with ambiguity. In her upbringing the young narrator has been confronting the inconsistencies and contradictions that lead to her constant confusion and her questioning of tradition and identity. She finds herself suspended between memory and reality. As Kingston writes, "Chinese Americans, when you try to understand what things in you are Chinese, how do you separate what is peculiar to childhood, to poverty, insanities, one family, your mother who marked your growing with stories, from what is Chinese? What is Chinese tradition and what is the movies" (5–6)? In this sense, *The Woman Warrior* is not "another in a long line of Chinkie autobiographies by Pocahontas yellow blowing the same old mixed up East/West soul struggle," as Frank Chin has accused (qtd. in David Li, *Imagining the Nation*, 45). The multiple stories told in Kingston's mixed genre portray the particular bond between Chinese American women and cultural memory. The female characters, actively involved in remembering history, play a major role in building up a talking-story community. At the same time, their narrative undermines the totalizing "American Orientalist discourse."

"Besides bringing Asian America into the national consciousness and activating the quest for the ethnic anecdote, lore, and myth, *The Woman Warrior*'s enduring contribution lies perhaps just in its foregrounding of representational issues that have accompanied the growth of Asian American creative and critical production" (David Li, *Imagining the*

Nation, 61–62). Kingston's efforts in seeking female empowerment push the critical investigation of Chinese American identity from the cultural nationalist stage to that emphasizing the "gender-ethnicity nexus" (to borrow Sau-ling Wong's words, "Ethnicizing Gender," 111). She, therefore, plays a key role in the critical transition of Chinese American identification. With new waves of Chinese immigrants arriving after the 1965 Immigration Act, the altered demography provoked a change in the landscape of Chinese American literature.[26] The lines between Chinese and Chinese American, Asian and Asian American, "so crucial to identity formations in the past, are increasingly blurred" (Kim, Preface, xi). New gender and ethnic relations in the 1980s and 1990s required scholarship to "denationalize" Chinese America and to revisit the formation of Chinese American site.[27] The essays in the special issue *New Formations, New Questions: Asian American Studies* (1997) collectively resituate the cultural, historical, and social dimensions of Chinese America within the new context.[28] In her assessment of this significant switch of emphasis in Chinese American literary studies in the 1990s, King-kok Cheung points out:

> Whereas identity politics—with its stress on cultural nationalism and American nativity—governed earlier theoretical and critical formulations, the stress is now on heterogeneity and diaspora. The shift has been from seeking to "claim America" to forging a connection between Asia and Asian America; from centering on race and on masculinity to revolving around the multiple axes of ethnicity, gender, class, and sexuality; from being concerned primarily with social history and communal responsibility to being caught in the quandaries and possibilities of postmodernism and multiculturalism. (*Interethnic Companion*, 1)

The critical landscape of Chinese American identity politics has evolved from addressing the identities of Chinese Americans as the "Oriental problem" and claiming America (Chun, "Go West"; Henry Yu) to recent scholarship toward transnational perspectives. "Mobilized by historical, conceptual, and institutional forces" (Xiaojing Zhou 3), cultural heritage and identity politics in Chinese American literary studies have stepped beyond the dichotomy of the "real" and the "fake" to a new focus on the Chinese America in a transnational and multicultural context. The "reterritorialization" of Chinese American studies during the past decade or so opens the field to multilingual, international, and interdisciplinary perspectives, or to use Lisa Lowe's words "the international within the national" ("The International within the National," 29). In 2004 Maggie Ann Bowers envisioned two possibilities: "The future of Asian American Studies is at a crossroads that will lead it either towards a split in the field of study into the two areas of Asian diasporic global studies and local immigrant American studies, or towards a comparative inclusive approach that not only allows for differences of history, the gradients of ancestry and connections with Asia itself, but also encourages us to gain insight by comparison" (116). Since we entered the new millennium, we see the field's movement toward, to borrow Youngsuk Chae's words, a "politically conscious Asian American multiculturalism." The discourse of hyphenated identity of Chinese America, and by extension Asian America, has evolved "beyond hyphen" (Ty "Rethinking the Hyphen"; Ty and Goellnicht). Different creative and critical strategies are used to contest or escape the identities imposed on Chinese Americans "by history, by the media, by high and low culture, by political and legal discourse" (Ty and Goellnicht 10). The "both/and" and "either/or" approaches to self-definition have developed into the transnational and multicultural lens.[29] As Rajini Srikanth stated in her "Presidential Meditations" (2008), the field has "widen[ed] beyond a focus on the U.S. nation state to consider the Americas (Canada, Latin America, and the Caribbean); to engage transitional allegiances spanning the United States and ancestral homelands in East, Southeast, and South Asia; and more recently, to explore West Asia (what is known in the United States as the Middle East)" (1). She sees the ever-expanding Asian America as "a sign of vibrancy, as evidence of the field's confident assertion of its value in studying and responding to changing conditions locally and globally" (Srikanth 1).

When asked about the potential audiences for her writing, Kingston pointed to three groups: herself, Chinese Americans, and all readers in general. By writing for herself, Kingston finds a voice to articulate taboos, such as the family secret of the "no name woman," and in the process she is able to take stock of her bewildered girlhood. Next, "by writing for her fellow Chinese Americans, she introduces to that group one voice that she hopes will inspire others to speak out" (Huntley 29). Regarding the third group, Kingston obviously achieved her goal: advocating for a Chinese American voice in American literature through both creative and critical writing. Showing a strong awareness of the double burden of her ethnicity and gender, Kingston has clearly stated that her mission as a writer has been to insert a new voice into American culture, a voice not only female but also Chinese American. She says, "I'm doing with this womanly, feminine narrative voice . . . something quite revolutionary in Western literature. . . . It's usually a white man. And I'm saying, 'Look, the omniscient narrator is a Chinese woman'" (qtd. in Hurley 85). Not articulated in her initial expectation, Kingston's readership has expanded to include Chinese-speaking audiences as a result of the publication of *The Woman Warrior* in Chinese translation.

Chinese readers' responses to *The Woman Warrior* began earlier than its Chinese translation. For instance, Ya-Jie Zhang, a Chinese academic, published probably the earliest reading of Kingston's book from the vantage point of a Chinese woman and at first felt offended by Kingston's book. After taking an American Ethnic Literature course with Amy Ling at Rutgers University during her stay in the United States, however, Zhang concludes that "*The Woman Warrior* is indeed a good book" (Ya-Jie Zhang 107). Two decades later, numerous Chinese readers have become familiar with Kingston (by her Chinese name Tang Tingting) and *The Woman Warrior* (by the slightly different Chinese translations of the book title: *Nü yongshi, Nü doushi,* and *Nü zhanshi*). In addition to reviews and newspaper articles, scholarly studies of Kingston and her works, particularly *The Woman Warrior,* have proliferated in China. Within the rising interest in Chinese American literature among Chinese scholars, critics, and general readers, *The Woman Warrior* holds a particularly important position. In China the popularity of Kingston and other Chinese American writers, such as Amy Tan, belongs to the new intellectual engagement with the internationalizing Asian American literary studies.

No Chinese American literary work has gained greater acceptance from general audiences or such enduring attention from critics than *The Woman Warrior.* This work has widespread distribution: Kingston is said to be "the most anthologized of any living American writer," and her work is read by "more American college students than [the work of] any other living author" (Skenazy and Martin vii).[30] Thus, the White Tiger mythology, inspired by the Mulan lore yet recreated by Kingston, represents a Chinese American woman warrior avenger autobiographically in a cross-cultural context and leads the way to Mulan's international fame and further transformation in visual representations in the post-Kingston era. After the late 1970s, this character continues to thrive, rewritten as a Chinese American icon whose influence has exceeded the realm of literature outside the geographical boundaries of North America.

5 / One Heroine, Many Characters: Mulan in American Picture Books

Mulan's story is so well known and so beloved, I wanted to do what I could to preserve the heart of her story, present it honestly, while making it interesting to the widest possible audience. . . . There are many positive values youngsters can take from both the movie and book. Male or female, everybody has dreams and potential inside them.

—ROBERT D. SAN SOUCI, "ROBERT D. SAN SOUCI HOMEPAGE"

Robert D. San Souci, author of the children's picture book *Fa Mulan: The Story of A Woman Warrior* (1998) and the film story for Disney's animated feature *Mulan* (1998), leads the reader to another valuable creative engagement with Mulan's story in contemporary America.[1] Writers and artists of children's literature have reimagined this character and represented her tale in many ways.[2] Although their texts arguably target young readers, they include elements for adult readers to comprehend in an attempt to appeal to adult mediators, such as parents, teachers, and librarians. Although the visualization of Mulan is not a contemporary American invention, the assorted images of her character that are portrayed in picture books and animated films in the United States since the 1990s are of particular significance in expanding the heroine's international reputation as well as embedding new meanings into her tale through textual and visual retelling in a cross-cultural context.[3] Leaving the examination of the cinematic versions of Mulan's story for chapter 6, I focus here on children's picture books that help foster Mulan's iconic characterization in China and North America.[4]

In addition to San Souci's work, six picture books had been published in the United States before 2008: Wei Jiang and Cheng An Jiang's *The Legend of Mu Lan: A Heroine of Ancient China* (1992); Charlie Chin's *China's Bravest Girl: The Legend of Hua Mu Lan* (1993, illustrated by Tomie Arai); Jeanne M. Lee's *The Song of Mu Lan* (1995); Song Nan Zhang's *The Ballad of Mulan* (1998); Janet Hardy-Gould's *Mulan* (2004, illustrated by Kanako Damerum and Yuzuru Takasaki); and Gang Yi and Xiao Guo's

The Story of Mulan: The Daughter and the Warrior (2007, illustrated by Xunzhi Yin).[5] All seven books are unrelated to Disney's animated film and display different approaches to visualizing the character of Mulan and representing her story in verbal and visual narratives.[6] Like earlier artists who produced illustrations and paintings to capture the character of Mulan, picture book writers and artists have the added task of transforming a literary work into visual images when they digest, modify, or rewrite her tale. "Picture books," argues David Winslow, "are documents and witnesses which can furnish us with a guiding thread, supplementing the complementing textual and oral materials. Furthermore, they allow us to recognize and establish the continuity of traditions and to trace the directions in which they are extending" (142). Although the picture books I examine in this chapter either are written and drawn based on the Chinese folk "Ballad" or refer to it as a cultural inspiration, each distinctively alters the plot as well as Mulan's characterization, and at times the books go well beyond the parameters provided by the poem; thus, the books react to the cultural context from which they come and implant their authors' varied critical and political agendas.

Jack Zipes's scholarship on the social function of the fairy tale has redirected critical attention of children's literature to cultural patterns in traditional tales and their ideological implications. Like many fairy and folk tales, Mulan's story is elastic: its evolution reveals "a process of organic reshaping around a set of core elements in response to historical and cultural influences" (Tosi 384). The abovementioned pictorial presentations, though quite distinctive from one another in terms of textual narrative and artistic style, in general retain the "core elements" established by the "Ballad" while still realizing the imaginative potential of Mulan's tale within the context of contemporary children's culture. Therefore these authors and illustrators all revitalize traditional values, develop new meanings, and visualize the characters and episodes. Because these picture books are targeted primarily to children and their families, they imagine Mulan in visual languages as well as in text narratives that are accessible to young readers through highlighting, amplifying, or rewriting specific aspects. In this process, they add another layer to the palimpsest of Mulan's story. As has long been realized, in most picture books neither the pictures nor the texts can stand by themselves: they work with one another in a bound sequence of image and narrative that is inseparable in the readers' experience (Moebius 141). These bound sequences featuring Mulan offer variations in storytelling and illustrations, thereby providing differing conceptualizations of the protagonist's story and visualizations of her appearance and behavior. Thus these texts, in their utilization of both words and images to construct Mulan's tale, strive not only to capture the cultural legacy of traditional China but also to convey new messages and implications within the context of contemporary America.

To limn a more visible and sensible image of these Mulan picture books that have come out within the last two decades, we need to situate them within the critical landscape of Asian American children's literature. If children's literature in general is a powerful vehicle for delivering messages regarding cultural awareness and national identity, then ethnic children's literature in particular provides "cultural barometers" for measuring social trends (McNarmara 77). For Asian American children, identity pursuit becomes especially pressing because they are caught in a triple bind: they are "pressured to remain faithful to ancestral heritage, while at the same time admonished to assimilate and become fully American, but ultimately finding that because of their Asian genes, many Americans will never give them full acceptance" (de Manuel and Davis vi-vii). Despite the need for Asian American children's literature to be read "as a multilayered and nuanced attempt to establish the place of Asian American writers for children in American culture, and to creatively engage their marginal positioning," in-depth criticism and analysis of this field as a whole are rare (de Manuel and Davis vi-ix). *The Lion and Unicorn* special issue, "Asian American Children's Literature" (2006), is the first critical volume that focuses specifically on Asian American writers and works for children.

As Katherine Capshaw Smith has stated, one primary factor that distinguishes ethnic children's literature from adult literature is its "complexly layered audience": children's literature reaches child readers as well as various adult mediators, and the latter read and evaluate the texts in anticipation of a young audience and often influence what and how children read (3). Asian American children's books, like works of other ethnic children's literature, belong to "a particularly intense site of ideological and political contest, for various groups of adults struggle over which versions of ethnic identity will become institutionalized in school, home, and library settings" (Katherine Smith 3). As Mulan's story evolves and changes, it lives with different writers, artists, and audiences. "A function of picture books for children, as with other kinds of literary production, is to constitute social and cultural identities by addressing the challenge to resignify established assumptions and meanings of identity" (Stephens and Lee 1). These texts lead the reader to scrutinize the important questions of the "layered audience" as well as their social function and cultural influence in the United States and beyond.

Recognizing children's picture books as significant educational tools on two levels, Clare Painter reminds the reader of the "initial literacy" and the "critical literacy" that are created visually and verbally in such texts. Picture books not only provide implicit lessons in literacy for young readers, but they also operate as "powerful ideological tools in their social function of 'naturalizing' (or, less frequently, challenging) prevailing values about childhood, home and family" (Painter 40). Within the many Mulan versions, an analysis of the implications that are facing children allows the reader to discern both the texts' discursive significance and the writers' and artists' strategies in the contexts of Asian American children's literature, criticism, and multicultural education. "Although debates about legitimacy often undergird discussions of adult ethnic texts, authenticity becomes a particularly potent issue for children's literature because of the didactic imperatives both embedded in the texts and imposed contextually by adult arbiters" (Katherine Smith 6). My discussion centers on two important questions: How do some authors adopt a bilingual layout to present a heroine's tale of triumph to both English-speaking and bilingual readers, a complex process that involves the further dimension of audience? How is the character's female identity, particularly her cross-dressing (implied in the "Ballad"), reimagined and visualized in the picture books?

Bilingual Picture Books and Multicultural America

In a three-part series published in *The Horn Book* magazine in 2002 and 2003, Barbara Bader provides a comprehensive overview of multiculturalism and children's literature in the United States. According to Bader, the overwhelming success of Sandra Cisneros's *House on Mango Street* (1984) and Amy Tan's *The Joy Luck Club* (1989), both of which are suitable for young adults, has inspired writers and awakened publishers; after a grass roots period in the 1980s, multicultural children's books flourished in the 1990s ("Multiculturalism in the Mainstream," 273). The promotion of multiculturalism in the U.S. school curricula as well as among the general public has provided a favorable climate in which adaptations and translations of traditional tales from different cultures have found their ways into the publishing houses.[7] In particular, publishers, writers, and artists have adopted bilingualism as a strategy to engage with the multiculturalization of children's literature. In 1974, Congress passed the Bilingual Education Act. During the next three decades, the increasing amount of bilingual publications has pointed to the complex agendas and values of such texts: second language acquisition; cultural, folklorist, and historical preservation; helping ethnic minority children cope with self-esteem issues and socialization; and enhancing the diverse cultural environment (Smith and Higonnet, "Bilingual Books," 217). Bilingual texts play a significant role in the emerging as well as the growing amount of multicultural literature for children.

Presumably the aforementioned picture books of Mulan, bilingual or otherwise, belong to the surge of multicultural books for children and young adults since the 1990s. "Like any other form of cultural expression," says Asian American scholar Sheng-mei Ma, "children's literature displays a particular relationship among the producers, the consumers, and the products" (*Deathly Embrace*, 97). Credit for the publication of this bundle of picture books goes as much to writers and artists' as it does to publishers in their efforts to participate in the "ongoing multiculturalization of children's literature" (Bader, "Multiculturalism in the Mainstream," 275). Some publishers, unique in their editorial vision and mission of publishing bilingual and culturally diverse texts, have been recognized for their contributions to the development of multicultural children's literature. Founded in 1975 with a grant from the U.S. Department of Education, San Francisco-based Children's Book Press, the country's first publishing house to "focus exclusively on quality multicultural literature for children," aims to promote cooperation and understanding through multicultural and bilingual literature by offering children a sense of their culture, history, and importance ("Children's Book Press homepage"). Among its guiding principles are the dedication to telling authentic stories through publishing texts that provide "an intercultural understanding of the reader's own, and of other, cultures" and the commitment to bilingual literature and literacy by promoting "the value of knowing more than one language and the mind-expanding power of reading"("Children's Book Press homepage"). During the past three decades, the Children's Book Press has published Asian American, African American, Native American, Latino and Chicano, and multicultural children's books. Being marketed as a picture book in full color for children ages six and up, Charlie Chin's *China's Bravest Girl* belongs to the Press's bilingual Asian American picture book list.[8] Recommended by the Elementary School Collection, this title has won high praise from reviewers.

In addition, Victory Press, based in Monterey, California, publishes a "Heroines in History" series that features books on famous women throughout the world. Their program has published titles about famous female scientists, modern day heroines, heroines of ancient China, heroines in America, and famous women writers and artists. The publisher's website includes a press release of *The Legend of Mu Lan*, Mulan as a Unit Study, and links to books and sites on heroines, information about Mulan, multicultural distributors, other multicultural children's books, and parenting resources. Written and illustrated by a Beijing-based father-daughter team Wei Jiang and Cheng An Jiang, *The Legend of Mu Lan* has been published in five bilingual editions: English/Chinese, English/Vietnamese, English/French, English/Spanish, and English/Khmer.

Front Street Books, founded in 1994 and joined Boyds Mills Press in 2004, features a unique line of art and design-driven picture books that strive to "expose young readers to the best literature available in other countries, cultures, and languages" ("Front Street Books homepage"). Published in 1995 as one title to help fulfill such a mission, Jeanne Lee's *The Song of Mu Lan* has received strong praise from reviewers, critics, and general readers alike.

In comparison to these presses, California-based Pan Asian Publications has a more specific approach in shaping their publication program. Devoted to bridging east and west through publishing bilingual picture books, this publishing house states that its mission is "to promote Chinese culture and to encourage children to learn a second language" ("Bridging East & West"). This company not only publishes books that adapt classic Chinese stories, legends, and folktales for English and bilingual editions, but it also distributes bilingual books in thirty-five languages published around the world.[9] In 2007, Pan Asian Publications launched a new project to develop its picture books into DVDs, CDs, and eBooks. Song Nan Zhang's, *The Ballad of Mulan* that has been published in English, English/Chinese, English/Spanish, English/Vietnamese, and English/Hmong editions, now has a DVD version under the same title. The DVD was released in 2008 in Mandarin and English with subtitles in Mandarin, classic Chinese, *hanyu pinyin* romanization, and English. The bonus feature of this DVD includes a recitation of the "Ballad" in Mandarin and historical notes on the "Ballad."

Most likely reflecting the mission of multicultural education, bilingual children's books target general readers as well as audiences from specific ethnic and cultural backgrounds. Children's stories, when they include such an active construction of a bicultural identity in Asian American literature, may take on the role of social empowerment (Celestine Woo 250). For example, as an integral part of Asian American children's literature, bilingual picture books of Mulan present to the general reader a cultural heroine who is celebrated not only in China, but also among Chinese American communities. If pictures "take on the role of models which allow children to experiment with actions internally" (Harper 402), then Mulan's character in children's books provides a positive representation for Chinese American youngsters, a female heroic image for all children, and an imaginative cultural adventure for all readers. One might argue that the genre in which these writers and artists participate and the messages they seek to convey help shape their choices about what specific aspects from the "Ballad" to include, what elements to expand or rewrite, and how to represent them. In retelling Mulan's tale for children, four of the seven picture books chose to utilize an English/Chinese bilingual layout: Lee's *The Song of Mu Lan* and Zhang's *The Ballad of Mulan* present the "Ballad" with English translation alongside visual representations; Jiang and Jiang's *The Legend of Mu Lan: A Heroine of Ancient China* and Chin's *China's Bravest Girl: The Legend of Hua Mu Lan* narrate stories of Mulan with expanded plots and themes in bilingual texts as well as in full-color illustrations. San Souci's *Fa Mulan: The Story of A Woman Warrior*, Hardy-Gould's *Mulan*, and Yi and Guo's *The Story of Mulan* are published exclusively in English.

Jeanne M. Lee's *The Song of Mu Lan* and Song Nan Zhang's *The Ballad of Mulan*

Both Jeanne M. Lee's *The Song of Mulan* and Song Nan Zhang's *The Ballad of Mulan* present the "Ballad" in Chinese alongside an English translation while supplying visual narratives to envision Mulan's story and to convey the cultural environment of traditional China. The editor's note on the dust jacket of Lee's book states: "*The Song of Mu Lan* is closely translated from an ancient text and echoes the rhythms of Chinese, which is here faithfully reproduced in original calligraphy by Chan Bo Wan, the artist's father." The placement of this statement before the title page of this pictorial adaptation for children stresses its close connection to its traditional Chinese source. Moreover, the author's note at the end further explicates the origin of this picture book and clarifies the cultural climate that the artist strives to convey in the drawings: "It is believed that this Chinese folk poem originated during the Northern and Southern Dynasties, A.D. 420–A.D. 589. It was recorded in court anthologies as early as the Tang Dynasty. . . . The verses of the poem are still taught to children in China today and are sung in Chinese opera in different dialects" (Lee). As Maria Nikolajeva and Carole Scott have pointed out, endpapers of a picture book "can convey essential information" and "contribute to a word-image tension" (241). Insofar as she is aware of the historical source for her literary and artistic creation, Lee self-consciously positions her work as a means of introducing a Chinese cultural legacy to English as well as bilingual readers.

Not only does Lee's claim that her work is a "faithful" reproduction emphasize its cultural affiliation to Mulan's story, as narrated in the "Ballad," but this assertion also introduces the artist's interpretation through her reimagining and reconstructing the cultural past. Strategically, the graphic and topographical design plays an effective, significant role in Lee's *The Song of Mu Lan*. First, the author divides the "Ballad" into several sections within the narrative in accordance with the English translation and a series of drawings. Second, she presents the poem as a whole on the endpapers, right before and after the storytelling and retelling in words and images. The rhymed "Ballad" presented in calligraphy appears as part of the image on these pages. The layout of the verse is designed in the form of pages from a block-printed edition or an engraved plate with the fresco-styled decoration embellished at the edges. Interestingly, the poem as a whole appears more like a drawing than a text on the endpapers. Through her bilingual and graphic designs Lee's version of Mulan's tale is thematically framed within the milieu of classic Chinese culture. In this sense, her book is a children's text that "foreground[s] the possibilities of linguistic hybridity, bilingualism, and biculturalism" (Katherine Smith 6). Although Lee's verbal and visual revisioning is grounded in China's cultural past, it still is able to create a new structure within the context of contemporary Chinese American literature.

Another picture book, *The Ballad of Mulan*, provides a similar case. The author Song Nan Zhang, an artist born and educated in China and working in Canada when the book was published, writes on the dedication page: "For everyone with an interest in ancient Chinese culture and literature." This statement clearly indicates the author's intention for undertaking this project: to introduce not only Mulan's tale but also traditional Chinese culture to a broad range of audience beyond China's geographical borderlines. The publisher's introduction on the dust jacket further specifies the targeted picture book's readership—the dual audience of children and adults:

Artist Song Nan Zhang spent over two years researching the daily life and culture of the Northern Wei dynasty. His watercolor paintings for this book include exquisite details of armaments, architecture, painting and decorative arts, fabric and clothing design, all to evoke this far-off time. Mr. Zhang's retelling of the legend is a faithful elaboration of the original Sung dynasty transcription of the poem—which itself has been rendered by him in Wei Tablet Style calligraphy in each illustration. In *The Ballad of Mulan*, Western audiences of all ages will discover the poignance and splendor of this classic work of Chinese literature. (Song Nan Zhang)

The placement of these words before the opening page of Zhang's story highlights the book's roots in Chinese tradition and its endeavors to express the cultural environment from which Mulan's story grew. *The Ballad of Mulan* not only translates the "Ballad" in textual and visual narratives, but it also portrays the historical and cultural setting of the Northern Wei Dynasty. By emphasizing Zhang's translation as a "faithful elaboration" of the Chinese "Ballad" the publisher explicitly claims the book's cultural heritage and innovative approach. Not only does this gesture underscore the book's affiliation to the classical story of Mulan, but it also points to the artist's creative interpretation and reimagination in English narrative and visual images that extend beyond the wording in the "Ballad." Thus, Zhang grounds his revisioning in China's historical past and presents the glory and richness of the Northern Wei tradition to readers of all ages.

Furthermore, in his presentation of Mulan's tale as part of the representative legacy that came out of its time as well as a guide to readers to understand the legend within its cultural context, Zhang's map and list of images on the endleaves introduce the Northern Wei Dynasty and its culture. On the map he demonstrates the national borders of the Northern Wei and the historical routes for this Xianbei regime's rise and migration and reconstructs Mulan's military journey to the frontlines based on the place names found in the "Ballad." While the map occupies the center of this spread, the right and left columns are filled with images of ten artifacts from that period in smaller panels: calligraphy, a porcelain jar, stone carving, sculptures from Grottos, excavated baked clay figurines, a painted lacquer screen, a wall painting, woven silk brocade fabric, and other artistic and historical relics. The captions on these pages are in classic Chinese and English. After briefing the reader with the cultural background of the Northern Wei, Zhang starts his retelling

of the "Ballad" in classic Chinese characters while his English translation is accompanied by watercolor drawings on each page. Similar to
Lee, Zhang divides the classic Chinese verse into several sections within
the narrative along with the English rendition and a series of images. After presenting Mulan's story line by line, Zhang adds a full-text citation
of the "Ballad" in simplified Chinese characters at the end of the book.

Zhang adds his commentary after he translates the last line of the
"Ballad," and he concludes the story and elucidates his interpretation of
the moral values implied in Mulan's tale: "Mulan's glory spread through
the land. And to this day, we sing of this brave woman who loved her
family and served her country, asking for nothing in return." Zhang's
approach offers an opportunity for readers, children as well as adults,
to enjoy the cross-references of Mulan's legend in traditional Chinese
and English, both in storytelling and visual presentation. To reinforce
his intention of introducing Chinese culture to the reader, the author's
"Historical Notes on Mulan" provides additional information of the
Northern Wei government and its culture as well as a brief introduction to Mulan story in premodern and modern times. Song Nan Zhang
states that Mulan's heroism, loyalty to country, and devotion to family
"continue to provide the basis for countless Chinese poems, essays, operas, paintings, and more recently, animated films and comic books."
Through such multifaceted approaches, he gives Mulan's tale a specific
and clear location within the complex historical and cultural environment of the Northern Wei.

In light of Lee's and Zhang's demonstrations of the cultural connection of Mulan's story within their contemporary reimaginings, the authors' linguistic strategies play an important role. Both artists choose
to design their books in a manner that privileges the bilingual layout:
beginning on the cover page and continuing throughout the book, the
"Ballad" in classic Chinese characters and English translation and the
series of reenvisioned images are presented side by side. The front and
back covers of Lee's book compose one scene, in which the book title in
Chinese characters, *Mulan ge*, is displayed on the right while the title in
English, *The Song of Mu Lan*, appears on the left. This dichotomy establishes from the beginning her cross-cultural and bilingual format. The
storytelling through words and images executes this pattern: two pages
form one plot, whereby a few lines of the Chinese verse is on the right,
while the revised English translation is on the left. The design of the text
in Chinese follows the style of classic language; namely, the characters
are read from top to bottom and from right to left, while the typography

of English text reads from left to right, line by line according to Western usage. Zhang's text employs the same pattern in adopting a bilingual format. Such a design presents the text narrative principally as a translation of the classical Chinese poem while the artists create interpretive images to multiply or expand its meanings and implications.

Given their bilingual designs, the reader might consider Lee and Zhang's adaptations to be faithful, albeit creative, renditions of the classical Chinese "Ballad." Besides introducing Mulan and Chinese culture to an English-speaking audience in general, one might argue that their books address concerns regarding cultural dilution that plague Chinese diaspora communities. They may be a response to immigrant Chinese fears that later generations will lose touch with their cultural heritage. This ethnic group has taken upon itself to operate children and youth-oriented organizations in its communities to offer Chinese language and specialty classes after regular school hours.[10] Katherine Capshaw Smith has pointed out:

> Many ethnic children's texts also refuse to "fix" their stories within a single genre or mode. Aware of the various cultural influences that create identity, texts combine folklore, oral histories, songs, school knowledge, memories, and family stories, moving seamlessly through various strategies and narratives. In this way, texts imagine a sophisticated and multiply literate ethnic child reader, one who can speak the language of the schoolhouse as well as the language of the folk, one who can negotiate the traditions of family life as well as the demands of school institutions. (7)

Lee and Zhang's works, in the form of pictorial storytelling, carry on this educational task by reminding younger generations of their cultural origin and by creatively linking such origins to the paradigms of their American lives.

Lee's decision to recast the "Ballad" into primarily the heroine's first-person narrative gives the story a sense of coherence and enables the reader to make connections and to identify with the character; Zhang's book, by contrast, adopts a generally omniscient purview and creates dialogues between characters at different moments as the plot develops. Lee's use of the first-person "I" reveals Mulan's concern about her father's enlistment, her departure from home, military experience, and homecoming. Moreover, the author's text uses quotation marks to specify the protagonist as the speaker who leads the reader throughout the story. For instance, when introducing the conflict at the opening, Lee's text reads:

Click, click. Click, click.
Mu Lan is at her loom.
We no longer hear her weave.
Now we only hear her sigh.
Why does Mu Lan sigh?
Why is Mu Lan sad?

"I do not sigh.
I am not sad.
Last night I heard the call to arms:
The Emperor is raising an army.
Twelve times I heard the call to arms,
And each time, my father's name."

The first spread image portrays Mulan sitting in front of her loom, think-ing instead of weaving; the following spread shows Mulan standing among fellow villagers and listening to the enlistment call announced by two service men on horseback. Perry Nodelman has discussed the dual narrative perspectives in picture books that adopt a first-person point of view. He argues that, while the text in a picture book may use first per-son, the pictures "rarely convey the effect of an autodiegetic first-person narration" (Nodelman, "The Eye and the I," 2). Lee's pictures make the reader aware of things happening around the protagonist while the ver-bal texts allow considerable expansion of the narrator's observation. Be-cause Lee centers her narrative largely on Mulan, the female one-person point of view is dominant in the text throughout the book whereas the visual narrative sometimes provides an omniscient view of the situation and the character's surroundings.

In his translation of the "Ballad," Zhang's approach diverges through a mainly third-person narrative voice. Unlike Lee's work, Zhang's pic-ture book presents the beginning of the story as a dialogue between Mu-lan and her mother:

Long ago, in a village in northern China, there lived a girl named Mulan. One day, she sat at her loom weaving cloth. *Click-clack!* *Click-clack!* went the loom.
Suddenly, the sound of weaving changed to sorrowful sighs.
"What troubles you?" her mother asked.
"Nothing, Mother," Mulan softly replied.
Her mother asked her again and again, until Mulan finally said,
"There is news of war."

"Invaders are attacking. The Emperor is calling for troops. Last night, I saw the draft poster and twelve scrolls of names in the market. Father's name is on every one."

The first spread image of Zhang's book depicts a young woman dressed in pink (Mulan) sitting next to her loom and an older female character dressed in yellow and brown (presumably her mother) standing next to her. The face-to-face position of the two characters indicates a conversation in progress. The next page is framed in a cloud, in which the draft posters hanging on the wall in a marketplace attract a crowd; this suggests that the scene is a flashback in Mulan's mind as she reveals her concern to her mother. This image portrays a large group of villagers who focus on the military scrolls. The reader cannot tell the position of the main character.

The quotations above also point to another distinction between the two picture books. Lee's English version translates almost literally yet smoothly the diction and wording of the "Ballad" and retains the generic format of the poem by presenting the English translation in rhymed verses, while Zhang's rendition takes more liberties to follow the main storyline and remain true to the "Ballad" in its narrative prose, albeit adding, omitting, or changing some phrases at times. Mulan's initial hesitation together with her mother's insistence in Zhang's text provides a good example of these distinctive approaches.

Furthermore, in terms of artistic design, Lee's illustrations feature soft lines without border frames, which call attention to the characters; the bilingual text is incorporated into each spread page. Zhang's drawings, by contrast, use border frames on each page to separate the visual representation from the textual narrative in English. The classic Chinese characters framed in borderlines with colored backgrounds sometimes interrupt the wholeness of the drawings. In translating the lines of Mulan's homecoming and redressing, Lee's text reads:

"I go to meet my comrades.
Together for twelve years,
My comrades will be startled.
They do not know I am a woman."

The drawing foregrounds the characters by featuring Mulan, now a beautiful woman in feminine clothes, standing by the door on the left side while her fellow soldiers and family sit around a feast table on the right. Mulan's comrades dressed in military uniform are clearly distinguished

FIGURE 5.1. From *The Song of Mu Lan* by Jeanne M. Lee. Copyright © 1995 by Jeanne M. Lee. Published by Front Street, an imprint of Boyds Mills Press. Reprinted by permission of Boyds Mill Press, Inc.

from her family members who wear civilian attire. This illustration also suggests that Mulan's re-dressing happens right after her honorary discharge from the army and homecoming. The English translation and the corresponding lines in Chinese characters on each side of the spread page are integrated into the background without disturbing the characters' portrayals. To the reader this combination of text and image communicates a sense of coherence because they work together toward a common end (see figure 5.1).

In comparison, Zhang translates the same lines from the "Ballad" and portrays the same episode in a different manner:

> What a surprise it was when Mulan appeared at the door! Her comrades were astonished and amazed. "How is this possible?" they asked.
>
> "How could we have fought side by side with you for ten years and not have known you were a woman!"

His illustration provides a detailed portrayal of the characters' clothing and the household decorations. The Chinese characters, framed in straight borderlines, cover part of the drawing. On this spread, Mulan stands on the right side and the other characters on the left. Only one man appears in armor; the rest of the group is in civilian attire. The facial expressions, however, of several characters indicate surprise, thus making it unclear which comrades' voices narrate the text on the same page. Although both Lee and Zhang's books offer strong text with appealing visual narrative, Lee's work provides greater smoothness and coherence. Inventive as it is, Zhang's work, without as much text-image interaction, thus shows more disconnection between the verbal narrative and the visual presentation (see figure 5.2).

One might argue such usage of bilingual text by both Jeanne Lee and Song Nan Zhang is a discursive strategy that multiplies ways of digesting, embellishing, and retelling Mulan's tale and inscribing new messages for the audience outside of China. Both artists seek to produce historical renditions of the cultural environment, and at the same time they aim at a certain audience while reflecting their own stance. Their bilingual approach, which presents Mulan's tale in a cross-cultural setting, distinguishes their books from both the Disney publications produced as companions to the Disney Studio's film *Mulan* and picture books published in Asia.[11] The bilingual layout of Lee's and Zhang's picture books is particularly effective in integrating the traditional Chinese verse into their literary and artistic recreations. In this sense, Lee and Zhang have

What a surprise it was when Mulan appeared at the door! Her comrades were astonished and amazed. "How is this possible?" they asked.

"How could we have fought side by side with you for ten years and not have known you were a woman!"

made their fair share of contributions to grounding young children in "accurate, culturally sensitive images" before these youngsters encounter more complex representations (Mendoza and Reese). By contrast, in presenting Mulan's story the Disney publications are modeled primarily on the 1998 feature animation. For example, Gina Ingoglia's *Disney's Mulan* (1998) opens with the dragonlike image of the Great Wall and the invasion of the Huns to emphasize that national security is in jeopardy. Such an opening not only sets up specific circumstances to emphasize the female protagonist's glorious achievement in her one-woman show but also marks the orientalism and exoticism that dominate cultural representations produced by the Disney Company. Similar to the film on which they are based, such publications represent commercialized recreations of Mulan. Naturally, most Disneyfied pictorial texts do not include the Chinese "Ballad" in the body of their texts or images, nor do they introduce the historical and cultural background to situate the heroine's tale. Instead, they largely adapt certain episodes and graphics from Disney's animation feature, which children worldwide have seen and memorized.[12] These picture books, marketed for child viewers and their families, therefore are adaptations based on Disney's contemporary American adaptation.

Similar to Lee's and Zhang's works, in terms of tracing the history and incorporating the "Ballad," three other picture books were published in Asia around the same time: Chen Quansheng, Tang Yongli, and Huang Miaozi's *Gu shi wen jinghui: Luo shen fu, Mulan shi* (The Pick of Classic Poetry and Prose: Ode to Goddess of Luo River, Ballad of Mulan, 1989) published in mainland China; C. C. Low and Associates' *Mulan Joined the Army* (1995) published in Singapore; and Li Xiang's *Hua Mulan* (1998) published in Taiwan. Like Zhang's book, these pictorial versions draw on the "Ballad" as their historical inspiration and the basis for their visual presentations. Nevertheless, the artwork in each of them caters to distinct audiences and therefore requires a readjustment in storytelling to accommodate different cultural contexts and viewers. *Mulan shi* belongs to a series of "Artistic Appreciation" that presents the folk "Ballad" in simplified Chinese characters together with traditional Chinese watercolor paintings. The book ends with the complete text of the "Ballad" in the rapid cursive style of Chinese calligraphy, but the

FIGURE 5.2 (OPPOSITE PAGE). From *The Ballad of Mulan* by Song Nan Zhang. Reprinted with the permission of Pan Asian Publications (USA) Inc. Copyright © 1998 by Song Nan Zhang.

book includes neither introduction nor background information about the "Ballad."[13] As one of the books in "the pictorial series of Chinese legends in Chinese and English," *Mulan Joined the Army* includes the "Ballad" at the beginning of the book to highlight the source of its bilingual adaptation (Low and Associates, *Mulan Joined the Army*, viii). Unlike Jeanne Lee's and Song Nan Zhang's books, though, the "Ballad" is presented here in simplified Chinese characters, which are read from left to right following Mandarin usage. The authors may have made this choice to accommodate Chinese-speaking children who are educated in modern-style simplified characters rather than in classic Chinese. In the Taiwanese version *Hua Mulan*, the folk "Ballad" is included as an appendix attached to the visualized retelling of Mulan with national phonetic alphabets on the side (a romanization system used in Taiwan) to mark the pronunciation of each character. The verse, appended at the end, carries the precious tradition from the past that enables the illustrated modern version to convey the legacy of an age-old history in the form of a family storytelling. The words on the book's back cover are directed to parents who tell bedtime stories to their children. Hence, *Hua Mulan* is clearly designed for pedagogical purposes to educate child-age readers and to preserve cultural traditions.

Given the fact that Mulan is well known to readers who speak Chinese or who are knowledgeable about Chinese culture, the aforementioned picture books published in mainland China, Singapore, and Taiwan are not burdened with the urgency to claim cultural heritage for their adapted version. Instead, because the authors and publishers probably have Chinese-speaking or Chinese-learning children in mind as their expected audience, these texts are more concerned with the transmission of history and tradition. In fact, all three picture books belong to children's classical literature series, aimed at continuing and popularizing traditional culture among young readers. In contrast, Lee's and Zhang's texts, geared toward readers who are not necessarily familiar with Chinese culture, put more weight on the legacy of ancient Chinese culture. The artistic design of the bilingual and visual presentations in their books addresses the heroic legend in a manner that permits geopolitical and cultural crossings and in the process might appeal to a Western audience as well.

Unlike Lee's *The Song of Mu Lan* and Zhang's *The Ballad of Mulan*, *The Legend of Mu Lan* by Wei Jiang and Cheng An Jiang along with *China's Bravest Girl* by Charlie Chin present adapted bilingual stories of Mulan that transform the characterization and narrative well beyond the parameters and plots in the "Ballad." With watercolor illustrations Jiang and Jiang's book presents a story based on the "Ballad," yet they greatly expand the narrative sequence to showcase Mulan's military lineage and outstanding performance. This picture book belongs to Victory Press's Heroines in History series.[14] Distinct from Lee's and Zhang's texts in which Chinese characters are printed in calligraphy that requires training in classic Chinese to understand the text, *The Legend of Mu Lan* includes simplified Chinese characters in typeset font alongside an English translation. In terms of encouraging second language acquisition in children's education, Jiang and Jiang's reader-friendly book may be adopted for Chinese language training at beginning and intermediate levels. The publisher specifies the values of this bilingual children's book: the text makes it possible for children to excel at their natural interests, regardless of gender, of patriotism and respect for one's elders, or of women's effectiveness in martial arts. "In publishing this book," stated Eileen Hu from Victory Press, "it was crucial . . . to break down stereotypes of submissive Chinese females. Unlike the Disney movie, the historical Mu Lan did not need the help of a boyfriend" ("Mulan, the Actual Legend of Chinese Heritage").

Children's Book Press marketed another picture book, *China's Bravest Girl*, as a story in which "a contemporary Chinese American poet and storyteller recounts the legend of Hua Mu Lan, who goes to war disguised as a man and becomes a great general" ("Children's Book Press homepage"). In this work, Charlie Chin retells Mulan's story in the form of a folk song sung to a melody played on a pipa (a traditional Chinese string instrument); poet, author, critic, and classical Chinese literature specialist Wang Xing Chu translated the song into English. Both the Chinese text and the English translation are in rhyme. The Chinese text appears through inserts with border frames against backgrounds that feature a dragon, phoenix, butterfly, peony, and crane, all commonly recognized cultural images related to China. The narrative begins and ends with the pipa player/storyteller singing the legend to the emperor, which functions as a bookend to frame the heroine's tale.

In addition to the four bilingual works mentioned above, three other picture books of Mulan were published in English in the United States since 1998. Illustrated by the husband-and-wife team Jean and Mou-Sien Tseng, the first picture book is San Souci's *Fa Mulan: The Story of A Woman Warrior*, which presents a retelling of Mulan's story whose cover page includes the book's title and the names of the author and illustrators in English as well as in Chinese characters. The second picture book is Hardy-Gould's *Mulan*, which includes adapted stories of the character with new twists and settings. As part of Oxford University Press's Dominoes series, this version is useful for reading and learning English language at the beginner's level. A teacher of English for many years, Hardy-Gould adapted Mulan's story with 250 headwords and designed exercises for young readers to practice different words and improve their reading comprehension skills. The illustrations are drawn in Japanese manga style.

Published in 2007, the third picture book *The Story of Mulan* by Yi and Guo is U.S. Sunny Publishing's first book in its Courage and Wisdom series in English in the United States, United Kingdom, Canada, Germany, and France. The company's publishing plan, listed on its homepage, is straightforward: "One of the purposes of publishing this serial is to introduce some true historical figures and their interesting stories to the western world, so that they will be able to understand the Chinese people, the Chinese culture, and the Chinese way of thinking. Above all, to help the western people to appreciate the unique wisdom that Chinese people apply in dealing with complicated problems and dangerous issues." The eleven books planned for this series, accompanied by oil paintings drawn by Chinese artists, retell Chinese stories in English for easy understanding. Yi and Guo's *The Story of Mulan* retains the basic storyline of the "Ballad" yet sheds new light on the heroine's tale, which I examine in more detail below.

Cross-Dressing, Performative Gender

In the bundle of the picture books published in the United States, each writer employs differing strategies to present the storyline of Mulan and to depict the characters and the events. To explore in depth the range of approaches they use, I examine how each work handles one particular aspect of Mulan's tale: her female identity with and without male disguise. After all, this character's attractiveness to writers, artists, and readers lies in Mulan's combined attributes of being heroic and female. Even though the theme of Mulan's cross-dressing is not emphasized in the "Ballad," it has become a significant feature, making her tale so striking and responsive to repeated literary, artistic, and critical interest. In the Chinese legacy in late imperial and modern times, as Joseph Allen has argued, the image of Mulan in male disguise on the battlefield dominates the majority of the narratives and illustrations (353). Despite her primary motivation—to save her frail father from going to war—Mulan's decision to dress up as a man transgresses the boundaries of socially and culturally defined gender roles in traditional Chinese culture, a move that invites further discussion and reconsideration of the permutations of Mulan's identity. In the particular field of children's literature, her story is one of triumph that not only offers a female role model but also points to alternative codes of behavior for boys and girls. Moreover, her substantial and glorious success in a heroic discourse leads the reader to some important questions about her female identity and cross-dressing. As noted, cross-dressing is not an uncommon topic in publications for children. "Despite any suspicions that cross-dressing and transgender issues are topics unsuitable for children's literature, a rich history of cross-dressing exists in that literature" (Flanagan, *Into the Closet*, 78). The reader can find prevalent examples from the traditional tales collected by Brothers Grimms, seventeenth century French fairy tales, folktales from Russia, the Balkans and the Middle East, as well as from contemporary children's books and films (Flanagan, "Cross-Dressing as Transverstism," 5). Among them the most commonly occurring model is female-to-male cross-dressing.[15]

When examining retellings of the story of Joan of Arc for children, Victoria Flanagan argues that contemporary versions often minimize the significance of Joan's cross-dressing for the purpose of "sanitation" because her refusal to abandon masculine costume accounted at least in part for her trial and brutal execution. Texts in children's literature generally structure Joan's story to affirm and celebrate female experiences and values in a heroic discourse. They applaud Joan for her character and behavior while leaving "her subjectivity and spiritual convictions largely unexplored or underdeveloped" and thus diminishing the subversive effects of her gender transgression (Flanagan, *Into the Closet*, 63–64). Different from adaptations of Joan's story for children, picture books that retell Mulan's tale address the heroine's gender identity and cross-dressing, and some even probe the character's subjectivity as well. These works collectively present transformed storylines, and the reconfigured textual and visual presentations that thus recap the heroine's legend invite the reader to contemplate the heroine's female identity and her performative gender in disguise.

As part of the "paratexts" of a picture book, the cover page is "often an integral part of the narrative. . . . The narrative can indeed start on the cover, and it can go beyond the last page into the back cover. Endpapers can convey essential information, and pictures on title pages can both complement and contradict the narrative" (Nikolajeva and Scott 241). Despite their varied artistic designs and writing styles, all but one of the aforementioned picture books portray Mulan as a warrior dressed in (presumably male) armor on their cover pages (see figure 5.3).[16] The only exception is Jeanne Lee's *The Song of Mu Lan* whose cover page is a collage of the book's images, providing a synopsis of the story in visual presentation. Pictures can convey two sorts of information more readily than words: "what *type* of object is implied by words and which particular *one* of that type is being referred to" (Nodelman, "Relationships of Pictures and Words," 719). In these cover images, Mulan appears as a fully dressed service (wo)man, riding a horse with a spear, a sword, or a long knife in hand. At first glance, a reader, Chinese or otherwise, who is familiar with Mulan's legend can identify the theme of cross-dressing easily before starting to read these picture books. Horses and weapons, together with the warfare and martial exploits that they embody, are symbols commonly associated with male prowess, while the name "Mulan" is a synonym for "heroine" among Chinese speakers. For readers who do not have much knowledge of Chinese culture and are unfamiliar with Mulan, from these front covers they could anticipate a story about war and heroes. The words "heroine," "girl," "woman warrior," and "daughter" used in book titles indicate the twist of gender and the heroic discourse of a brave woman in Jiang and Jiang's, Chin's, San Souci's, and Yi and Guo's works, respectively.

One key question in examining the particular emphasis on cross-dressing in these picture books is how certain behaviors linked with male or female are socially determined and symbolically represented by clothes. In the light of theorizing gender as a cultural and social construction, Simone de Beauvoir initiates the widely cited idea that one is not born a woman but rather becomes one (301). Furthermore, Judith Butler's contention that gender is produced performatively highlights how gender constitutes its purported identity (*Gender Trouble*, 24–25). One way to investigate gender as a social and "performative" edifice is through examining the function of dress in constructing, deconstructing, and reconstructing gender identities. Valerie Hotchkiss's study of medieval female transvestites suggests that "[t]he focus on clothing, which covers the body (sex), or more specifically, change of clothing, which refashions the body (sex), reveals the impermanence and liability of gender constructs" (126). Similarly, Marjorie Garber analyzes the power inherent in dress and cross-dressing and explores how "clothing constructs (and deconstructs) gender and gender differences" (3). Following such scholarly leads, I argue that during the process of making a (wo)man dress functions as a considerable symbol in defining one's

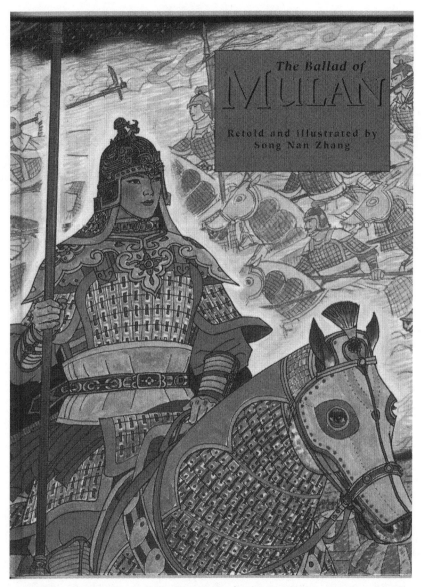

FIGURE 5.3. From *The Ballad of Mulan* by Song Nan Zhang. Reprinted with the permission of Pan Asian Publications (USA) Inc. Copyright © 1998 by Song Nan Zhang.

gender identity. "Central to children's cross-dressing narrative is a pre-occupation with the relationship between gender and sex, particularly in the context of how gender is socially inscribed upon the human body" (Flanagan, *Into the Closet*, xv). If gender is viewed as a social construct, then dress significantly represents the "constructedness" of gender. By extension, cross-dressing supplies a way to cloak one's sex (body) and assume a "performative" gender (clothes) in a particular social setting.

Thus one might argue that the female body of the cross-dressed daughter Mulan portrayed in these pictorial works articulates "'other-ness' within the accepted discourse . . . through a 'mixed process of ac-ceptance and resistance'" (Robertson 66). Through donning male clothes the heroine acquires an opportunity to venture "outside" into men's space where she exceeds the achievements of her male contemporaries. Resorting to male attire obviously crosses the boundary drawn between men and women and abuses the dress code, yet dressing as a man indi-cates acceptance and support for the existing ethical values that define maleness and femaleness in Chinese society by performing as a male when in the men's realm. Similar to the female transvestites in literary and historical documents in Europe, this Chinese heroine "conform[s] to androcentric models by assimilating maleness" (Hotchkiss 3). Hence, costume change is represented as both a violation *and* a conformation of the dress code that delineates divisions between men and women.

In exploring cross-dressing in children's literature from the particu-lar angle of gendered dress and dressed gender, I follow Joanne Eicher and Mary Ellen Roach-Higgins's definition of dress as "an assemblage of body modifications and/or supplements displayed by a person in com-municating with other human beings" (15). Cross-dressing becomes a "performative" action to cover one's sex with an adopted gender. Tak-ing the cue from Marjorie Garber's statement that male and female are culturally marked categories, I analyze how clothes function as "a sign of the constructedness of gender categories" (Garber 9, 47) and examine the possibility of reconstructing one's gender identity through cross-dressing. Within this framework, these pictorial stories of Mulan show that through manipulating, modifying, and supplementing the body with clothes (Johnson, Torntore, and Eicher, Introduction, 1), a woman can forge a new gender identity: namely, through changing costume, a biological female "performatively" becomes a cultural male. Such trans-gressions enable her to present herself as equal to (if not better than) her male contemporaries, even if only on a temporary basis. If dress "makes the human body culturally visible" (Silverman 147), then cross-dressing enables Mulan's biological female body to be perceived as a cultural male in the military realm. In other words, the heroine's transgressions are certified by hiding her female body under male attire, namely forging a male image in the social arena by way of cross-dressing and therefore being judged by such criteria generally applied to measuring a man's abilities as valiance.

Thus dress, as reflected in the recreated texts and images of Mulan, is what Howard Morphy calls "both an indicator and a producer of gender" (qtd. in Barnes and Eicher, *Dress and Gender*, 7). Gender distinctions encode different dress for men and women to wear in accordance to their biological sexes; dress, in turn, decides how one's gender is perceived socially. Carol Gilligan tells the reader: "The sex differences depicted in the world of fairy tales . . . indicate repeatedly that active adventure is a male activity, and that if a woman is to embark on such endeavors, she must at least dress like a man" (13). In this sense, cross-dressing is both an extravagance and a necessity for the heroine. In these picture books, unlike Disney's rebellious protagonist, Mulan's departure from home is granted with her parents' permission; her military career is carried on only under male disguise. "The cross-dressing heroine's ability to master an authentic masculine performance is celebrated and validated as a legitimate response to prescriptive definitions of masculinity and femininity" (Flanagan, *Into the Closet*, xv-xvi). Once she sheds men's attire, Mulan simultaneously loses her legitimate access to the martial arena and returns to the inner quarter, a female terrain. Regardless of their varied plots, all the pictorial versions conclude with Mulan's change from a warrior back to a woman: re-dressing in female attire and restoring her displaced gender identity.

Picture book artists portray Mulan's gender in differing manners. Through one strategy, artists demarcate her female and male life with clear signs and thus separate her femininity from her performative masculinity in terms of space. In discussing the "gendering process" in children's literature, John Stephens has pointed out: "to understand how gender is inscribed within various genres common in children's literature, criticism must pay close attention to discoursal representations, as well as to elements of story" (29). As particular discourses enriched by both text and image, some picture books for children clearly present the heroine's female and male identities in different settings through depictions of Mulan's costume change and shifting space as the transition moments. In Jeanne Lee's *The Song of Mu Lan*, for example, the drawings juxtaposed with the narrative use the feminist paradigm of spatial division to construct the contrasting scenarios for Mulan's double roles: the domestic space with a wooden-structured bungalow, lattice windows, doors, curtains, and feminine dresses denotes her female life as a daughter at home in contrast to the outside space with mountains, rivers, soldiers, horses, and armor that connotes her "masculine" role as a warrior in the battlefield.[17] The drawings on the first two pages sketch Mulan's domestic condition as she sits in front of a weaving machine. Dressed in feminine clothes with bright colors and soft lines, the heroine's hair is worn in a sophisticated style with decorations. She is holding a weaving shuttle in her hand. Not only is Mulan dressed in the attire and makeup customary for young women of her time, but she is also performing a traditional female chore: weaving cloth in a domestic setting.

As the plot develops, the dramatic spatial change is displayed in both text and image. After Mulan persuades her parents to allow her to disguise herself as a man in order to liberate her father from military service, she prepares for enlistment. One drawing shows how another woman helps Mulan change her hairdo. Once the costume change is completed, her hair, a significant symbol of feminine beauty, is covered under the helmet and will remain hidden until the heroine's triumphant homecoming that closes the episode. The next drawing reinforces the female protagonist's alteration of her gender role (from a female to a male) by illustrating her movement from an "inner" location to an "outer" space. In the farewell scene before her departure to the martial expedition, Mulan appears as a male soldier in armor, riding on horseback with a sword attached to her, ready to join her companions for the defensive warfare at the frontier. In the farewell scene, Mulan is dressed as a soldier, moving from the inside to the outside. On the left side of the page stand Mulan's father and mother by the gate of their house while the right side shows an open area extending to the distance filled with soldiers, armor, weapons, flags, and military camps. Directing her stallion toward the "outer" space, the heroine turns around to face her parents to bid farewell. The spatial division and the gender shift are stressed by the image, thus indicating Mulan's movement from the inside to the outside. As the informed characters, the parents know about Mulan's cross-dressing; in their gaze, the heroine continues to be a woman. But her fellow soldiers are unaware of her transgression; in their eyes, her female identity is and will be suspended under the disguise of male attire until the end of the war. As such, Mulan leaves the familiar domestic surroundings in which she has performed the role of a young woman, mounts her horse, and heads to the battlefields to fulfill her duties as filial child and loyal subject.

After years of harsh life in the battlefield, Mulan returns home in triumph. In the scene of her return, the drawings incorporate into the narrative structure another spatial transition to represent the reversal of Mulan's gender role transformation (this time, from male to female). In contrast to the farewell scene, Mulan now withdraws from the outside loci into the inside space with success and honor. While her fellow soldiers wait on horseback and camelback on the left side of the picture, the drawing on the right side portrays Mulan, still dressed in military uniform but without horse and sword, running toward her parents who welcome their daughter with open arms by the family gate. The next image illustrates how Mulan takes off her armor, re-dresses in her feminine clothes, changes her hairdo, and sits in front of a mirror to put on make-up to adorn her face. Until this moment, neither has the heroine's hair been visible under the helmet, nor is her female identity exposed to her fellow companions. When she presents herself as a beautiful woman in the domestic space, the other soldiers are astonished at first; upon learning she is a woman, however, the soldiers demonstrate an even greater admiration and respect for Mulan's courage and capability.

Symbolized by the spatial change, Lee's picture book thus begins with Mulan's life as a daughter, throws a twist at the moment when she transgresses her gender role to enact her filial piety and loyalty, climaxes at the exposure of (as well as return to) her femininity, and concludes with her ideal fulfillment. In the final scene, the female image of Mulan represents a reconciliation of the conflicts incurred by her boundary-crossing action and a restoration of the social norms: the heroine returns to the inner quarter and restores her woman's life immediately after accomplishing the mission to save her father and serve her country. When she is a woman, she is no longer a warrior. Similar divisions of Mulan's gender roles—biological female and adopted male—marked by feminine dressing, hairdo, and weaving machine and armor, spear, and horse respectively also appear in Chin's *China's Bravest Girl*, Zhang's *The Ballad of Mulan*, and San Souci's *Fa Mulan*. This strategy downplays the subversive aspect of Mulan's cross-dressing and highlights the nonthreatening nature of her action. In contrast to this approach, Wei Jiang and Cheng An Jiang's *The Legend of Mu Lan* adds a prelude that suggests the character's possible combination of femininity and masculinity and dramatizes the transgressive side of Mulan's cross-dressing.

The Legend of Mu Lan therefore retains the basic storyline of the "Ballad" while enriching the narrative with new plots that become important threads in the Mulan lore and influence later transformations of her story. Instead of following the "Ballad" and introducing the character as a young woman sitting in front of a loom, Jiang and Jiang start off their book with Mulan's characteristics and her upbringing. They introduce the main character as a "smart and brave" girl who lives in a farming village in ancient China. "Since she was young, her father taught her to fight with swords, spears and poles. She also learned to ride horseback and shoot with a bow and arrow. She was good in all different types of martial arts" (Jiang and Jiang). The accompanying illustration shows Mulan practicing martial skills with a spear under the guidance of her father. This addition foreshadows Mulan's outstanding performance in military service, which is portrayed in great detail later in the book. In addition, *The Legend of Mu Lan* teases out the subversive and transgressive nature of the character's enlistment in disguise. When Mulan proposes to take her father's place and answer the imperial call, her father "shook his head as he replied, 'The law says females are not allowed to join the army. It is impossible.'" After Mulan resorts to men's clothes, "Tears rolled down the faces of Mu Lan's parents. They nodded and agreed to let Mu Lan fight against the northern invaders" (Jiang and Jiang). The two illustrations suggest the dual implications of Mulan's action. As a young woman in a feminine dress, Mulan's proposal meets her father's disapproval, which spells out the subversive aspect of her plan. Her decision to cross-dress transgresses the division between men and women institutionalized by "the law." On the next page, however, Mulan's act of putting on men's clothes gains not only parental permission but also a certain legitimacy in her act of bending the law. A similar case appears in San Souci's *Fa Mulan*, in which Mulan's father protests against Mulan's suggestion that she serve in her father's name: "the Khan does not let women serve as soldiers." These episodes call the reader's attention to the heroine's female identity and the implications of her cross-dressing. The dramatized risk of resorting to male disguise also adds more heroic glory to Mulan's character.

In Jiang and Jiang's picture book, once Mulan joins the army she thrives in performing masculinity, which seems a logical development from the previous training sequence. "Whether wielding a sword in hand-to-hand combat, galloping on horseback with a spear or shooting an arrow, she always could frighten the enemy. Her companions all admired her ability." The authors take liberties to speculate about Mulan's training and military lineage that lead to her success. Furthermore, the artists develop another aspect of Mulan's character by emphasizing her wisdom. "Because of her courage, intelligence and ability, she was successful in many battles . . . [and] was promoted to the rank of commanding general" (Jiang and Jiang). The plot of the decisive battle at Mount Mo Ten reveals that the heroine is not only soundly trained in martial arts but also well versed in military strategy. Mulan's idea to use goats with lanterns hung on their horns for the night attack confused the enemy officers and soldiers and directly led to the final victory of the imperial army. Despite taking liberties of this sort, Jiang and Jiang's narrative follows the poem's storyline and includes Mulan's homecoming and re-dressing as the closure.

Jiang and Jiang subtly represent Mulan's female identity during her military career in disguise. Whether on the battlefield or during the intermission, the color of Mulan's military outfit presents a contrast to that of the other service men. Although dressed as a man, Mulan's hat, robe, and clothes are generally in such warm colors as red, pink, and yellow whereas her fellow companions are usually dressed in cold colors like green, blue, and brown. As a result of using different hues, even in group portraits the heroine stands out visually. To the reader, the image of Mulan always embraces a sense of softness and warmness suggesting her femininity during the course of her cross-dressing. This artistic strategy constantly reminds readers about Mulan's female identity, distinguishing her from other soldiers and officials throughout the book. Like many other picture books designed for both young children and sophisticated adults, *The Legend of Mu Lan* communicates to audiences at various levels of reading skills and comprehension. The array of characters and episodes "addresses a spectrum of ages and experience" (Nikolajeva and Scott 21). The combination of texts and images in Jiang and Jiang's *The Legend of Mu Lan* thus effectively presents Mulan's story to child readers while it simultaneously provokes adult readers to examine the main character's gender identity and performance.

If Jiang and Jiang's picture book begins to fill Mulan's premilitary life with familial tradition and training, then San Souci's *Fa Mulan* further establishes a lineage of female heroism in Chinese culture and encourages the reader to imagine Mulan's tomboyish nature. Beginning with the scene that opens the book, San Souci's narrative refers to the swordswoman Maiden of Yue repeatedly:

"Fa Mulan! Stop!" Elder Sister ordered as the two walked from the family farm to the market. But Mulan sliced the air with a bamboo stake. "I am a swordswoman like the Maiden of Yueh!" she cried.

"Proper young women do not play with swords!" scolded Elder Sister. "They do not go to war!"

"War may come to me," Mulan said. "The Tartars have crossed the northern border and are burning many towns."

The illustration portrays Mulan, though dressed in feminine clothing in pink, orange, and red with floral patterns, as taking a martial art stance with a bamboo stake in hand, pretending she is wielding a sword. Her elder sister, framed in the same picture, holds a basket of cloth and reinforces the code of "proper" female behavior. The dialogue between the sisters indicates that instead of following the rules and presenting herself as a young woman, Mulan self-consciously seeks to follow the path of the swordswoman Maiden of Yue. Such an opening establishes a connection between the character Mulan and the female heroism in Chinese tradition. This lineage is revisited throughout the story. At first glance the tomboy image of the heroine foreshadows the upcoming plot of her military service in disguise.

Different from the "Ballad," which includes little about the heroine's inner thoughts, the picture book *Fa Mulan* portrays Mulan's internal mind. At the beginning of her military career, "[l]eading her stallion to the water, Mulan whispered, 'I am afraid, but also excited.' She pointed her sword at the setting sun" (San Souci). To cope with her anxiety and uncertainty, Mulan again turns to Maiden of Yue for inspiration and courage. Once on the battlefield, Mulan "fought fearlessly and wisely, breaking the enemy's defensive line" by imagining how Maiden of Yue would have reacted in such a situation (San Souci). In contrast to Jiang and Jiang's approach of suggesting Mulan's female identity through the use of colors, San Souci's book takes a more direct route to envision the heroine's female sensibility and mindset. This book depicts how Mulan misses her family, guards her secret, and keeps her womanly dreams in private while serving her country: "She kept apart from the soldiers of her squad, her 'fire companions,' because of her secret. But sometimes one or another of the brave, handsome young men would touch her heart. She would dream of leaving the battlefield for the fields of home, of becoming a bride, a wife, a mother. However, duty to family and country, and her sense of honor, pushed all these dreams aside" (San Souci). Positioned in the midst of images that are portraying intense combats, this illustration features a setting that creates a different moment in the story and helps to display the mood and characterization. The dark blue background with tents, lanterns, and moon suggests a sense of peace and quietness. The soldiers keeping watch offer a picture of life at the frontiers. Mulan, though dressed as a man, is holding a scarlet scarf and appears to be lost in her thoughts of home and longing for a womanly life in a sleepless night.

The combination of Mulan's biological sex (female) and adopted gender (male) are emphasized as a privilege in San Souci's book. The author describes such an advantage using the words of a veteran who fights side by side with Mulan and witnesses her achievements: "You excel because you balance female and male energies. . . . A good swordsman should appear as calm as a fine lady, but he must be capable of quick action like a surprised tiger" (San Souci). Such a combination "substantiates the feminine by making it interchangeable with the masculine, resulting in a conception of gender that transgresses the conventions of masculinity and femininity and carves its own gender niche" (Flanagan, *Into the Closet*, 45). With her wisdom, courage, and skills, Mulan outlines a strategic plan and leads the soldiers to conduct the decisive strike that defeats the enemy and wins the final victory for her country. At the denouement, Mulan, now re-dressed as a young woman, exchanges words with the companion whom she feels closest to in her heart. Their words hint at "a bright, shared tomorrow," suggesting the foreseeable realization of Mulan's womanly dream that she put aside during cross-dressing (San Souci). San Souci closes the story with the father's words: "We have all heard of famous warrior women, like the Maiden of Yueh. But my daughter's fame will outshine and outlive them all." These words once more connect Mulan with the heroic female lineage explored in chapter 2.

A parallel example to San Souci's picture book in terms of balancing male and female roles and filling the character's service life with her feelings and thoughts, Yi and Guo's *The Story of Mulan* emphasizes the distinction between Mulan's female sensibility and the all-male military environment. The opening narrative portrays Mulan as a character with the perfect balance of male and female roles by stating that she learns sewing and embroidery from her mother as well as archery and horseback riding from her father. Yet, the first image reveals to the reader only her feminine side by showing a young woman sitting in front of a window working on a piece of embroidery. The curtain, the vase of flowers on the end table, and the countryside background outside the window create in the picture a setting of softness and tranquility. "The counterpoint between textual and iconic narrative is an important point of tension in communicating that book's theme" (Nikolajeva and Scott 23). Because the verbal text and visual characterization are complementary with counterpoint details on the opening page, there is room for expansion by the reader's visualizations. The information conveyed by

As a girl, Mulan encountered inconveniences that the young men did not. She hid her secrets with clever excuses. None of the young soldiers had a problem with her and nobody suspected her true gender.

FIGURE 5.4. From *Courage and Wisdom: The Story of Mulan the Daughter and the Warrior* by Gang Yi and Xiao Guo, illustrated by Xunzhi Yin. Reprinted with the permission of U.S. Sunny Publishing Inc. Text and illustrations copyright © 2007 by Gang Yi.

pictures is not entirely duplicated by words. Instead, both words and pictures carry the load in the narrative.

Yi and Guo share a presentation of the character's martial skills acquired through family lineage with Jiang and Jiang, but the former authors go further to portray the institutionalized preparation. Before engaging in combat, Mulan and other new recruits undergo demanding prebattle training at the campsite. "As the visual semiotic is not inherently time-based in the same way as language is," argues Clare Painter, when reading children's picture books "the essential relation between any two juxtaposed images is not one of addition or sequence but of comparison and contrast. Two successive images invite comparison and any further semantic relation must be inferred by attending to sameness and difference" (49). The textual and visual narratives portray a sharp contrast between Mulan's public life as a soldier and her private life as a girl. During the training "she did not mind pain and showed no sign of weakness. Her skills in fighting improved rapidly and rivaled those of the young men" (Yi and Guo). The corresponding illustration portrays Mulan and fellow soldiers as dressed in armor and practicing

FIGURE 5.5. From *Courage and Wisdom: The Story of Mulan the Daughter and the Warrior* by Gang Yi and Xiao Guo, illustrated by Xunzhi Yin. Reprinted with the permission of U.S. Sunny Publishing Inc. Text and illustrations copyright © 2007 by Gang Yi.

person-to-person combat with swords, knives, spears, and shields against a background of woods, mountain, and sky in green, blue, and gray. The next page, nonetheless, uses soft lines to depict a girly Mulan sitting in front of a mirror at night with her army uniform hung on the wall behind her. The lamp casts a reddish color on the entire page. The character is visibly female. The flowers decorating her hairdo, her facial features, and gesture all reinforce this picture's female image. "As a girl, Mulan encountered inconveniences that the young men did not. She hid her secrets with clever excuses. None of the young soldiers had a problem with her and nobody suspected her true gender" (Yi and Guo). In portraying Mulan's military career, most images in the painting present groups of soldiers without distinguishing the protagonist and further emphasizing Mulan's successful disguise. This spread, however, uses a contrastive setting to illustrate Mulan's feminine side (see figure 5.4).

Similar to San Souci's version, Yi and Guo's book also shows a glimpse into the heroine's mind during the long-lasting warfare: "Whenever there was a break in the fighting, she could not help thinking of home. She often dreamed about her parents and siblings." The contrast between

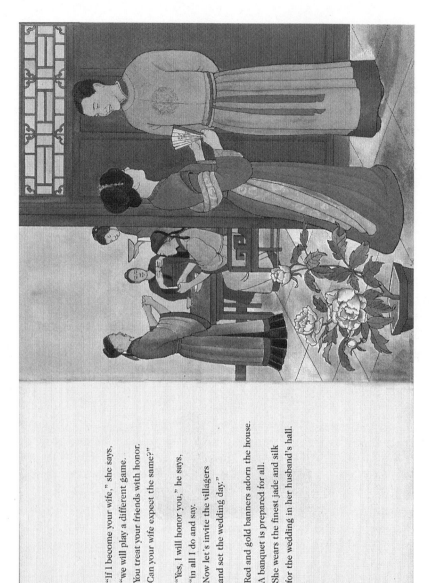

"If I become your wife," she says,
"we will play a different game.
You treat your friends with honor.
Can your wife expect the same?"

"Yes, I will honor you," he says,
"in all I do and say.
Now let's invite the villagers
and set the wedding day."

Red and gold banners adorn the house.
A banquet is prepared for all.
She wears the finest jade and silk
for the wedding in her husband's hall.

"如果要娶嫁給你，
從此關係不尋常，
做為朋友你尊重，
待妻能否一個樣？"

"如果我倆結連理，
夫妻恩愛賽鴛鴦，
今日把婚期訂定，
宴請鄉親共舉觴。"

五彩繽紛造旗飄，
親朋好友裝一堂，
木蘭披紗又戴玉，
夫婿美人世無雙…

Mulan's thoughts about the peaceful life at home described in words and her image of holding the helmet and spear in her sleep shown in the picture effectively demonstrates the contrast between the ferocity of war and happiness of home. Thanks to Mulan's wisdom and courage, the brutal war ends after twelve years, but her tale was to live for a long time (see figure 5.5).

If San Souci's book suggests the possibility of Mulan's marriage, Charlie Chin's version brings this hint to the level of realization. Mainly based on the "Ballad" in terms of storyline, Chin's *China's Bravest Girl* provides a twist at its resolution. After Mulan's homecoming and re-dressing, one of her comrades proposes to her. The conversation between the two brings the heroine's awareness of her female identity to the surface:

> "We were always the best of friends.
> Why not become husband and wife?"
>
> . . .
>
> "If I become your wife," she says,
> "We will play a different game.
> You treat your friends with honor.
> Can your wife expect the same?" (26–28)

Mulan's words express her concern about the male-female relationship in marriage. She self-consciously seeks for a wife's position with respect and honor. With the comrade's promise to honor Mulan as a wife, the story ends with their wedding ceremony. The drawing presents Mulan and her friend-turned-husband standing face-to-face, a position suggesting mutual respect and harmony. This spread is in contrast to the images portraying her departure and return, both of which present Mulan in a deferential position in front of her father (kneeling down or bowing), an indication validating the hierarchy based on gender and age. Such an ending is meaningful for the evolution of Mulan's tale on two levels. First, it gives the heroine a socially appropriate position by concluding her heroic tale with marriage. Second, it indicates that the relationship between the husband and wife is based on honor and respect, thus probing for the reader's contemplation of the protagonist's female subjectivity (see figure 5.6).

The picture book versions of Mulan discussed in this chapter are

FIGURE 5.6 (OPPOSITE PAGE). Text and Illustrations from *China's Bravest Girl: The Legend of Hua Mu Lan*. Story 1993 by Charlie Chin. Illustrations 1993 by Tomie Arai. Reprinted with permission of the publisher, Children's Book Press, San Francisco, CA, www.childrensbookpress.org.

shaped by not only the writers and artists' approaches to her story but also the conventions of the particular genre and the growing awareness and critical work of ethnic children's literature in the United States. In his author's note to *Fa Mulan*, San Souci addresses his understanding of retelling Mulan's legend: "I follow the traditional sequence of events, but retelling (as opposed to translating) allows me to fill out briefly sketched scenes and to 'read between the lines,' by drawing on my study of the poem in its historical and cultural context." This statement reflects a common understanding shared by other picture book authors whose works have drawn inspiration from the "Ballad." Trying to be faithful yet creative, the bundle of picture books that we are considering, in the forms of cultural translations and revisions of Mulan's tale, have facilitated this heroine's travel across geopolitical and cultural boundaries and have enabled her story to be embraced by an international audience. In these artists' contemporary versions, storytelling and retelling are reflected in both their textual narrative and reenvisioned drawings. The incorporation of words and images in these picture books affixes more visualized representations to the palimpsest of the heroine and distinguishes their visions from Disney's commercial fantasy. These cross-cultural variations of Mulan's tale therefore create, through the intersection of text and artwork, reimagined stories of Mulan. Derived from the "Ballad," their reinventions in narrative and illustration add new layers to Mulan's evolution from a "national" heroine in a folk ballad into a transnational character embraced by readers worldwide.

> First there was an unusual and compelling story and distinctive
> characters. It also contained a universal theme—that often the individual
> must sacrifice for the greater good, and that the path of important
> personal discovery lies in that sacrifice. Finally, it was a legend that was
> developed enough to contain those strong elements, but spare enough to
> invite further elaboration of character and motivation.
> —PETER SCHNEIDER (QTD. IN KURTTI 23)

In Asia, film versions of Mulan's story appeared through much of the twentieth century and long before the animated versions. In China, for example, two films appeared in 1927: the Minxin Film Company's *Mulan congjun* (*Mulan Joins the Army*) and the Tianyi Film Company's *Hua Mulan congjun* (*Hua Mulan Joins the Army*). In 1939, the Huacheng Company in Shanghai released *Mulan congjun* (*Mulan Joins the Army*). In subsequent decades, two films with the same title appeared: the Beijing Film Studio released a film of the Yu opera performance titled *Hua Mulan* in 1956, featuring the famous opera singer Chang Xiangyu in the leading role, and the Shaw Brothers in Hong Kong released their film *Hua Mulan* in 1964. These early live-action adaptations interpret Mulan's tale in different ways to serve particular purposes: for example, the 1939 film boosted people's spirits with the image of a patriotic heroine during the anti-Japanese war, and the 1956 film promoted the political agenda of "women holding up half of the sky" with a strong female character. These films, all revising Mulan's character and enriching her story, are little known outside China.

Although Disney Company's animated film *Mulan* (1998) has enjoyed worldwide distribution, publicity, and popularity, the Disney Studio is neither the first nor the only production company to undertake such an effort. In the 1990s a few other animated direct-to-video U.S.films adapted Mulan's legend. *The Secret of Mulan*, a feature animation produced by United American Video Entertainment in 1998, incorporates Mulan's tale within the world of nature by portraying the characters as six-legged caterpillars and depicts a defensive war in which Mulan protects her kingdom against the invading troops led by the evil Mala Khan. The choice of animal characters, a noticeable departure from the "Ballad," is a creative and friendly way of retelling Mulan's story to children, especially within younger age groups; the specific choice, however, dramatizes gender difference, cross-dressing, and the main character's entry to adulthood through the natural process of transformation: a caterpillar turns into a butterfly. The voiceover at the beginning of this sixty–minute long film tells the viewers: "This is a tale of one of the most famous heroes of all, Mulan, born in a small village to a family of warriors." Although the narration does not indicate the film's adoption of animal characters, the visual on screen displays two sisters in the animated and humanized form of caterpillars. The first sequence features Mulan defending the necessity for a girl to master warrior skills such as strength, endurance, and speed, and her sister reminds her that "no man wants a rebellious headstrong girl who doesn't know how to behave." The conversation between the sisters points to the differing cultural expectations of boys and girls. Mulan's words and actions against social norms foreshadow her later capability to participate in military service.

To save her father from going to war, Mulan covers her hair, curls up her antennae, impersonates a male caterpillar, and adopts a new name Hu-A (in Chinese the word "hua" literally meaning flower and "Hu-A" also resembling the sound of a grunt made by some U.S. infantrymen). Due to her extraordinary leadership skills, outstanding military strategic plans, and brave spirit, Mulan/Hu-A quickly climbs the ladder from a soldier to a captain and then to a general. Modifying the cross-dressing element in the "Ballad," *The Secret of Mulan* dramatizes Mulan's transformation from a cross-dressed prepubescent caterpillar to an adult female butterfly while she is in the midst of warfare. Thereafter she wins the decisive battle in her female form. At the end the prince, a male butterfly who is also the military commander-in-chief for the kingdom, tries to make sense of the combination of the courageous, loyal Hu-A and the intelligent, beautiful Mulan. The closing shot of the two butterflies flying and dancing side by side suggests a promising future for Mulan and the prince. With the target audience of children in mind, the filmmakers avoid direct portrayal of violence even though the film is about war, which echoes the condensed depiction of Mulan's military experience in the "Ballad." Instead of showing bloodshed and the brutality of the combat, *The Secret of Mulan* depicts the battles in a suggestive and symbolic manner, a technique that makes it suitable for young viewers.

In the same year when Disney premiered *Mulan*, Django Studios produced *The Legend of Mulan*, an animated film adapting Mulan's story. Springboard Home Entertainment released the DVD with a worldwide distribution that includes such bonus features as music, puzzles, games, and screen savers. This film presents an interesting combination of inadequate film presentation and creative plot elements in terms of reimagining Mulan's tale. Overall, the production quality of this animation is poor. The film lacks dynamic images; the pictures on the screen are quite static. For most of the film, the sound effects are almost inaudible compared to the characters' dialogue. The pace is very slow, presumably for the sake of young children, yet the use of profanity and the direct portrayal of violence and bloodshed on screen suggest the film's unsuitability for a young audience. Moreover, the film's characters are portrayed in problematic two-dimensional ways. Individuals are either evil or good. Except for Mulan's father, all the male characters look the same and resemble the derogatory racial stereotypes of Chinese and Chinese Americans prevalent in the nineteenth- and early twentieth-century United States: the art portrays them with exaggerated pigtails, buckteeth, and slanted eyes. Despite these flaws that make the film inappropriate as children's entertainment, *The Legend of Mulan* includes innovative narrative elements that enrich the development of Mulan's story in meaningful ways.

The opening narrative introduces Mulan as the courageous daughter of a worthy warrior and sets the story in South China near the Himalayas. Mulan's sun hat, the mushrooms in the forest, along with the lotus flowers and leaves in the pond all suggest a southern setting, which differs from all preceding and subsequent versions of Mulan's story in which her tale stems from a northern tradition. Moreover, *The Legend of Mulan* depicts the main character's growing process through three images of self-reflection in the pond. In the first part of the film, Mulan is portrayed as a little girl before puberty. She is shown as child-sized in the way that she does not reach the height of her father's shoulders. While sitting on the bank of the pond, Mulan sees her first reflection, in which her image of a young girl changes to resemble an adult in armor. Her father's words, adding more meaning to this reflection, reveal two messages to Mulan as well as to the viewer: one's heart can be stronger than one's muscles, and seeing a warrior's reflection does not make one a warrior. After the training sequence following her father's guidance that turns Mulan into a skilled warrior, her physical features change from those of a girl to those of a young woman. Similar to some previously discussed Chinese versions, Kingston's *The Woman Warrior* and Disney Company's *Mulan*, *The Legend of Mulan* add the plot of martial training to establish a connection between the main character's daughterly life at home and her military career; there is no trace of this link in the "Ballad." The second reflection in the pond marks Mulan's departure from home to join the army as well as her leaving childhood to enter adulthood. The portrayal of Mulan's physical growth and acquired skills indicates the filmmaker's effort to fill in the blank left in the "Ballad" with imagination and colorful incidents.

It is interesting that, throughout Mulan's journey of becoming a "dragon warrior" in the military, her cross-dressing is neither mentioned in the film narrative nor clearly displayed on screen. There is no specific reference to costume change upon her departure from home. When the character is dressed in military uniform, her hairstyle is visibly different from other male soldiers, which seems to suggest a female identity, thus leading to ambiguity regarding Mulan's gender. The final shot of the film is the third reflection of Mulan in the pond in which the rippling water mirrors a tough-looking soldier in uniform transforming into a young woman in a feminine dress with sophisticated hairdo portrayed in soft lines and warm colors. This scene suggests a similarity between the film, *The Legend of Mulan,* and the "Ballad"—cross-dressing is reflected through the heroine's re-dressing, although the film leaves out the revelation of Mulan's secret to her fellow soldiers.

In the 1999 film, *Mulan*, released by Burbank Animation and Studios PTY Limited and distributed in DVD by Canada-based Madacy Entertainment Group, the plots of the heroine's home-based martial training and her friendship with another soldier Liu Gang during her service receive extensive treatment. The on-screen introduction depicts Mulan as a girl sitting in front of a weaving machine and spinning, recalling the opening lines in the "Ballad." This film, depicting Mulan's training from a young age, immediately underscores the sixteen-year-old protagonist's acquired skills at fighting, running, shooting, and riding like a boy; she is capable of taking on any male opponent. The conversation between Mulan and her mother clearly distinguishes between social expectations of men and women. Mulan's unusual combination of male and female roles prepares the storyline to follow. Different from the "Ballad," the film presents in detail Mulan's cross-dressing in preparation for her departure. Her parents' initial resistance to her scheme reinforces the differing social positions of men and women. Eventually Mulan gains their permission to embark on her journey as if she were a "son." The film emphasizes her disguise solely as a provisional measure to save her father and the family honor, thus downplaying its subversive functions. This message becomes particularly clear to the viewer when juxtaposed with the sequence in which Mulan and her soldier friend Liu Gang disguise themselves as girls in order to spy on the rebels' camp and acquire their military plans. As the film narrative clearly indicates, Mulan's female-to-male cross-dressing as well as Mulan and Liu Gang's male-to-female disguise are handy ways to accomplish their respective missions.

Although Burbank Animation and Studios PTY Limited's film *Mulan* differs from Disney's production in character design, usage of animation technology, and target audience, it does nonetheless include some similar plot elements. The battle scenes in this fifty-minute-long film avoid showing bloodshed and violence directly and thus provide a sanitized version to the target audience of children at the age range of four to nine. In addition to her physical prowess, this film highlights Mulan's wisdom and courage, both of which ensure her success in service life and the ultimate victory of the imperial army. Mulan designs a plan to ambush the enemy troops and catch them off-guard. Furthermore, she, together with Liu Gang, infiltrates the rebels' campsite, steals their strategic plans, and directs a surprise attack to win the decisive battle that ends the war. As the plot develops in the film, the viewer sees the character Liu Gang turning from a friend and companion to a love interest during Mulan's military career. In one of their conversations Mulan specifically expresses her wish to marry someone she loves who is also her best friend, a subtle suggestion of her fondness of Liu Gang and the possible shared future. The film ends with Mulan's joyful yet painful homecoming: she is happy to see her family again after being away for many years, but she is sad to bid farewell to Liu Gang. They both decline the offer to become officials in the imperial court and set off for their respective homes. Before taking their separate ways, Mulan removes her helmet and confesses her secret to Liu Gang. The closing shot indicates a shared future for these two best friends; the implied "happily-ever-after" makes this production resemble the Disney Studio's *Mulan*.

None of the animated adaptations I have discussed has attracted much attention from film critics and viewers. Compared to these animated visualizations with limited distribution and a primary target audience of young children, Walt Disney Pictures' film *Mulan* introduced the character to a significantly broader range of viewers through its wide circulation in the international film market and its promotion aimed at the whole family, a strategy that advanced Mulan's international fame.

As the Disney Studio's first animated feature containing a Chinese lead character, *Mulan,* since its premiere at the Hollywood Bowl in 1998, won success at the box office and exerted a strong cultural influence. Earning more than $120 million in the United States, the film has grossed about $300 million revenue worldwide, making its way onto the list of the Disney Corporation's most profitable movies. It was ranked sixty-sixth on the list of the top-hundred all-time box office successes worldwide in 2004 (Wang and Yeh 191n3). Moreover, *Mulan* has won a number of awards and nominations.[1] As companions to its theatrical release on June 5, 1998, picture books using the images, characters, and plots from *Mulan* were published in the United States around the same time; chapter 5 briefly addressed these titles in the discussion of Disney publications. These picture books, together with toys, games, clothes, and other products for children, were part of the marketing strategy for the Disney enterprise to publicize its new film.[2] The Disney Company has led the way in revolutionizing folk and fairy tales into a modern competitive and profitable business through the process of what Jack Zipes has called "commoditization" (*Fairy Tales,* 197). The presence of Mulan-themed products in chain stores, shopping malls, fast-food restaurants, and superstores has maximized potential customers' exposure to the Disney universe's film commodity. The film *Mulan* has been released in many countries and regions, including the Chinese-speaking regions of mainland China, Taiwan, and Hong Kong and has been dubbed into thirty-five languages, including Mandarin and Cantonese, therefore significantly promoting Mulan's international fame.[3]

The popularity of this Walt Disney feature animation is overwhelming. Critical reaction, however, is mixed. Articles and reviews published shortly after *Mulan*'s release speak to the merits and success of the film. David Sterritt, a reviewer for the *Christian Science Monitor,* for example, considers the film the product of a foolproof recipe that combines a feisty heroine and a spunky sidekick with songs, action scenes, and an exotic historical setting, thus representing the Disney formula at its best (B3). With a specific focus on the main character, Corie Brown and Laura Shapiro's *Newsweek* article praises the film's messages of female empowerment in portraying a strong-willed heroine who takes action and successfully saves the day (64). Mimi Nguyen's essay for the *San Jose Mercury News* goes further to praise the film character Mulan to be a skilled martial artist, an intuitive strategist, and a girl of action and intelligence; she considers such an image in contemporary popular culture a strong role model that offers a positive impact on youth. Addressing the universal notions and pedagogical values of the film that is "part traditional war saga, part modern-day feminist fable, and a total delight," Richard Corliss's review for the *Times* points to the embedded messages for children: family love and duty, personal honor and group commitment, obedience and ingenuity (69). Grounded in a thorough scholarly discussion, Joseph M. Chan similarly views the film as a positive product of transculturation and globalization that adapts a traditional Chinese legend onto the screen while keeping in mind an international market.

Writing for *Time* magazine, Labi, McDowell, and Park, nonetheless, argue that Mulan's male disguise sabotages the film's theme of female heroism and confirms a male-dominant rule (60). In a similar vein Kathi Maio's article for the *New Internationalist* not only criticizes the Disney version of Mulan for aspiring to be a homemaker who is looking for a man and identifying with male authority instead of seeking her own empowerment, but she also argues that such characterization has become "an agent of a U.S. conglomerate's ambition to dominate the culture of Asia and the entire globe" (12). Among Asian American scholars, the criticism primarily centers on how Western popular media eroticizes the Orient in the name of cultural authenticity. For instance, Shengmei Ma criticizes the film's re-orientalizing China and Chinese sources for American viewers to consume (*Deathly Embrace*, 126–43). Vincent Cheng similarly argues against the Disney Studio's approach of taking "Orientalism-for-consumption for cultural 'authenticity'" (76). Dolores de Manuel and Rocío G. Davis consider the film to be a "totalizing and homogenizing" version that exploits the martial arts caricature and reverts to the stereotypical Fu Manchu-like villains, despite its claim for cultural authenticity (Editor's Introduction, viii, xi).

Although some of these observations valorize the film for its gestures toward transcultural adaptation and feminism, others demonize it for its cultural appropriation and false feminist sentiments. By looking more closely at the Disney Studio's claims for the film's cross-cultural and feminist aims, I develop a fuller picture of the hybrid characterization of Mulan in the transformation of a classic Chinese folk story into a Western family-oriented animated feature film that is targeted to a global market. Specifically, by looking closely at the preproduction stages, production mechanisms, particular sequences in *Mulan*, and critical reactions to the film in the United States and China, I can address the two crucial questions about the film's claims: Is it a cultural adaptation rooted in Chinese tradition, or is it a hybrid product packaged for an international market? Is it a feminist text endorsing a female role model,

or is it an early twenty-first-century postfeminist discourse reflecting a
false feminist consciousness? Finally, I assess what happens to Mulan's
story after its global distribution by the Disney Company, a media giant
with multinational resources and distribution networks.

A Cultural Product, a Hybrid Product

An innovative production, Disney's *Mulan* wins the viewer's heart
with its captivating storylines, attractive characters, and intricate setting and landscape design. An animated film that incorporates many
musical elements for children usually requires a process of acculturation
that resounds across not only cultures but also the ways children are
meant to read and interpret the film text. As a modern media genre,
"[a]nimation self-evidently reaches large audiences, appeals to them, and
has an effect," whereas the audiences reclaim and revise the meanings
of animated films with regard to "their own gendered, ethnicised [sic]
or sexual gaze" (Wells, *Understanding Animation,* 223). As many commentators have noted, in the "Magic Kingdom" well-known tales from
different cultures are reconstituted and sanitized to attract a large number of viewers, primarily children along with their families. In the cyber
age, Disney.com presents itself as "The Web Site for Families." Similar
to other Disney productions like *Pocahontas* and *Aladdin, Mulan* reshapes a traditional tale for contemporary viewers.[4] Joseph Chan calls
such an approach "transculturaion," a process by which one culture is
transformed by another in their mutual encounters and a form of cultural borrowing in which one culture reconfigures another for its own
purposes (225, 228). Georgette Wang and Emilie Yueh-yu Yeh describe it
as "deculturalization," a process through which a familiar narrative pattern not only deemphasizes all the elements that are culture specific but
also guarantees comprehension across viewer groups (178). As the multinational studio's first animated feature film that stems from a Chinese
story *Mulan,* together with its sequel *Mulan II* (2005; direct to video),
transforms Mulan's character and story to accommodate contemporary
young audiences as well as their families, American and international.

The company uses what has become the Disney fairy or folk tale formula to structure the story line: an adolescent protagonist disappointed
by his or her present life embarks on a journey or process in search of
a true sense of self. After a confrontation with a certain embodiment
of evil or challenge as the climax, the hero or heroine finally achieves
individual fulfillment and proves his or her value to the world. He or she

is usually rewarded with a marriage or a promising coupling that closes the film narrative (Zipes, "Once Upon a Time," 110–12; McCallum 118). In the past, such a formula has proved successful for Disney's entertainment enterprise, which is aimed at a predominantly white, middle-class American family audience. At the turn of the twenty-first century, international circulation of such a childhood or young adulthood adventure was systematically continued. Modern technology, advertising, and promotional channels help accelerate the speed of the fashion cycles and ensure the global reach of the charm and enchantment packaged by the "Magic Kingdom." Although *Mulan* does adapt some basic elements of the Chinese folk "Ballad" to structure its narrative, it modifies the plot elements and reimagines the characters to highlight such timely and common agendas as family honor, an individual's successful adventure, and issues related to cultural and ideological struggles over gender, all of which make it more likely to resonate with viewer groups from different cultures. As the epigraph to this chapter suggests, the Disney production's further elaboration of character and motivation highlight the "universal theme" of Mulan's story: realization of the greater good and important personal discovery are often linked to an individual's sacrifice (Schnedier qtd. in Kurtti 23).

Joseph Chan elaborates, "[t]he adaptation of foreign stories serves at least two organizational functions: It adds variety to Disney's productions, giving it a more global image; and it reduces the risk of production because these stories have stood the test of time in their home cultures" (231). As one of Disney's endeavors to move beyond the musical comedy formula initiated by *The Little Mermaid* (1989) and repeated by *Beauty and the Beast* (1991), *Aladdin* (1993), and others, *Mulan* helps widen and diversify the subject matter of Disney's productions (Canemaker 231). In this film, the Chineseness within the character Mulan and her story has been retained strategically while readjusted to cater to the international film market.

When making the film *Mulan*, the company undertook a strategic plan to validate the film's cultural heritage. "The pre-production period ... involves the key personnel—producer, director, designer and art director—defining the proposed 'style' of the film, and determining the nature of the characters, their personalities and design, and possible voice-casting options" (Wells, "I Wanna Be like You-oo-oo," 145). As part of an approach established by *The Rescuers Down Under* (1990) production team, who went to Australia for research, the Disney Company systematically sends, whenever possible, a creative group to the actual location of a screen story; this component has become an integral part of its preproduction filmmaking process (Kurtti 45). In June and July 1994, the Disney Studio sent out a team of ten employees to China for a three-week trip to conduct the research. The core production crew of *Mulan*—Pam Coats (producer), Barry Cook (codirector), Ric Sluiter (art director), Mark Henn (supervising animator for character animation of Mulan), Robert Walker, and others—attempted to discover and recover the cultural environment in which Mulan and her legend are rooted. They visited the Great Wall, Datong, Luoyang, Xi'an, Jiayu Guan, Dunhuang, and Guilin to see the generally renowned tourist sites as well as particular historical relics of the Northern Wei Dynasty and trace the cultural heritage of Mulan and her heroic deeds.

On one level, the preproduction trip was a way to show "respect" to the cultural origin of the upcoming film and to help claim a Chinese atmosphere for this new feature animation. On another level, these direct observations of the traditional landscape and architecture inspired many aspects of the film's artistic design. The use of the "poetic simplicity" (to use Pam Coats's phrase) that pervades traditional Chinese painting appears to have served as a general guidepost in designing the background setting of the film. The reproductions of the curved lines of the rooftops in traditional Chinese architecture infuse the construction of the Fa family house and the Imperial Palace with colors and shades in Chinese painting. Although a small detail, the Moon Gate construction leading to the Fa family's garden contributes to the Chinese flavor of the film's setting. The artists on the production team created the settings and costumes based on not only their research but also the Chinese architecture and landscape that they observed and absorbed on the trip. Mark Henn, a key animator who joined the touring team to experience its cultural adventure in China, remarks: "The trip to China gave me a chance to be in Mulan's home country and imagine how she would have lived and felt about her family and country. This was key to my understanding and development of her character" (qtd. in Schroeder and Zoehfeld 56). Henn's words state clearly that this direct encounter with the local culture and traditional sites in China stimulated his imagination. Thus the scenery, stories, records, and experiences gathered on this preproduction trip indeed served as sources of inspiration in the film's design.

During the production process, the Disney Studio utilized the so-called "cross-cultural referencing mechanisms" by hiring Asian and Asian American artists and cast with the purpose of adding more Chinese touches to the film (Joseph Chan 236). For example, the Taiwan-born artist Chen-Yi Chang played a key role in shaping the character designs that utilized "ancient Chinese paintings, drawings, and sculptures for inspiration" (Schroeder and Zoehfeld 45). Moreover, the Chinese American scriptwriter Rita Hsiao was part of the screenplay team and helped arrange the film's narrative as well as the characters' speeches. Furthermore, the production used Asian American actors and actresses as voice talents for most characters (Ming-Na Wen as the speaking voice of Mulan, Lea Salonga as the singing voice of Mulan, B. D. Wong for Li Shang, Soon-Tek Oh for Fa Zhou, Freda Foh Shen for Fa Li, for example), with the exception of Eddie Murphy as the comical sidekick Mushu, a travel-size dragon from the Fa family temple who tries to make Mulan a hero so that he can resume his job as the family guardian.[5] In the film, the characters' names follow the Chinese tradition of the family name coming first and the given name second.

Disney's effort in claiming cultural authenticity is effective to some degree as confirmed by many reviewers and scholars. For example, Li Yinsu wrote an article in Chinese and published it in China; Li views *Mulan* as a successful animation within an international cultural context that "escapes the narrowness of orientalism":

> *Mulan* gives up Disney's traditional structure. The female protagonist's ultimate "mission" is no longer searching for her true love, searching for her final destination; instead, [she] makes a determined effort to defend against foreign invasion and to protect family honor. [This] upholds filial piety in Chinese tradition as well as panders to the social ethos emphasizing traditional moral principals in recent years in the United States. . . . Different from the oriental myths made in the past, *Mulan* does not demonize China purposely. Rather, [it] shows a *sincere effort in understanding Chinese culture.* (90; italics added)

Drawing on the successful experience of Disney's remake of Mulan, Li Yinsu also calls for producers to attend to transculturation in their future productions so that Chinese animation may thrive.

Despite the Disney Studio's efforts to highlight cultural legitimacy, many film images and designs fail to represent China and Chinese culture. Instead, they "reflect the American concept of 'Chinatown', i.e. a globalized China, wherein acupuncturists, panda bears, the Great Wall, the Imperial City, Chinese calligraphy and Chinese martial arts are used in the Disney version of Mulan as elements conveying an Americanized index of 'Chineseness'" (Jun Tang 153). In this sense, regardless of the company's labor to market it as culturally authentic, the film *Mulan* is as much a hybrid product as many of its Disney Studio predecessors. In conveying a culturally inflected story through an animated visual presentation, Disney's film incorporates the icons of Chinese culture that are familiar to non-Chinese audiences. The film begins with the image of the Great Wall and climaxes in the Imperial Palace, both of which are commonly recognized symbols of China. The prevailing dragon image unmistakably marks Chineseness to English-speaking audiences. For instance, the design of the film's title shows Mulan's name above a crouching dragon. The lamps, shields, and pillars in the Fa household as well as the canons used by Chinese soldiers all carry variations of the dragon image, not to mention Mulan's trickster helper Mushu who himself is conceived as a compact-sized and lizard-looking dragon. Although a non-Chinese audience probably would associate these images with China, the film's usage of the dragon is problematic.[6] Furthermore, the inclusion of kung fu replicates abundant examples in the American film business that use martial arts elements to appeal to the American imagination of China.[7] For example, at the military camps in the Disney film, Mulan and her fellow new recruits are trained to become skilled martial artists under the guidance and leadership of Captain Li Shang. Moreover, at the final showdown with the barbarian chieftain Shan-Yu in the Imperial Palace, the heroine, by using her outstanding martial skills and wits, beats her opponent who is physically larger, stronger, and more muscular. This repeated emphasis coincides with viewers' association of martial arts with China.

An effort to expand the Disney Company's Asian market (Maio 12; Byrne and McQuillan 163; Wells, "I Wanna Be like You-oo-oo," 149), *Mulan* experienced a journey to its home culture.[8] Although initially banned in mainland China, *Mulan* is reported to have been a hit in the film markets of Taiwan and Hong Kong.[9] In mainland China, however, *Mulan* was not as successful as expected. It is estimated that the film grossed only about $1.3 million, equal to one-sixth of the anticipated box office income (Joseph Chan 242). According to the statistical data gathered by the China Film Corporation in February 1999, *Mulan*'s box office revenue in mainland China was the lowest among the thirty-four imported American "megafilms" since 1994 (Rosen 5). That poses a sharp contrast to the success of *The Lion King* (1994), which, at that time, generated one of the highest revenues among Western films in China. Two major reasons have been cited for the film's box office failure in mainland China: it was released shortly after the Chinese New Year when most children were just returning to school and starting a busy semester, and the Chinese audience disliked the film (Xiang 28).[10] The first reason seems to be a problem in the marketing research and planning; the second is a failure to anticipate how the film would play in the specific cultural setting and how the Chinese audience's familiarity with Mulan's legend shaped their expectations of the film. However, the political underpinnings surrounding the release of *Mulan* in China also have played a significant role. The Chinese government considered *Kundun* (1997, a film funded by the Disney Company and distributed by Touchstone Pictures) politically problematic because it is based on the life experience and writing of the Dalai Lama, the political and spiritual leader of Tibet who has been in exile for decades. The political controversy over *Kundun* most likely affected the business negotiations between the Disney Company and China, which eventually approved *Mulan's* release in the Chinese film market but not until about a year later, with limited release, and after the holiday season. Stanley Rosen has suggested, "[a]s a Hollywood film made for an American audience Chinese viewers had no difficulty identifying flaws of a cultural and historical nature in the film" (5). In mainland China, Disney's *Mulan* never attracted as many adult moviegoers as the company anticipated; these included parents who bring young viewers to the movie houses and school teachers and administrators who make decisions about what films to choose for the collective screening in primary and secondary schools.

Despite its less-than-satisfactory box office record, Disney's animation has shown such a strong cultural influence in China that it has become a topic for review articles, scholarly publications, and graduate-level theses with mixed responses. On the positive side, Fei Li praises the film as a new breakthrough from the scope of traditional interpretations of Mulan's legend: "it is the first Chinese folk tale to be interpreted completely anew, refurbished, and repackaged by the Americans, and it will naturally attract audiences if the publicity for it is properly carried out" (16). Similarly, Bi Geng and Li Dongqing's article analyzes the major reasons for the film's appeal and speaks highly of it as "a vivid model and salutary lesson for Chinese literature and arts to enter the global stage" (36). Li Shuying, a college teacher specializing in language and literature in English, remarks: "Even though there are some changes in Disney's *Mulan*, the appraised filial piety true to the story of Mulan's enlistment taking her father's place remains intact. Yet because of the inclusion of the values and morals in Western culture, the Hua Mulan defined by Eastern tradition is presented with a new image and new meanings" (134).[11]

The negative reviews criticize the Disney version of the tale for vio-lating the main theme of the Chinese folk "Ballad." The following re-marks found in Chinese popular magazines and film journals offer a few examples:

> Since the creators [of *Mulan*] gave first consideration to the view-ing preferences of American audiences, everything in that film is tied to the Hollywood pattern; the inclusion of Chinese cultural elements exists merely to satisfy the novelty-seeking mentality of those same viewers. . . . The film therefore has flaws that immedi-ately strike Chinese audiences—the nuptial ceremony, the anachro-nous use of firearms, and so forth. (Shao 12)
>
> In the minds of the Chinese people, she is a far cry from the traditional female hero; she is a Western lass who grew up eating bread and butter. Admittedly, this Westernized Mulan is quite lov-able as she dashes across the ancient battlefields of China, but she evokes little sense of identification in a Chinese moviegoer. (Yang Zhang 26)
>
> [E]verywhere in the film one sees the Americans' disfigurement of Chinese history, their lack of understanding of the Chinese envi-ronment, their eternal inability to understand Chinese culture, and their skewed comprehension of Chinese people. . . . [A]s Chinese moviegoers with a conscience, we are clearly unable to comment with equanimity on the film's strengths and weaknesses in light of the West's misunderstanding of us. Nor is it possible to counte-nance the film's disrespect for our cultural tradition. (Renjie Zhang 31–32)

Similar scholarly studies that point to the westernization and otherness of the heroine as flaws of Disney's film are abundant.[12]

These reviews and essays collectively reflect the film's cultural influ-ence in China, even though it has not become one of the main imported American blockbusters. More important, the comments speak to the hy-brid nature of *Mulan*. Despite their varied opinions and comments, most Chinese scholars agree that the image of Mulan revitalized by Disney Empire has been instilled with a modern ideology that sustains most productions from this media corporate. While adopting plot elements from the Chinese folk "Ballad," the new visualization is branded with Disney's characteristic atmosphere (Zhongshun He 24).[13] Political per-spectives underlie these comments. The positive remarks tend to view the film as an opening for cultural dialogue whereas the negative ones seem to interpret the film as an imperialistic appropriation and distortion of Chinese culture. The reactions among Chinese moviegoers and critics should not go unnoticed and warrant a close examination because they provide a window to Chinese perspectives on the implications of and challenges to film adaptation in the global era. *Mulan's* reception in China provides another interesting layer of the character's cross-cultural journey—that is, not only from East to West but also from West to East. The embrace or rejection of the Disneyfied *Mulan* by mainland Chinese audiences largely speaks to its acculturated character, plot, and theme. Wang Lei's comparative review of *Mulan* and *Lotus Lantern* (1999), a Chinese animated production, points to universalized themes as the main reason for Disney's success in the international film market. Wang states: "in order for viewers worldwide to enjoy this Chinese story, *Mulan* actually only borrows the structure of the traditional story and reveals global ideas upheld by the United States. Therefore, [the film] finds favor in audience's eyes" (17). In comparison, *Lotus Lantern* is a cultural product bearing too many Chinese values to appeal to an international audience.

The Disney film's codirector Tony Bancroft stated: "We knew we had to respect the material. This is a beloved story to the Chinese people. We also knew that we weren't going to make a Chinese picture. We couldn't. We're not Chinese. We have a different sensibility, a different storytelling style" (qtd. in Kurtti 24). To make the film appeal to a broader range of moviegoers, the Disney version portrays a Chinese heroine and her story with a new spin. Overall, the film shows saving one's family honor as the first and foremost priority and incorporates the heroine's personal discovery during the process. The newly invented character Mulan helps connect children to the product through emotional identification. By transforming the theme of filial piety indicated in the Chinese "Ballad" to the idea of honoring one's family, Disney's *Mulan* presents a broadly appealing concept that is more readily understood by people of different cultures (Joseph Chan 233). The film narrative starts with two emergencies that endanger the Fa's family honor: Mulan's failure at the bride selection and the imperial order that calls her disabled veteran father to enlist. The urgent situation leads to the further development of the plot and provides an opportunity for the young protagonist to carry out a military adventure and prove her dedication to her family as well as her individual value, both important themes that invite many viewers' empathy.

Despite the outright claim for cultural authenticity, the Disney Corporation does not venture beyond its well-established formula with

Mulan and in the end presents a hybrid product that is neither Chinese nor American. Looking at the film within the character's cross-cultural transformation, *Mulan* is a homogenized invention. Drawing on different resources, the Disney Studio transforms the traditional Chinese story of Mulan into "a timeless legend aimed at Disney's family audience, which celebrates universal acultural values of love, courage and independence" (Wang and Yeh 182). In spite of the production team's efforts to make the artistic design, characters, and storyline culturally "authentic" or the film's success in establishing the heroine's international fame and providing a cross-cultural version of her tale, the film is predominately hybrid. Such a combination of different cultural elements designed to appeal to a wide range of audiences represents the very process of Disneyfication.

A Feminist Text, a Postfeminist Text

To Mulan's traditional portrayal as a loving, considerate daughter and a wise, courageous soldier who defends her country and returns home with honor, Disney adds a new element by making her a role model for individual accomplishment. This kind of individuality does not appear in the "Ballad" or the variations of her story in Confucian China. The Disney film's portrayal of a young woman whose free spirit and strong personality enable her ultimately to save her family honor as well as achieve individual satisfaction encourages a feminist reading. Nevertheless, in the films made by the Disney Corporation, as Jack Zipes has argued, the imagination is instrumentalized to formulate and disseminate the "Disney American ideology" and to domesticate traditional tales and sanitize their rebellious and progressive features or potentials (*Fairy Tales*, 193, 212). *Mulan* is no exception. Though seemingly different, given her tomboy personality and physical strength, Mulan shares some basic qualities and functions with other Disney princesses.[14] Despite the main character's transgressive and rebellious actions in the film *Mulan*, "independence functions not as an indication of female power or self-determination, but rather as a strategy for seduction: Reluctance functions in a Disneyfied courtship as the lure with which the chosen woman finally attracts a husband" (Bean 54). Ultimately the audience is guided to harness Mulan's social outcomes in a film construction of a "proper womanhood." Hence, despite its appearance of being a feminist text that promotes female empowerment, the film's profeminist plot elements actually represent a false feminist mentality.

Overall the classic disruption-resolution narrative structure described by Annette Kuhn drives the plot of *Mulan* (258). The story embarks on the character's journey from her life as a daughter to an alternative world as a soldier (disruption) and concludes with her return home (resolution).[15] Besides developing some basic elements from the "Ballad" for theatrical effect, this film narrative also fills the old tale of Mulan with many new Disney features. Mulan's rebellious behaviors and feminist spirit, exemplified by her disastrous interview with the matchmaker, the training and combat sequences in her military career, and the final showdown against the foe, eventually are contained by the promising romance of Mulan and her love interest Captain Li Shang. At its beginning the film *Mulan,* setting the stage for plot and character development, introduces three crises at different levels: national, familial, and personal. The opening scene of the film is set at the Great Wall, the defense system at the Chinese border where the invading Huns undertake a surprise night attack. Then they march rapidly, crossing the northern borders and imposing an imminent threat to the capital city as well as to the vast interior land of China that is identified as "the Middle Kingdom." The film then crosscuts to the Imperial Palace. To protect his empire and his people, the emperor issues an order to recruit one man from each family to reinforce the defense army. This opening sequence, a departure from the "Ballad" that begins with a peaceful setting at Mulan's home, poses an emergency for the nation's security as well as for the Fa family's well-being, for the imperial order calls for the enlistment of Fa Zhou, Mulan's disabled veteran father. The next transition leads the audience to the Fa family house on the day of Mulan's interview with the matchmaker.

To emphasize its feminist interpretation, the film *Mulan* highlights the main character's struggle in coming to terms with the conflict between her expressions of individuality and her society's expectation of young women. Mulan, as the only child and daughter, has to impress the matchmaker by presenting herself as a well-groomed maiden so that she can be properly betrothed, thus bringing honor to her family. The protagonist's first appearance on screen indicates that she does not conform to the standards of behavior and appearance demanded of a young woman interested in obtaining a marriage proposal. In contrast to the opening image of the "Ballad" where a weaver sits at her loom and contemplates, this Mulan not only tricks her dog "Little Brother" into helping her feed the hens, which results in much disorder at the family temple, but also rushes into town on horseback and arrives late for the dressing-up preparation before her interview.

The newly invented plot element of Mulan's interview with the matchmaker also relays the social expectation of women. The song "Honor to Us All" underscores the point that as a daughter Mulan can bring honor to her family only by way of finding herself a decent family-in-law through the approval and arrangement of the matchmaker. Mulan shows her willingness to fulfill her duty by secretly writing reminders on her wrist: "quiet, demure, graceful, polite, delicate, and punctual," but she is unable to follow these behavioral instructions for a proper bride-to-be. After all, she is a girl who stands out with her determination and articulates her opinions, but, according to the film narrative, the "ideal" woman—calm, obedient, and beautiful—should aspire to her main role in reproducing and extending her husband's family line. Regardless of the painstaking process of bathing, dressing-up, and making-up arranged by her mother and grandmother along with her efforts to be passive and demure, Mulan's meeting with the matchmaker ends in disaster. Infuriated, the matchmaker declares: "You are a disgrace. You may look like a bride, but you will never bring your family honor." These remarks shatter Mulan's hope of both supplying a "perfect daughter" and thriving in womanhood. Feeling humiliated and frustrated, Mulan cannot face her father after she returns home.

The thematic thread emphasizing the feminist aspect of film is further developed in the heroine's solo rendition of "Reflection," a song that drives the plot through lyric. After her failed interview with the matchmaker, Mulan returns home and sings the song while walking in her family garden and staring at her image reflected in the pond, all part of her contemplation. Her inability to pass for a perfect bride makes it impossible for her to be a perfect daughter, no matter how hard she tries. This song expresses the vital internal conflict that the young protagonist confronts: on the one hand, she should abide by social dictates and fulfill her duty to honor her family; on the other hand, she yearns to realize her individuality and be true to herself. As has been made clear in another song, men and women have different positions in society and different duties to fulfill: a man's duty is on the battlefield; a woman's rightful position is at home where she bears male heirs for her husband's family. Mulan wants to make her family and primarily her father proud, but at the same time she wants people to recognize her value for who she really is. It is worth noting that the promising marriage at the film's closure, which returns Mulan to "proper womanhood," cancels out this seemingly feminist thematic thread.

As the film goes on, other threads enrich Mulan's character. For example, Robert San Souci, one author of the film story for Disney's *Mulan*, published a 1998 picture book, *Fa Mulan: The Story of A Woman Warrior* that portrays Mulan as a tomboy.[16] As I discussed in chapter 5, San Souci begins his book with Mulan slicing the air with a bamboo stake and pretending to be a swordswoman while her elder sister scolds her and reminds her, "Proper young women do not play with swords." The reimagination of Mulan being tomboyish that appears not only in San Souci's book but also in Disney's film is of particular significance in the transformation of her tale. Because tomboyism for a girl is often associated with the heroine's desire for freedom and mobility, it is considered "a sign of independence and self-motivation" as long as it is linked to "a stable sense of a girl identity" (Halberstam 6). In the film Mulan's tomboyism is crucially portrayed as tolerable and nonthreatening because it is harbored within safe boundaries, which her motivation (to save her father and to honor her family) emphasizes and the ending (to bring home not only honor but also a love interest) confirms. These reconfigured elements help build up the feminist appearance of the film, yet a careful examination suggests otherwise.

Opening the film narrative with a desperate protagonist who is trapped in a disappointing reality and thus longs for adventure is not unique to the Disney production of *Mulan*. According to Eleanor Byrne and Martin McQuillan, "Disney's renaissance in the 1980s was marked by the birth of a new breed of newly born women who have desires to escape the prisons of domesticity" (67). Embarking on her unusual adventure with courage, young Ariel (*The Little Mermaid*) trades her voice to the Sea Witch Ursula for a pair of legs and is determined to make her dreams come true. Princess Jasmine (*Aladdin*) and Pocahontas are similarly bright, beautiful, free-spirited, and adventurous. Like them, Mulan is shown to have a mischievous side. Even before going on an adventure, she shows herself to be a strong, smart, and skillful young woman who neither dreams about a prince nor waits to be rescued; instead, she takes up action to save the day. Hence, *Mulan* differs from the Disney prefeminist Alice (*Alice in Wonderland*, 1951). Mulan does not simply fantasize or dream about a young woman's life filled with adventure, excitement, and freedom;[17] rather, she moves to the level of action to protect her family's honor and in the process achieves extraordinary success and outshines her male contemporaries.

When Mulan runs into the conflict between social expectations for females and her strong personality, her father's conscription order provides an opportunity for her to reconcile the conflict—that is, she can uphold the family honor and prove "her worth" by defying convention. Mulan dresses in her father's armor, steals away from home, and rushes to the military camp. Her actions unmistakably show her love for her father and her dedication to her family. Yet at the same time leaving home without her parents' knowledge, another departure from the "Ballad," is also a daring personal adventure for the young heroine.

In contrast to the "Ballad," which describes the heroine's military career in only a few lines with hardly any detail, the film develops a number of episodes to portray Mulan's wisdom, courage, persistence, skills acquired through intensive training, and success in the military expedition. Departing from the conventional cartoon female who is often defined as feminine through dazzling ball gowns and high-heels, Mulan resorts to men's clothes and invades a male territory to tantalize the viewer with the transgressive nature of her behavior. Cross-dressing is an important theme that enables Mulan's story to have been transmitted in China for centuries and to have attracted much attention in the United States. This subject is also in the spotlight of Disney's *Mulan*. Gender and sexuality in animated films are represented particularly through the encoded body. This Disney adaptation demonstrates a reconstruction of the heroine's female body and identity. For most of her military life in the film, Mulan is Ping, a name she adopts hastily upon reporting for duty in the recruitment camp.

Ping's/Mulan's military adventures are important innovations of the film. In particular, the production team designs the new feature of the training sequence, in which Mulan must hide her female body and toughen up. The film shows the challenges that Ping/Mulan faces due to her lack of skills, strength, and military experience before displaying her innate characteristics such as persistence, wisdom, and courage. At the military camp, Ping/Mulan refuses to give up, rises above the adversity, and retrieves the arrow from the top of the pole while carrying two heavy weights that represent discipline and strength. Together with other new recruits, she gains new combat skills, such as fighting with rods, archery, artillery, and hand-to-hand battle. Toward the end of the training sequence, the chorus of "I'll Make a Man Out of You," together with a series of fast-paced jump cuts, points to the promising result. The lyric describes the swift moves and mighty forces of the soldiers while the visuals emphasize the impressive martial skills that Ping/Mulan and her fellow recruits have acquired. These scenes not only showcase the main character's physical strength and skills in martial competition and confrontation as an equal to her male peers, but Ping's triumph in training also contrasts with Mulan's failure at the matchmaker interview. At the camp her determination and strong will no longer make her a misfit;

rather, she thrives as a young "man." The training episode is also of particular significance in the film narrative because it introduces Mulan's love interest, Li Shang. During the course of intensive training, Mulan develops respect and affection for Li Shang who, despite his initial tough, arrogant appearance, guides the cadets with knowledge and patience and successfully trains them into capable and confident soldiers. In addition to her physical prowess, the film casts the spotlight on Mulan's wisdom and courage, which enables her success without necessarily forfeiting her femininity.

After the new recruits complete their field lessons, Ping/Mulan and her fellow combatants march into the frontline full of energy and confidence, only to discover that the main force of the imperial army led by General Li, Li Shang's father, has been completely wiped out by the Huns. When she finds herself in an unanticipated confrontation with the Hun troops, who overwhelmingly outnumber the remaining cohort of the imperial soldiers, Ping/Mulan's courage and wisdom play a key role in defeating the enemy. While the Hun horse cavalry spreads out everywhere and presses forward, Li Shang gives the orders that soldier Yao aim the last canon at the Hun chieftain Shan-Yu and all soldiers prepare for combat and death in honor. Understanding the urgency of this dire situation and seeing a snow-covered overhang on the mountain, Mulan snatches up the last cannon and runs with it toward the Hun troops. She fires into the overhang just as she approaches Shan-Yu, causes an avalanche that buries the entire Hun army, and thus single-handedly saves the imperial soldiers. Ping's/Mulan's exceptional military performance is displayed side by side with her attraction to Li Shang that implies the possibility of the future development of their relationship. When Li Shang gets lost in the snowstorm, Ping/Mulan rushes without hesitation to his rescue at the risk of losing her own life and eventually saves him. When the soldiers praise Ping/Mulan as their hero, "the bravest of us all," and cheer about her victory, she wins not only the battle but also the captain's trust and, as the audience later discovers, his heart. Ping's/Mulan's glorious triumph also leads to the revelation of her secret. Ping/Mulan has been slashed by Shan-Yu's sword; she loses consciousness and is treated by a military doctor, who discovers her female identity.

Disney's film is the first version of the story in which the protagonist's gender is revealed to her fellow soldiers before the end of the war. Violation of the dress code is repeatedly portrayed as a capital crime in the film, underscoring the transgressive aspect of Mulan's action. It is first articulated in Fa Zhou's words when he finds out that Mulan ran away in disguise: "[i]f I reveal her, she will be [killed]." Mulan is thrown into a desperate situation in which she could let her family down once more and even lose her life. The image of Mulan kneeling down on the snow-covered ground, hunching her female body under a thin blanket, is a sharp contrast to the previous celebration in which everybody is cheering for the military success attributed to Ping. Suddenly the war hero Ping, who had been admired by other soldiers and officers, has turned into Mulan, a condemned "treacherous snake" who has committed "high treason" and "ultimate dishonor," to use the counsel's words that reinforce the transgressive nature of the protagonist's behavior. Li Shang, sword in hand, stands high and looks down at Mulan. At this intense moment, the law that elevates masculinity and belittles women takes over the plot, creating tension around the possibility of severe punishment. Later on, after the showdown in the Imperial Palace, the counsel reiterates the charges against Mulan: "[t]hat creature's not worth protecting. . . . 'Tis a woman. She'll never be worth anything." The indiscretion of Mulan's gender identity through resorting to male garments, despite (or because of) the potential severe punishment, undoubtedly sharpens Mulan's role as a good daughter who would risk her life to save her father and her family's honor in the Disney adaptation. Such a portrayal of cross-dressing as a fatal taboo is not included in the "Ballad," nor is it a noticeable trend in the Chinese variations of Mulan's story. Female cross-dressing, as a matter of fact, is a repeated phenomenon in premodern Chinese literature.[18]

In both the "Ballad" and Kingston's retelling, Mulan's cross-dressing is represented as a border-crossing behavior that is justified by her motivation (filial piety and revenge, respectively) and its legitimacy is reinforced by the resolution of the tale (that is, the victorious heroine resumes her womanly role). In addition, numerous variations of Mulan's tale do not reveal Mulan's gender identity until the end of the story.[19] Disney's film takes a different approach by revealing the heroine's female identity much earlier, which creates a moment for the leading character to reflect on her decision as it foreshadows her journey of adventure in her female self. After the battle in the film, Captain Li Shang spares her life as a way of showing his gratitude, yet, because she has been identified as a female, Mulan is not allowed to march with the rest of the troops to the capital city where they will be welcomed as heroes and saviors of China. Left behind in the snowy mountain area, Mulan, still in male disguise, admits her failure to Mushu: "Maybe I didn't go for my father. Maybe what I really wanted was to prove I could do things right. So when

I look in the mirror, I'd see someone worthwhile. But I was wrong. I see nothing." Mulan's confession echoes her solo "Reflection" sung in the earlier sequence, articulating her desire to become a dutiful daughter as well as a valuable young woman.

More important, this early revelation of the character's sex enables Mulan to achieve success at the climax as a woman instead of a male, thus adding another profeminist thread to the film before closing the story with the heroine's domestication. In other variations of Mulan's story that begin with the "Ballad," the heroic and the female features of the character are separated. When Mulan is a woman, she is not heroic; when she is a hero, she is wearing men's clothes and appears to be male. In this sense, the military achievement and honor Mulan receives still belong to a hero. In contrast, in Disney's film Mulan confronts the foe and wins final victory as a heroine. Mulan's desperate situation as a young woman begins to improve when she learns that the recently defeated Hun army is planning an attack. The surviving Huns have broken through the snow and are marching with Shan-Yu to the capital city intent on capturing and overthrowing the emperor. They will attack while the Chinese are celebrating their military victory and unaware of their enemies' survival. Instead of going home and facing her father with yet another failure and dishonor, Mulan-as-woman decides to journey to the Imperial Palace to save the emperor and the empire, an expedition that also restores honor to her family and proves her worth.

In the film, three fellow soldiers—Ling, Yao, and Chien-po—follow Mulan's lead and rescue the emperor as a team; furthermore, they dress as women so that they can catch the Huns off-guard. This episode, another invention of Disney's production team, has no trace in the "Ballad." Different from Mulan's disguise, the three soldiers' cross-dressing appears to be a device for comic effect in the film. The men's disguise makes them look like "ugly concubines" in the words of the Hun soldiers. Their attacks with watermelons, apples, bananas, and oranges, all fake breasts pulled out of their dresses, add more humor to the film narrative and enable the potentially violent fighting to appear comical and entertaining and thus appropriate for its target audience.[20] As Victoria Flanagan has argued, male cross-dressing in children's literature is mostly depicted in negative ways and diverges sharply from female cross-dressing in that "the issue of gender performance is seldom raised as a serious concern" (Into the Closet, 53). Male cross-dressers are typically portrayed in a comic mode that emphasizes their inability to behave convincingly as women (Flanagan, Into the Closet, 53). It further emphasizes the "constructed-ness" of one's gender identity. Through these two kinds of cross-dressing (female-to-male and male-to-female), the social significance of dress is highlighted. In other words, gender identities are culturally (re)constructed concepts and symbolized in particular by clothes. Valerie Hotchkiss's study of medieval female transvestites suggests that "[t]he focus on clothing, which covers the body (sex), or more specifically, change of clothing, which refashions the body (sex), reveals the impermanence and liability of gender constructs" (126). If gender is viewed as a social construct, then dress serves as a significant sign in representing the "constructed-ness" of gender. By extension, cross-dressing provides a way to cloak one's sex (body) and in the meantime to take on a "performative" gender (via clothes) in a particular social setting. The soldiers' cross-dressing accentuates how daring and impressive Mulan's disguise is because hers is dangerous and institutionally forbidden while theirs is merely a distraction for the purpose of humor. This addition also demonstrates the privileged sex would be ridiculous when performing as the inferior one. A woman dressing as a man potentially poses a threat of usurping male power while a man dressing as a woman is taking a sexually submissive position. This episode, together with the firework-like explosion that destroys Shan-Yu, turns violence into festival entertainment and thus maintains the film's suitability for children and family audiences.

After rescuing the emperor from the Huns and defeating Shan-Yu in one-on-one combat in the Imperial Palace, Mulan stands in front of the emperor, who himself affirms Mulan's victory as a woman. He speaks to her: "I've heard a great deal about you, Fa Mulan. You stole your father's armor, ran away from home, impersonated a soldier, deceived your commanding officer, dishonored the Chinese army, destroyed my palace, and you have saved us all." These words are an apt summary of what the maiden has done, but they also offer official approval for her unusual conduct. Given the emperor's position as the symbol of supreme authority, his judgment represents society's reaction to the protagonist's unconventional behavior. When the emperor bows to Mulan to show his gratitude for saving him and his Middle Kingdom, his people have no choice but to acquiesce and approve her behavior. It is acceptable for Mulan to adopt a masculine persona when in the service of her country. Because of her success, Mulan is perceived as a heroine instead of an offender. Moreover, the counsel, Captain Li Shang, and Mulan's fellow soldiers inside the palace as well as the huge mass of Chinese people outside the palace prostrate themselves to her, a woman, to show respect and gratitude. This approval of Mulan's unusual behavior on different levels is another unique aspect of Disney's version. Next, the emperor offers Mulan an official position in his council, another territory commonly reserved for men and forbidden to women. Expressing her wish to go home and return to her parents, Mulan politely declines the offer. Instead, she is willing to conclude her adventure by resuming a daughter's position. She is then granted the sword of Shan-Yu and the crest of the emperor as gifts to honor her family. Perhaps because of her extraordinary achievements, the young heroine is allowed to cross yet another boundary: she hugs the emperor to show her joy and appreciation before she departs for home in triumph.

Commenting on the specific scene of bowing as the confirmation of Mulan's achievement in the "Bonus Features" of *Mulan* DVD, the producer Pam Coats remarks, "[Mulan] has changed the way society thinks about the role of women. This is made very clear in that final sequence where the Emperor bows. And then she turns around and you see this entire sea of people bowing to her." In the film producer's view, what distinguishes Mulan from other Disney heroines is her ability to think on her own and to speak her mind. Coats considers the story to be about "a woman who uses her brain and reacts with the combination of physical and mental prowess" (qtd. in Lyons 7). The film's portrayal of a successful able-minded and able-bodied protagonist cannot help but remind readers of Kingston's *The Woman Warrior* that transforms Mulan from a Chinese folk heroine to an Asian American woman warrior. Given its popularity among general readers as well as its far-reaching influence on a number of scholars, Kingston's text not only made Mulan a familiar name to many English-speakers but also prepared the ground for reading this character from a feminist perspective. Kingston's version and other retellings may not have influenced Disney's film directly, but they were available to the Disney Studio's production team.

Regardless of Mulan's daring spirit and skills, it is noteworthy that "one of Disney's most vigorous heroines literally has to disguise herself as a boy" (Labi, McDowell, and Park 60). Even though Mulan achieves success after she resumes her female self, her victory as a woman is portrayed as a onetime measure to save the day. The film *Mulan* reinforces "hegemony of gender ideology" in that the character Mulan belongs to the "latest sexist and xenophobic messages churned out by the Disney apparatus for the purpose of swaying children to conform to Victorian Western notions of gender behavior" (Ayres 48, 49). Despite the pro-feminist elements featured in the Disney film, Mulan does not represent a feminist character because her adventures and accomplishments are motivated by filial duty to her father and family rather than by righting a wrong or seeking female empowerment and glory. Mulan is respected because she is "prepared to give up her life in order to save the life of her father and later the life of her lover" (Ayres 48). After all, like many of its Disney predecessors, the film ends with the likelihood of a good marriage for the protagonist. "Ultimately, her demonstrated feats of bravery, fighting skill, and intelligence serve to bring honor to her father and prove her worthy of the captain's love" (Ayres 48). At the closing scene, Mulan returns home with the sword of Shan-Yu and the crest of the emperor and meets her father in the family garden. Fa Zhou's words, "The greatest gift and honor is having you for a daughter," ultimately join together the family honor with the heroine's personal achievement. Not all the family members are satisfied, however. Mulan's grandmother re-marks with sarcasm, "Great. She brings home a sword. If you ask me, she should've brought home a man." Mulan's grandmother trivializes Mu-lan's heroic experience and signals that the rest of the film is pure Disney. Getting a hint from the emperor that "a flower that blooms in adversity is the most rare and beautiful of all. . . . You don't meet a girl like that every dynasty," Captain Li Shang shows up at the Fa's house to bring over Mulan's helmet. Mulan, now bashful but obviously pleased, asks him, "Would you like to stay for dinner?" Her grandmother's line, "Would you like to stay forever," puts closure on Mulan's adventure outside home and emphasizes her return to the appropriate social position for a young woman: marriage. Thus this film version is compromised by Mulan and Li Shang's potential engagement at the end. In this sense, Mulan does not transcend the gender conventions, and her defiance does not include a political agenda calling for women's equal rights. Boys are still the ones who lead active lives and engage in military combat, and girls can do so only when they pretend to be male—and this pretense can last only for a limited period of time. One thus might argue that Mulan's nonthreaten-ing combination of masculinity and femininity has contributed to her emergence as a role model in contemporary times.

Disney's *Mulan* is a hybrid film in many ways. The inspiration for her character and story comes from a non-Euro-American tradition and therefore ensures the heroine's exotic attributes. Codirector Barry Cook explains the way Disney remodels Mulan's tale into a hybrid product:

Mulan is not just someone who accomplishes something in spite of the restrictions placed on her because she is a woman, but she is a person who achieves something extraordinary. Seeing her as an individual who was able to alter society's views and affect a positive change in those around her clarified the story for me. It was her strong personality traits that made the story happen; she's the catalyst. (qtd. in Schroeder and Zoehfeld 56)

Disney thus has attempted to authenticate Mulan for its market value as an "Asian" story in order to appeal to American and international audiences. Cooks's remarks as well as Disney's animated production portray Mulan as, above all, a successful individual who saves her family honor. Thus, the animation feature *Mulan* "sings the praises of an individual who defies tradition out of an unselfish devotion to family, who uses the strengths of her spirit and mind to achieve the seemingly impossible, and whose unique courage earns her the respect of her contemporaries and the love of succeeding generations" (Schroeder and Zoehfeld 72). The emphasis placed on Mulan's dedication to family independence, responsibility, and individual choice therefore mirrors contemporary values in the format of an ancient Chinese legend. The film's protagonist is still a typical Disney teenager equipped with hybrid traits and situated in an international context. Mulan's mindset and actions in the film clearly convey the Western message of individual realization. Because she is "Chinese-looking yet American-acting Mulan" (Ma, *Deathly Embrace*, 142), U.S. as well as international teenagers are able to identify with Mulan's adventurous journey away from home in the sense that it mirrors their quest for adolescent self-realization.[21] The film's conclusion with the young protagonist successfully saving her country and family while realizing her individual identity arouses admiration among young viewers across cultures. Through the use of different elements Disney reconfigured the heroine's tale and thus enriched the film: adding new threads about the protagonist's personality, expanding the plot of her military adventure, and developing feminist elements in the narrative, among others.

Perhaps most important in terms of its infusion of non-Chinese values, Disney's film differs from all other transformations in the sense that the protagonist's gender secret is exposed earlier, and therefore she wins the final battle as a "modern" young woman who does not need to resort to male disguise. At the victorious finale in the Imperial Palace, the emperor as well as the Chinese people bestow recognition on a heroine, a successful female, and thus one might suggest—using such "cross-cultural referencing mechanisms," to borrow Joseph Chan's words—that the Disney version has inserted a hybrid characterization to the Mulan gallery. In the process of this cultural hybridization, the film transforms Mulan's tale for children as well as their families and thereby reaches a large audience. Disney's film presents a transnational transformation of the heroine's tale that is a result of bricolage. In keeping with literary trends, future reinventions of Mulan will probably draw on or react to this transformed, hybrid Disney text.

The Continuation of Mulan's Charm

It seems that Mulan's charm in the United States did not stop with Disney's 1998 animation. In February 2005, Disney released a sequel, *Mulan II*, going directly to DVD and VHS. On the whole, the new sequence continues its predecessor's story and focuses on how Mulan deals with the dilemma between fulfilling her social responsibility and being true to her heart. Through the relationship between Mulan and Li Shang that undergoes tests, the film introduces the lesson of *yin* and *yang* to the audience: namely that the balance between the opposites will "create harmony and life," using Fa Zhou's words. The producer of *Mulan II*, Jennifer Blohm, comments that Mulan is "such a great role model because she's a very modern, creative, strong, brave woman" (*Mulan II* DVD "Bonus Features"). If the heroine's position as a role model had been established in the 1998 film, then this function is confirmed even further in the sequel. At the opening of the second film, the village girls display admiration for Mulan's power, and they follow her to the fields to learn how to "be tough" and directly articulate "we want to be like you."

In the sequel, Mulan's way of bending the rules has contaminated other characters, female and male alike. The three Chinese princesses, Ting Ting, Mei, and Su, who practice Mulan's motto in the film—"My true duty is to my heart"—discard their initial vow to serve the emperor and the Middle Kingdom by way of marrying the princes of the Kingdom of Qui Gong in order to create a stronger alliance to defend against the Mongols' impending invasion. By releasing themselves from the mission to unite the two kingdoms through marriage, the princesses choose to follow their hearts and seek true love. In this film, the heroine Mulan defiantly continues her way of "winging it" instead of following the regulations, but the film lacks character development. Moreover, the order of the leading and supporting characters seems to be reversed. The minor roles—the gang of three comprised of Mulan's soldier friends Yao, Ling, and Chien Po along with the princesses—occupy a large portion of plot time. Probably owing to these defects, one Chinese film review published immediately after its release censured *Mulan II* as a wretched sequel to a fine work ("Hua Mulan II").

The interest in both Mulan and her story has not died out among American filmmakers; the heroine's long-lasting popularity in China continues to boom. A number of news reports describe adaptations of her story in the forms of live-action films, TV series, and other performance genres.[22] Most recently a live-action Chinese film, *Hua Mulan*, directed by Hong Kong director Jingle Ma and starring Vicki Zhao Wei, premiered in mainland China, Singapore, and Malaysia on November 27, 2009. According to the director, his version deals with the emotional depth of the character and focuses on her vulnerabilities and relationships, thus providing a sentimental human portrayal of the beloved heroine. Ma's statement that his first mission is "to tell a Chinese story for the Chinese," and at the same time he wants his film to "go global"—perhaps a challenge to the animated transformation presented by the Disney Corporation (Min Lee).

In addressing the questions regarding "whose story? Does it matter?" Joseph Chan concludes: "*Mulan* is not genuinely Chinese, nor is it all American. It has become a transcultural text: a combination of old and new, traditional and modern, East and West, collectivism and individualism, female submissiveness and women's liberation, filial piety and reciprocal love between father and daughter" (241). Just as the critical engagement incurred by Kingston's retellings of this woman warrior's legend did not mark an end to the scholarly discussion on cultural authenticity and ethnic identity in Asian American studies, the Mulan mania in media and performance genres will not stop at Disney. Instead, new representations of the heroine's tale add additional layers of interpretations and revisions to the palimpsestic imagery of this woman warrior for viewers to enjoy and for researchers to contemplate. Along the trajectory of boundary crossing, Mulan and her story provide a cultural locus in which the dichotomies—authenticity and transformation, nationalism and transnationalism, tradition and invention, misogyny and female agency, femininity and masculinity—are complicated, contested, and reconstructed. Structured mainly on conjectures instead of historical evidence, Mulan and her tale mirror the culture and ideals of the "self" and the "other" during their travels along the temporal and spatial lines across national and cultural boundaries. The legend of Mulan has been traveling inter- and intranationally for hundreds of years, and it appears likely that the tale will be journeying further among diverse cultures and in the process undergo more transmissions and transformations.

7 / Epilogue

When researching Mulan's character and lore, I started out with three touchstone images: the premodern Chinese heroine reflected in the "Ballad," the Chinese American woman warrior depicted in Kingston's *The Woman Warrior*, and the hybrid displayed in the animated Disney version. By tracing the cross-cultural transformation of Mulan's legend in this book, I have attempted to restore the connecting tissue among these images, and in the process I recovered many versions in-between and searched for the implications of the different variations. Although I mainly dealt with written texts and films, the oral tradition could not be neglected in the passage of the Mulan lore from one generation to the next and from one region to another. In fact, from the earliest dissemination of a folk ballad, to varied renditions in storytelling, stage performance, and other oral genres, to the mother character's "talk-stories" in Kingston's book, and finally to the picture books for parents to read to or with their children, the oral impact is crucial in the continuity and development of Mulan's story. The numerous representations of Mulan in literature and media are significant portraits in the long-lasting evolution of her story and contribute to building up a collage of images. During the course of reshaping and retelling, her tale has become a compatible vehicle for transporting and forming cultural traditions.

In premodern China, the heroine made her way from fiction into history. The extant written form of the "Ballad" came down from the thirteenth century, hundreds of years later than the commonly acknowledged composition date that places Mulan's first appearance in literature between the fourth and sixth centuries. Most likely rewriting and revision had already started before Guo Maoqian's anthology; later versions of Mulan's story have added colorful plots and underlined various values. Not until centuries after the written form of the "Ballad" had been in circulation did Mulan's name start to make its way into historical documents. The entries in local gazetteers and tablet inscriptions found in various regions provide strong evidence of the Chinese people's efforts to historicize and localize this exceptional character. There is a two-way interaction in the development of Mulan's image. History and ideology interrupt her legend in various social contexts, highlighting certain aspects and downplaying others, as well as decoding moral values from her story and adding new ones to it. The heroine's tale, in turn, makes its way into local history and China's cultural warehouse by representing varied messages that are either encoded into or deciphered out of it. In this sense, Mulan's tale serves as a cultural vehicle that carries portable traditions across time and space.

The analysis of the heroine typology posits Mulan as a paradigm coming out of a group and growing into a model that embodies a collection of the virtues of the Chinese warrior women. Despite their differences, stories about military women and chivalrous ladies supply ingredients that have enriched the kaleidoscopic collection of Mulan's lore. The enduring popularity of Mulan and her warrior sisters represents the long history of Chinese women's participation in the military and martial worlds. This unification of heroism and womanhood indicates the possibility for a woman to enter the space outside her family compound in Confucian China. These heroic women figures collectively reflect a coexistence of the unusual and the acceptable: femininity in a male world. What makes these heroines famous is their extraordinary yet in most cases temporary participation in the male territory. In many cases, this episode is neither prefaced by martial training, nor is it followed by continued female heroism.

The absence or omission of the training process suggests that military women were not intentionally prepared to become warriors; they merely happened to become heroines in active duties under special circumstances. Later literary imagination, especially in martial fiction, filled such a gap. Similarly, the training scene, although not found in the "Ballad," starts to appear in literary variations of Mulan's legend during a much later period. When Mulan's fame travels across the Pacific Ocean, the fact that the maiden has undergone a particular training process to acquire martial skills is highlighted in multiple rewritings.

In premodern texts, celebrated Chinese heroines, including Mulan, are not portrayed as feminists fighting against gender inequality; rather, their transgression into male territory is often restricted within certain limits. Although the actions of such heroines are unusual, they are necessary and justifiable. Furthermore, in various renditions, Mulan's glory in action is presented as not only accidental but also temporary. Mulan redeems her transgression through loyalty and filial piety, and most versions also underscore the re-dressing as a return to her position as both daughter and potential wife/mother. Such restoration ensures a happy ending for Mulan's story: a perfect combination of masculinity and femininity. Even the contemporary American versions do not bend this rule. Fa Mu Lan is depicted as an ideal fulfillment in Kingston's *The Woman Warrior*—a filial daughter (stepping in to save her father from going to war), a good resident (taking up her sword on behalf of her village), a dutiful wife (keeping her husband company on the battlefield and giving him a son), a loving mother (looking after her newborn in the midst of warfare), and a devoted daughter-in-law (promising to serve her in-laws and bear more heirs for the family). The commercial production from the Disney Studio assures the audience that the heroine returns to her womanly life and suggests a potential marriage at the end of the film. Mulan, together with other Chinese heroines, is generally tamed or domesticated in the aftermath of her military and martial confrontation. Compared to western heroines, such as Joan of Arc, who end their journeys tragically, a Chinese heroine enjoys a successful and happy ending. Rather than fighting followed by death, Chinese heroines, exemplified by Mulan, succeed and survive, probably because they honor their timely retreat from male space and return to female life. If Mulan had accepted the official post and served the emperor in his imperial court, then the heroine's destiny perhaps might not be so optimistic.

Regarding Mulan's transnational journey, Kingston's *The Woman Warrior* plays a crucial role in attaching new plots and messages to the folk story, in giving the character a voice in an autobiographical narrative, and in popularizing the heroine and her story in the new world. *The Woman Warrior*, witnessing the narrator's personal journey of searching for an identity, starts from a girl's imagination of a warrior with swords and ends with a young woman's configuration of a warrior with words. When reading Kingston's version of the woman warrior in the context of Asian America, the task facing the reader is not, and should not be, the advocacy of a return to the so-called "origin" of the tale; rather, the reader must examine how Kingston's writing articulates the specific ways in which ethnicity and identity function (Rey Chow, *Women and Chinese Modernity*, xi). Similar to the "Eighteen Stanzas for a Barbarian Reed Pipe," in which Cai Yan rewrites the Xiongnu melody into Han Chinese songs that transport the message of sorrow, Kingston's revision representing the portable cultural traditions "translates" Mulan's story well through the retelling of a compatible legend. The centrality of Kingston's recreation in the cross-cultural transformation of Mulan lies in the fact that it establishes a bridge between two cultures that leads to Mulan's popularity in America followed by her international fame. The visual imagination of Mulan in contemporary American popular culture after the publication of *The Woman Warrior* further reveals that Kingston's influence reaches far beyond academia.

Overall, this book investigates how Mulan fits into the intellectual, historical, and cross-cultural contexts regarding heroic discourse and womanhood. In the diffusion of Mulan's story through generations and across languages and cultures, her tale has been imbued with new messages within different cultural milieu. In examining each rendition, its faithfulness to the "origin" is not important; the significant issue, instead, lies in what new aspects or messages are discovered or recovered in Mulan's story, in what context, and for what purpose. The divergence in various renditions is as important as the core element in the developing process of Mulan's legend. The evolving narrative and image of Mulan have gone through multiple modifications. Her story, like many other traditional folktales, has undergone and continues to experience a process of reshaping and retelling and lives with storytellers (both oral and written) and audiences. Mulan lasts and changes. During the course of erasure, addition, and revision of her story, the unchangeable ingredient—the narrative of a young woman's successful transgression—has filtered through all layers of her legend and provides a unique image that is both male and female.

The gender of this particular heroine is significant. Mulan's female body in male attire is an idealized combination of masculinity and femininity. In this respect, cross-dressing is simultaneously a transgression and a compromise: a transgression because resorting to men's garments violates the dress code and doctrines of gender segregation; a compromise because performing gender respects the social definition of male and female and follows the rules in playing the game. In this sense, as unconventional as Mulan's deeds are, they do not threaten the social order. Moreover, for Mulan, as well as for other cross-dressed heroines in Chinese culture, femininity is never forfeited. The category of cross-dressing women in Chinese culture embraces many well-known figures, whose unusual behaviors challenge the gender separation of Confucian ethics. Mulan's military life on the battlefield is only one such "invasion" into the male territory. In the stories of the "Butterfly Lovers" and the "Female Top Graduate," women disguise themselves as male students to attain access to education. In a number of chivalrous tales, lady knights-errant dress up as men for convenience in traveling. For example, the leading character Yu Jiaolong (known as Jen in English subtitles) runs away from home on her wedding day and travels in male disguise in Ang Lee's Academy Award winning feature film *Crouching Tiger, Hidden Dragon* (2000). Although the viewer, as an informed reader, can easily identify her femininity under male attire, the characters in the film appear to accept the fact that she is a "man" after costume change.

Part of Mulan's universal appeal resides with the humanness of her character. Different from the superhero, who is gifted with superhuman powers and can pass as human, in many variations of her story this heroine stands out by widely recognized values and virtues: filial piety, loyalty, courage, and wisdom. "The uniqueness of *Mulan* is not just in the time honored tale. Its uniqueness lies in the way it entwines so many tales, ancient and contemporary; so many lives, past and present" (Kurtti 7). Mulan's image reaches far across time and space. The narrative of a young woman's successful transgression becomes a comfort and encouragement for girls and women anywhere and any time. The Disney Studio's film *Mulan II* illustrates the universal influence and compatibility of Mulan's deeds. In this film her courage and free spirit affect the village girls as well as the three princesses. The village girls follow Mulan to gain wisdom and to learn "how to be tough." The princesses eventually discard the royal mission of arranged marriages for political purpose and choose their true loves. Mulan's words—"My duty is to my heart"—becomes a mantra for the princesses as well as for the film. The image of Mulan provides a cultural icon of heroines who belong to both future and past.

The multiple facets of Chinese heroines, exemplified by Mulan, cannot help but remind the reader of European figures such as Joan of Arc whose story also flourished in history and literature.[1] W.A.P. Martin called Mulan "a Chinese Joan of Arc" as early as in 1900 in his book *The Siege in Peking: China against the World* (172).[2] Culturally different as they are, these two heroic women defy conventionally assigned gender roles for females; they abuse and take advantage of the dress code. A brief juxtaposition of Mulan and Joan of Arc would suggest the following aspects of commonalities and differences. Despite coming of age in different sociohistorical circumstances, both maidens have cross-dressed; they have accomplished distinguished military achievements and have been cherished as cultural icons owing to their extraordinary courage; both have inspired a record number of variations in poetry, drama, and fiction; and the development of their stories demonstrates the process of constructing an archetype. Nonetheless, the cultural galleries of these two characters bear obvious distinctions. While Mulan's literary journey begins with a folk ballad, renditions of Joan of Arc often depart from the historical record (Astell xiii). Compared to the verbal reports of the proceedings of trial, letters, and public documents about Joan's military career and imprisonment,[3] Mulan's character embraces more legendary elements whose story cannot be located in any dynastic history. Furthermore, the reasons that motivate the two heroines to join the army are dissimilar: Joan is motivated by her own will (under the guidance of God, according to Ann Astell) while Mulan enlists for the purpose of saving her father. Likewise, their unusual action has incurred consequences that contrast sharply: Joan was punished brutally by the infuriated authorities while Mulan won acceptance and praise and later was able to return to a peaceful womanly life. The cross-dressing theme of both stories is followed by contrasting results. The trial records show that Joan was repeatedly questioned and charged about her wearing of male clothes (Astell xv); the revelation of Mulan's female identity, however, only increases the admiration and respect attributed to her. While Mulan re-dresses in feminine clothes and returns to her female life, Joan of Arc's testimony insists and defends cross-dressing and military service: "For nothing in the world, will I swear not to arm myself and put on a man's dress" (qtd. in Feinberg 35). Joan ends her journey in a significantly different way from Mulan, probably because Mulan as well as many other Chinese heroines return to their womanly life after a temporary invasion into male territory. In contrast, Joan keeps on marching forward and thus turns into a threatening force. Leslie Feinberg describes the situation: "Joan's position as military leader of a popular peasant movement threatened the very French ruling class she helped lift to power;" however, "[t]he more Joan of Arc was idolized by her followers, the more she posed a threat to the Church's religious rule" (33, 35). A comprehensive comparative study of heroines of Asian cultures with those of Euro-American traditions offers an unprecedented platform to undertake a cross-cultural exploration of gender identity and social ethics, which I leave for future scholarly pursuits.

Appendix: Selected English Translations of the "Ballad of Mulan," Listed in Chronological Order

Martin, W.A.P. (1827–1916). "Mulan, the Maiden Chief." *The Chinese Their Education, Philosophy, and Letters*, 316–19. New York: Harper & Brothers, 1881.

William Alexander Parsons Martin is probably the first person to introduce the "Ballad" to English readers. His translation was first published in 1881 when he was president of the Tungwen College in Beijing. Martin identifies the poem as "a Chinese ballad of the Liang Dynasty (502–556 A.D.)" with anonymous origin and uncertain date (316). He includes English translation on pages 316 and 318, and the poem in classic Chinese on pages 317 and 319.

Martin's translation appeared again in his 1894 anthology of Chinese poetry, *Chinese Legends and Other Poems* (Shanghai: Kellly & Walsh, 1894. 1–4). This anthology presents the poem in English translation only, except that poem's title is printed in both English and classic Chinese. The translator's introductory note sets the background of the poem: "An officer being disabled, his daughter puts on his armour, and so disguised leads his troops to the conflict. The original is anonymous, and of uncertain date" (1).

Later Martin included his translation again in the appendix of his other book, *The Siege in Peking: China against the World*, and changed the title into "Mulan, a Chinese Joan of Arc" (New York: Fleming H. Revell Company, 1900. 172–73). According to Martin's note to the appendix, the "Ballad" and two other poems he includes "throw much light on Chinese life" and are translated and published for the first time in the

United States (171). Then, it was collected in Book III "Legends from Chinese Folklore" in another anthology of Martin's, *Chinese Legends and Lyrics*, under the title of "Mulan, the Maiden Chief" (Shanghai: Kelly and Walsh Limited, 1912. 35–37).

Martin's translation "Mulan, the Maiden Chief" is collected in the first volume of the fourteen-volume *The World's Story* (Eva March Tappan, ed. *The World's Story: A History of the World in Story, Song, and Art*. Vol. 1: *China, Japan and the Islands of the Pacific*. Boston: Houghton Mifflin, 1914. 57–59). The editor adds three introductory paragraphs about the historical background of the poem with a particular focus on the chaotic warfare and fast shifting political power in China during that period. Tappan concludes her introduction by stating: "In these times of constant fighting, it happened more than once that a woman held a fort against an invading enemy. Such a warrior was Mulan. This poem was written between 502 and 556 A.D." (58). Now the reprint in Tappan's volume is available online through the Modern History Sourcebook http://www.fordham.edu/halsall/mod/556mulan.html.

Stanton, W. "Muk Lan's Parting: A Ballad." *The China Review (Notes and Queries on the Far East)* 17 (1888–1889): 171–72.

Stanton's translation appeared in a bimonthly periodical published in Hong Kong. The English translation was printed above the "Ballad" in classic Chinese in each stanza. The brief introduction at the beginning states: "It is not known who wrote this ballad, but some suppose the famous heroine herself wrote it. It is taken from the poetry of the Tang Dynasty" (171). Stanton does not provide any information about the reference to the Tang poetry.

Budd, Charles. "Muh-Lan." *Chinese Poems*, 124–29. London: Oxford University Press, 1912.

Budd's translation is included in his translated collection of Chinese poems. His "Preface," written in the Tung Wen Kwan Translation Office in Shanghai, states that many of the translations are "nearly literal, excepting adaptations to meet the exigencies of rhyme and rhythm" and "[a] few notes are given at the end of each poem to explain historical names" (4–5). In this collection, the "Ballad" only appears in English translation. Budd's brief note dates Mulan to the Liang Dynasty (502–556) without any supporting references. His translation was later reprinted under the title of "The Ballad of Mulan" in *Asian-Pacific Folktales and Legends* (edited by Jeannette Faurot. New York: Touchstone, 1995. 95–98) under the category of "Myths and Legends."

Waley, Arthur. "The Ballad of Mulan." *Chinese Poems: Selected from 170 Chinese Poems, More Translations from the Chinese, The Temple and The Book of Songs,* 113–15. London: George Allen and Unwin Ltd., 1946.

Waley's translation is included in his translated collection of Chinese poems. The "Ballad" only appears in English. The translator's brief note in parentheses at the beginning dates the poem to "northern China during the domination of the Wei Tartars, Sixth Century A.D." (113). Waley's translation is reprinted in *The Columbia Anthology of Traditional Chinese Literature,* edited by Victor H. Mair, 474–76. New York: Columbia University Press, 1994. The reprint identifies Mulan as "a member of the Särbi (Hsien-pei) people" and "often compared with Joan of Arc, although the two do not share much more in common than the fact that they were both women warriors" (474).

Jen, T'ai. "The Mu-Lan Rhyme: A Ballad, ca. A.D. 439–534." *United College Journal* 1 (1962): 1–6.

Jen's translation appeared in a bilingual annual periodical published in Hong Kong. The "Translator's Note" provides a comparatively long introduction to the "Ballad." Not only does it analyze the rhyme and the "delicate and powerful poetic utterance" of the poem, but it also briefly introduces the inconsistent biographical information attributed to the character and refers to a number of literary persons' notes regarding the "Ballad" (1). The translation is printed side by side with the "Ballad" in classic Chinese. The footnotes supplement additional explanation of specific phrases, place names, official rank, and the possible time period in which the "Ballad" came into being.

Frodsham, J. D. "The Ballad of Mu-lan." *An Anthology of Chinese Verse: Han Wei Chin and the Northern and Southern Dynasties,* 104–06. Oxford: Clarendon Press, 1967.

Frodsham's translation is collected in his anthology of Chinese verses, in which he provides English translation as well as annotations to selected works from the Han, Wei, Chin, and the Northern and Southern dynasties. The "Ballad" appears in English translation with footnotes to explain specific phrases used in the poem. The translator accredits the "earliest account of the legend of Mu-lan" to be found in the *Gujin yuelu* (104n1).

Sackheim, Eric. "Mu Lan's Song." *The Silent Zero, in Search of Sound: An Anthology of Chinese Poems from the Beginning through the Sixth Century,* 50–52. New York: Grossman, 1968.

Sackheim's translation is included in his anthology of Chinese poems before the sixth century. The "Ballad" appears in English translation with very brief endnotes to explain some wording.

Nienhauser, William H. "The Ballad of Mulan." *Sunflower Splendor: Three Thousand Years of Chinese Poetry,* Edited by Wu-chi Liu and Irving Yucheng Lo, 77–80. Bloomington: Indiana University Press, 1975.

Niehauser's translation is collected in an anthology of Chinese poetry. The "Ballad" appears in English translation with detailed endnotes that not only explain some phrases in the poem but also refer to scholarly publications on related topics. The translator points out: "[s]uffice it to say that Mulan was of northern, i.e., non-Chinese, stock and lived during the Six Dynasties period (A.D. 220–588)" (77n1).

Frankel, Hans H. "Mu-lan." *The Flowering Plum and the Palace Lady: Interpretations of Chinese Poetry,* 68–72. New Haven: Yale University Press, 1976.

Frankel's translation is included in his anthology of Chinese poetry that collects translation as well as analyses of a hundred and six poems. The "Ballad" is printed in English translation with classic Chinese in the footnote. Frankel's translation is followed by an interpretative essay, in which he analyzes the poem's word usage, character, and historical background. Frankel's translation is now available online under the title of "The Legend of Fa-Mulan": http://www.geocities.com/Hollywood/5082/mulanpoem.html.

Chin, Frank. "The Ballad of Mulan." *The Big Aiiieeeee! An Anthology of Chinese American and Japanese American Literature,* edited by Jeffery Paul Chan, Frank Chin, Lawson Fusao Inada, and Shawn Wong, 4–6. New York: Meridian, 1991.

In his introduction to the anthology *The Big Aiiieeeee,* Chin includes both the folk "Ballad" and Wei Yuanfu's imitative poem in classic Chinese and his translation of the "Ballad" in English. Chin uses the "Ballad" to support his criticism on Maxine Hong Kingston's reimagined heroine in *The Woman Warrior.*

White, Barbara-Sue, trans. "The Ballad of Mulan." *Chinese Women a Thousand Pieces of Gold,* 24–26. Oxford: Oxford University Press, 2003.

White's translation is collected in her anthology on Chinese women in "Part I: Exceptional Women." The translator includes the English translation and a brief introductory note at the beginning, in which White states that further tribute to this great folk heroine of China "was paid in the animated 1998 Disney movie and in the fiction of Maxine Hong Kingston" (24).

Notes

1 / Prologue

1. The transcriptions of the heroine's name "Mulan" in English are not consistent. In published materials, it has appeared as "Fa Mu Lan," "Fah Muk lan," "Mu Lan," and "Hua Mu Lan," to name only a few. Applying *hanyu pinyin* romanization, I transcribe her name as "Mulan" as it appears in the "Ballad of Mulan," the earliest existing written record of her story. Throughout this book, *hanyü pinyin* is used to transcribe names, places, and phrases in Chinese, with a few exceptions: (1) authors who have used other spellings for their names in publications in English, (2) place names well-known to English speakers (for instance: Taipei), and (3) transcriptions in quotations. Following the Chinese practice, I have rendered Chinese names with the family name first and given name after, unless the author has published with his or her name in English tradition.

2. As Andre Lefevere has laid out in his study, *Translation, Rewriting, and the Manipulation of Literary Fame* (1992), rewriting comes in many forms and plays a crucial role in addressing the issues of power, ideology, institution, and manipulation.

3. Maxine Hong Kingston's *The Woman Warrior* and *China Men* (1980) have added the phrase "talk-story" to the American literary tradition and English vocabulary. It first appeared as a verb: "Night after night my mother would talk-story until we fell asleep" (*Woman Warrior*, 19). In Kingston's usage, "talking-story" combines the Chinese folk genre of storytelling and the Hawaiian pidgin phrase in street language. She reshapes the "talk-stories" based on her mother's tales, the Chinese American community's anecdotes, cultural memory, and her own experience of growing up with a bicultural heritage. By inventing such a cultural form, Kingston engages with both her Chinese ancestry and her American existence and in the process seeks a balance between gender and ethnicity (Huntley 32; Brownmiller 178; Dong, "Maxine Hong Kingston," 1252).

4. In Spring 2003, Lilian Feitosa invited me to give a guest lecture on Kingston's

The Woman Warrior in her "Spiritual Autobiography" class at the University of Massachusetts at Amherst. I asked students to draw pictures of the heroine in their minds and then describe their portraits in class discussion. Frustrated, one student complained that her imagination was too dominated by Disney's film *Mulan* to create her own image. This response exemplifies how the narrative and visualization of the Disney production play an important role in preserving, presenting, and reconfiguring the story and image of this character.

5. Kingston's books have been translated into Chinese: *The Woman Warrior, China Men, Tripmaster Monkey: His Fake Book* (1989), and *The Fifth Book of Peace* (2003). The *Women Warrior* and *China Men* have more than one Chinese translation published in Taiwan, Hong Kong, and mainland China. Kingston and her writing, particularly *The Woman Warrior*, have become topics of doctoral and master's theses, scholarly journal articles, and academic conference papers in China.

2 / Heroic Lineage

1. The term "imperial China" is commonly used to refer to the last two dynasties: the Han Chinese-ruled Ming (1368–1644) and the Manchu-controlled Qing (1644–1911). For scholarship on literary women in China, see Waltner, Ropp, Carlizt, Mann "Learned Women," Mann *Precious Records*, Widmer and Chang.

2. The other figure is Yang Yuhuan (also known as Yang Guifei), one of the consorts of Tang Emperor Ming Huang (Xuanzong, 685–762; r. 712–756). Susan Mann singles out these two characters mainly because of their undying popularity, the historical ground, the consistent attraction to audience of their stories, and the "multimedia representations" they have inspired from ancient to modern times ("Presidential Address," 844–45, 854).

3. I use the term "Confucian ethics" as shorthand to refer to the social morality in Chinese culture since the Han Dynasty (206 B.C.-220) when Confucianism became the ideological, philosophical, and political mainstream of Chinese society. Confucianism, referring to a philological, semireligious, and ideological thought, is usually attributed to Confucius as its initiator. It has, nonetheless, a long history of development and transformation over the centuries in China. There is hardly a commonly agreed definition of Confucianism. In general, as "a worldview, a social ethic, a political ideology, a scholarly traditional, and a way of life," Confucianism functions as the rules and values that regulate the relations between individuals, families, communities, and nation-states for more than two thousand years in Chinese history (Tu, "Confucian Tradition," 112).

4. Gender segregation is by no means an exclusive Confucian thought in China. As a matter of fact, similar ideas have been stated by other philosophical groups: the Legalist Shang Yang (d. 338 B.C.) also has written about female business within the "inner" and male matters at the "outer" (*Shangjun shu* vol. 18).

5. For example, Mark Elvin's study of the social encouragement and governmental promotion of female virtues suggests: "the unusual feature about late imperial China" is precisely "the use of the *political* system to confer explicit honors for behavior defined as virtuous in private, everyday life" (151). Lisa Raphal's *Sharing the Light: Representations of Women and Virtue in Early China* (1998) further underlines the social functions of female virtues in early Chinese history. Taking on a broader view, the

collection, *Women and Confucian Cultures in Premodern China, Korea, and Japan* (2003) strives to position women "at center stage" and "to understand the concrete processes of female subject formation and to recover textures of female everyday lives in specific historical locations" (Ko, Haboush, and Piggott, "Introduction," 1).

6. The Chinese word *xia* does not have an exact English equivalent. I use knight-errantry and chivalry interchangeably when referring to *xia* in this book.

7. Given the obvious distinctions that the two groups represent in the light of their relations to the ruling power and their influences on the development of Mulan's tale, I analyze them separately here. There are other ways to divide heroines into subcategories. For example, Barbara Kaulbach has summarized four types of Chinese heroines in stage performances: female demons, bandits, generals, and women with magical powers (70). Sufen Lai addresses three kinds of warriors—women soldiers, wandering lady knights, and female outlaws—and emphasizes that cross-dressing daughters like Mulan and lady knights-errant are two complementary trends coexisting in forging the typology of warrior women.

8. Li's article was published in the *Social Education* special issue, "Homefront to Front Lines: Women in Wartime." As the editor stated upfront, the goal for this volume was to fill the need to understand "the many roles women have played in wartime that have been a general oblivion in various cultures" (Haas 65). According to the editor, up to 1994 Xiaolin Li is "the only person who has written in the English language about Chinese women in military" (Haas 65).

9. As demonstrated by the presence of 1,928 objects (among them weapons and ritual vessels) and approximately 7,000 cowry shells (currency at the time) in her tomb, Fu Hao must have been remembered and buried with the honors due a military leader. For English translation of selected inscriptions and commentary on Fu Hao's role as a royal consort during her life time and after her death, see Keightley 29–46; Robin Wang 2–3. For more information on the excavation of the tombs and the bronze vessels that include inscribed records, see Allan 6–18, 149–54.

10. For the role of women in spy craft, see Sawyer 109–11, 261–74.

11. I thank Ralph D. Sawyer for bringing these sources to my attention.

12. "Xiao" (filial piety) is usually considered the root of all virtues in Confucianism. Simply speaking, it refers to children's responsibility to respect and serve their parents when they are alive, and to honor and worship them through mourning and ritual sacrifice at their death (T'ien 149; Du and Mann 243n4).

13. All English translations of official titles in premodern China are based on Charles Hucker's *A Dictionary of Official Titles in Imperial China* (1985), unless otherwise specified.

14. No historical record indicates that the army under Princess Pingyang's command was an all-women regiment. The title of "female detachment" probably comes from the fact that this army's commander-in-chief is a woman. Later on this phrase usually refers to a military division of women soldiers in China.

15. Lady Liang's personal name "Hongyu" is not stated in the *Songshi*. Rather, it appears later in fiction, local topographies, and folk stories. These sourses contain more personal information about Lady Liang whose trace cannot be found in the dynastic history.

16. From the Three Kingdoms (220–280) to the Qing Dynasty, the imperial court had a system of Nine Ranks with the First Rank as the highest. These ranks were

categories into which all officials and the posts they occupied were divided for purposes of determining prestige, compensation, and priority in court attendance (Hucker
177).

17. In her book *Dangerous Women: Warriors, Grannies, and Geisha of the Ming*,
Victoria Cass includes Qin Liangyu as an exemplary of female warriors and identifies
her as having been raised in a Confucian family (81). Nonetheless, there is no record
about her family background in the *Mingshi*, except that she was born into a family in
Zhong Prefecture in Sichuan.

18. A book-length collection of historical and legendary accounts of Qin Liangyu,
titled *Qin Liangyu shiliao jicheng* (Collection of Historical Records of Qin Liangyu),
was published in 1987. This comprehensive collection in Chinese is organized into
seven sessions in chronological order that divides her life into different stages in which
a more colorful image of the heroine is illustrated.

19. For a study on the prevalence of female chastity and marital fidelity in the
Ming Dynasty, see T'ien 1–13, 39–69.

20. Even though the troops led by Lady Liang and her husband achieved multiple
military victories, their valor and skills were of no avail in saving the falling imperial court, given the overall weakness and malfunction of the Song government. In
the case of Qin Liangyu, her rejected defense plan and her consequent depression,
as documented in her historical entry, are obviously tragic results as well as pointed
reflections of the impotence of the Ming rule. When the Ming collapsed under the
smashing attacks of uprising, she could do no more than hold onto her home base and
establish a small patch of peaceful land, where she remained a Ming loyalist.

21. It is worth mentioning that female characters play a significant role in dramatic literature in Chinese culture, "as there are about as many heroine's plays as there
are hero's" (Qian Ma 33).

22. Chih-Tsing Hsia and Fan Pen Chen, for example, have discussed female warriors in Chinese fiction (Hsia 352–57; Fan Pen Chen 91–109).

23. Their stories appear in the Ming fiction, *Yangjia jiang zhuan* (Story of the Yang
Generals, Xiong Damu, fl. ca. 1522–ca. 1619) and *Yangjiafu shidai zhongyong yanyi
zhuan* (Story of the Loyal and Brave Yang Family, Qinhuaimoke, pseud. fl. 1606–1607)
as well as theater performance, storytelling, and poetry.

24. Kazuko Ono's *Chinese Women in a Century of Revolution, 1850–1950* (1989)
includes a fair amount of information about women rebels in the Taiping Rebellion
and the Boxer Rebellion.

25. Although difficult to be substantiated, it is possible that the historiographer
might have invented the plot of infidelity to condemn a disloyal woman like Yang Miaozhen. There is perhaps not a better way to denounce a woman in Confucian China
than emphasizing her unleashed sexuality.

26. For detailed discussion on how the "xia" was defined in early China in English,
see James Liu 1–17; in Chinese, see Cui Fengyuan 1–19; Chen Shan 1–14; Cao Zhengwen, *Zhongguo xia wenhua*, 7–14.

27. Little is known about the author Zou Zhilin. *Nüxia zhuan* is collected in an
anthology that was compiled around 1610.

28. James Liu's book *The Chinese Knight-Errant* includes some chivalric ladies
as supplement to the male knight-errantry. Chen Shan's book *Zhongguo wuxia shi*
(History of Chinese Martial Knight-Errantry, 1995) provides a comprehensive review

of Chinese knight-errant tradition from ancient to modern times. Cao Zhengwen's *Zhongguo xia wenhua shi* (History of Chinese Knight-Errant Culture, 1994) further develops the study of Chinese chivalry and includes valuable bibliographical sources of chivalric figures and works.

29. For exploration on sociopolitical and cultural background of the prosperity of chivalry in the Tang literature in English, see James Liu 86–87; in Chinese, see Cui Fengyuan 63–70. In his book on Chinese chivalric tradition, Cao Zhengwen summaries five attributes of the Tang stories as a new stage in the culture of Chinese chivalry (*Zhongguo xia wenhua shi*, 46–47).

30. Attributed to Huangpu Shi (fl. ca. after 840), this story is collected in *Taiping guangji* (Li Fang, 925–996, et al., comp., 193: 1450–51).

31. For an English translation of this story, see E. D. Edwards 2: 123–27.

32. This story is found in *Taiping guangji* (Li Fang et al., 149: 1456–59). For English translation of this story, see Chi-Chen Wang 98–103.

33. For an English translation of this story, see James Liu 96–97.

34. Literary renditions of women in military services, nevertheless, usually depict them as beauties.

35. Similar occurrences also can be found in Chinese literati tradition in which the records of literary women usually represent them as honorary men instead of talented women (Robertson 64).

3 / From a Courageous Maiden in Legend to a Virtuous Icon in History

1. I use "short essays" to refer to the *biji* or *suibi* (short sketches, casual notes, and casual essays), a particular genre in Chinese literature.

2. For example, Wang Yinglin (1223–1296), Ma Guohan (1794–1857), and Yao Zhenzong (fl. 1897) all include entries about the *Gujin yuelu* in their works. All three citations contain similar information about Zhijiang's living period and the compilation of the anthology: around the sixth century. Yet, none of the authors mentions the "Ballad" or the character Mulan. It is not clear whether these authors have seen the *Gujin yuelu* or have read about it in other sources. The *Gujin yuelu* is also mentioned in Shen Yue's (441–513) *Songshu* yuezhi ("Record on Music" in History of the Song). To read the records in Wang Yinglin, Ma Guohan, and Yao Zhenzong's works together with Shen Yue's account, I found an anachronous problem: if Zhijiang lived in the late sixth century, then how could his work be known by Shen Yue, a scholar predating him for almost a century? This kind of inconsistency is not uncommon when people refer to lost works such as the *Gujin yuelu* and depend on secondary sources.

3. Most Chinese scholars and writers are busy trying to locate a certain historical period for the "Ballad." It is, nonetheless, noticeable that as early as in the fourteenth century, Tao Zongyi (fl. 1360–1368) already acknowledges the obscurity regarding the origination of Mulan's story. He states that "[people] do not know exactly whose poem it is" (Tao Zongyi, *Shuo fu*, vol. 84a, in *Siku Quanshu*). Therefore, it is hard to decide the date of its first conception.

4. All references from *Siku Quanshu* were retrieved from the Intranet database Siku Quanshu, one of the Digital Resources for Chinese Studies at Harvard University in May 2007, http://hcl.harvard.edu/research/guides/chinese/part3.html.

5. Zhu Mu (fl. thirteenth century, *Gujin shi wen leiju houji* vol. 11, in *Siku*

Quanshu), for example, reiterated Pan Zimu's contention. A few centuries later, Hu Yinglin (1551–1602) supported this claim through a brief analysis of the phraseology and writing style of the "Ballad" (44–45). Among modern scholars, C. H. Wang also dates the poem to a period between the third and fourth centuries (32).

6. Xu Bo (fl. 1592–1639) considers the "Ballad" a work from the Qi and Liang dynasties (479–502, 502–557 respectively) (*Xushi bi jing*, vol. 3, in *Siku Quanshu*). The contention to accredit the "Ballad" to the Liang Dynasty is further supported by Shen Deqian (1673–1769) in his work (13: 326–27).

7. For instance, a number of Chinese scholars contend that the "Ballad" was composed in the Tang Dynasty (618–906) (Yao Darong; Xu Zhongshu; Luo Genze 151–55).

8. A partial list includes Zhang Weiqi; Yu Guanying 1–25; Wang Yunxi 119–22; Li Chunsheng; Wang Zhong 147–49; Xiao Difei; Chen Youbing; Che Baoren. The Northern dynasties include: Northern Wei (386–534), Eastern Wei (534–550), Northern Qi (550–577), Western Wei (535–557), and Northern Zhou (557–581).

9. Jiji: onomatopoetic word that imitates the sound of a sigh.

10. Xiyu, a Han Dynasty term literally meaning "western regions," refers to the area west of Yumeng Gate, including what is now the Xinjiang Uygur Autonomous Region in China and parts of Central Asia.

11. Interestingly enough, none of the variations, in Chinese or English, imagines Mulan at war with the Han Chinese, even though her story has a very likely non-Han origin.

12. The ellipsis of military combat is a poetic device commonly seen in early Chinese literature through which martial heroism is not celebrated as the primary theme (C. H. Wang 32; Allen 349–50).

13. Joseph Allen stresses the process of the heroine's undressing and redressing reflected in the "Ballad," which he views to be a story of returning home and a tale of domestication. See particularly 346, 350–53.

14. Collections such as *Wu Youru huabao* (Precious Drawings of Wu Youru, Wu Youru, ca. 1909), *Zhongguo bai mei tu* (Chinese Hundred Beauties, Yi Junzuo, 6th ed., 1975), *Ming ke lidai bai mei tu* (Ming Dynasty Block-Printed Hundred Beauties of all Times, Zhong Nianren, ed., 2003), *Wan Qing san mingjia hui bai mei tu* (Late Qing Hundred Beauties Illustrated by Three Masters, Fei Xiaolou, 1802–1850, Gai Qi, 1774–1829, and Wang Su, 1794–1877, 2005 ed.), and *Bai mei xinyong tuzhuan* (Hundred Beauties Illustrations and New Narrations, Yan Xiyuan, 1787–1804, Yuan Mei, 1716–1798, and Wang Hui, 2006 ed.) include drawings of Mulan as one of the famous Chinese beauties.

15. Some scholars, however, view gender equality as a significant theme reflected in the "Ballad." For example, Robin Wang contends that through forging their loyalties in the heat of battles "Mulan and her dumbfounded messmates have experienced the possibility of a new sense of gender equality and solidarity" (250).

16. In the *Wenyuan yinghua* (Outstanding Literary Works), a literary anthology compiled by a group of scholars allegedly under the lead of the Tang scholar Li Fang (925–996), the "Ballad" is included under the title of "Mulan ge" ("Song of Mulan") and incorrectly attributed to Wei Yuanfu (Li Fang et al. 3: 1773). Supposedly the version included in the *Wenyuan yinghua* should be the earliest written form of the "Ballad," since the collection was claimed to be compiled under Li Fang's lead and therefore came into being in the tenth century. However, the *Wenyuan yinghua* has

the following line under the title "Mulan ge": "Guo Maoqian *Yuefu* name unknown" (Li Fang et al. 3:1773). Here the *Wenyuan yinghua* refers to a collection that appeared in the thirteenth century as its source, from which it anthologizes the poem. That incurs an obvious anachronous problem. One possible explanation is that the *Wenyuan yinghua* was completed during or after the thirteenth century but alleged Li Fang to be its chief editor. Later, Peng Shuxia (fl. 1192) corrects this inaccuracy by stating that the "Song of Mulan" collected in the *Wenyuan yinghua* is the anonymous "Ballad," not a poem composed by Wei Yuanfu (in *Wenyuan yinghua* 5279).

17. One of the few exceptions, Margret Barthel's essay written in German, includes an analysis of Wei Yuanfu's poem and a comparison between Wei's work and the "Ballad" (459–64). More recently, Li Jingxin compares the two poems in a more detailed analysis in his article published in Chinese (48–50).

18. The tendency of interpreting cultural values out of the "Ballad" is quite common among Chinese persons of letters and continues in contemporary time. Some recent examples include analyzing the image of Mulan as not only "an embodiment of the benevolent and brave but also an incarnation of the wise and rational," and her character as a reflection of both Confucian and Daoist philosophies and thus explains Chinese cultural spirit well (Zhu Yingyuan 59), and discovering the "tragic ideology" and the yearning for a peaceful life embedded in the "Ballad" (He Chengfeng 37).

19. Fuyundui is a place name, referring to modern southwestern area of Baotou city in Inner Mongolian Autonomous Region in China, where memorial construction dedicated to Wang Zhaojun is found.

20. Wang Zhaojun, also titled the Ming Princess, is one of the famous beauties of ancient China. Her personal name is Qiang. As a historical figure, she was sent to marry Huhanye Chanyu of the Huns by Emperor Han Yuan (76–33 B.C.; r. 49–33 B.C.) and was titled Ninghu Yanzhi. In the Hun region, she bore children, stayed for the rest of her life, and was buried after her death. Her experience is one example of the *heqin* policy (to make peace with rulers of minority peoples in the border areas by marriage) in ancient China. Wang Zhaojun's story is an endearing and lasting topic in Chinese culture.

21. Other Tang poets such as Li Shangyin (813–858), Cen Shen (714–770), Li Yi (748–827), and Meng Jiao (751–814) also alluded to Mulan and/or the "Ballad" in their works.

22. There are examples where poetic references to Mulan bear more ideological weight. For instance, in the Qing Dynasty, He Chuguang wrote twelve poems under the general title of "Mulan ci sai shen qu" ("Ballad of Mulan in Honor of the Goddess," Zhu Maode and Tian Yuan 426–27). Alluding to a number of honorable women in ancient China, He Chuguang extolled Mulan as the highest model of female virtues. His poems were composed for the sacrificial rituals in honor of Mulan at the temple under her name and reflected the naturalization of the character to be a local heroine.

23. In another edition, this play is titled *Mulan nü* (Mulan Girl, Shanghai: Shangwu yinshuguan, 1958, 3, 1a–10b). The contents of the two plays are identical. There are several Ming editions of *Ci Mulan* still in existence. For a discussion on different editions of Xu Wei's collection, see I-Ch'eng Liang, Xu Wei, 74–76.

24. The other three plays are: *Kuang gushi Yuyang sannong* (The Mad Drummer's Three Songs of Yuyang; one act), *Yu chanshi cuixiang yimeng* (The Jade Monk's Dream

at Cui Village; two acts), and *Nü zhuangyuan cihuang defeng* (Woman Top Candidate Takes on the Man's Role; five acts).

25. Deng Mingshi (fl. 1134), in his *Gujin xingshi shu bianzheng* (Verification and Collection of Ancient and Present Family Names) records: "Mulan [is] sometimes simplified as Lan" (496). In this document, Mulan as a name is not necessarily related to the well-known heroine, but it points to the possibility that "Mulan" might be a family name that mostly likely belongs to a non-Han Chinese people.

26. Sanping Chen has studied the name "Mulan" and argued that it is neither a Han Chinese name nor a feminine one.

27. In Xu Wei's play, Mulan had a younger brother Yao'er and a younger sister Munan; both were still young when the enlistment draft came.

28. For more information on the tradition of women's footbinding in China, see Howard Levy; Jackson; Ko "Written Word and the Bound Foot," *Every Step, Cinderella's Sisters*.

29. Even when the Chinese drama entered the twentieth century, the most popular actors playing the female leads in large-scaled productions of the New Drama and the Reformed Beijing Opera were still men. Among such examples was the play, *Hua Mulan* (1914), in which the famous heroic female cross-dresser was performed by Wang Youyou (1888–1937), a male star (Bao 203).

30. For a study on boy actors and gender in Chinese opera, see Volpp.

31. Similar stories are also found in Yang Shen's (1488–1559) *Sheng'an waiji* (Extended Collection of Sheng'an 1971, 14: 449–50), Hu Yinglin's (1551–1602) *Shi sou* (Collection of Poetry 1973, 4: 15a-16a), and Wu Renchen's (ca. 1628–1689) *Shiguo chunqiu* (Annuals of the Ten Countries 902–979 1962, 45: 5a-5b). In *Chuogeng lu* (Notes Written after Stopping Tilling), Tao Zongyi (fl. 1360–1368) lists a play—*Nü zhuangyuan Chuntao ji* (Story of Woman Top Candidate Chuntao). Except for the title, no additional information about this play is included in Tao's work (9a), and it is not clear whether this play was available to Xu Wei in the sixteenth century.

32. Contemporary scholars have discussed the profeminist implications of Xu Wei's play. For example, in his foreword to Xu Wei's collection *Si sheng yuan* published in 1984, the editor Zhou Zhongming praises Xu Wei's emphasis on gender equality and women's rights, as reflected in these two plays (3–4). Que Zhen's article, "The Thinking of Recreation of Xu Wei's Drama Female Mulan" argues that in Xu Wei's writing "Mulan becomes a new type of image which criticizes the tradition of looking down upon women and manifests women's positive ideas of demanding for equality" (42). Viewing Xu Wei as an advocate for gender equality, in my understanding, takes him out of his time and interprets his writing beyond its social context. Mulan and Chuntao's stories do reveal the playwright's progressive ideas concerning women by recognizing and acclaiming their talent, but they also show the artist's syncretism to conform to social regulations at the time.

33. In Confucian doctrine, no physical contact is allowed between brothers-in-law and sisters-in-law. The analogy used by Mulan is meant to describe the urgent situation. Mencius said: "Not to help a sister-in-law who is drowning is to be a brute. It is prescribed by the rites that, in giving and receiving, man and woman should not touch each other, but in stretching out a helping hand to the drowning sister-in-law one uses one's discretion" (D. C. Lau trans. 164–65).

34. Qin Xiu: a woman named Xiu from the Qin family, wife of King Yan. To

avenge her family, she killed the foe in the middle of the market and was then incarcerated. Later she was remitted. Qin Xiu's story appears in the *yuefu* poem "Qin nü Xiu xing" (Ballad of Qin Xiu), written by Zuo Yannian. Tiying: daughter of a famous doctor Chunyu Yi. She lived during the Western Han dynasty. When her father was put in prison following other people's accusations, she appealed to become a slave for the government to save her father. Both figures are considered models of filial piety in China.

35. Dramatizations of Mulan's story flourished at the end of the Qing Dynasty. The three works, *Mulan congjun* (Mulan Joins the Army, 1903), *Hua Mulan chuanqi* (Legend of Hua Mulan, 1908), and *Mulan congjun* (Mulan Joins the Army, 1909), are just a few examples in a long list. These plays and opera scripts are mostly anonymous works or published under pseudonyms. Most of them are not available to the reader now, either having been lost or having become rare and hard to access. *Wanqing xiqu xiaoshuo mu* (Bibliography of Drama and Fiction in Late Qing, 1959), compiled by A Ying (pseud.), collects a number of Qing plays that have adapted Mulan's legend and has reserved precious materials of the heroine's tale in drama. One of the few exceptions, *Huitu Hua Mulan zhengbei guci* (Illustrated Story of Hua Mulan's Expedition to the North Sung to the Drum, ca. 1910–1919) is available to readers. In modern China, adaptations of Mulan on stage appear repeatedly. Chen Guohua's article, "The Transformation of Hua Mulan Stage Arts" examines the development of Mulan's image in stage plays and local operas (39–43).

36. For a brief introduction to *Xu Wei* in Chinese, see Zhou Zhongming. For comprehensive studies of Xu Wei's biography and his works in English, see Faurot; Liang, "Hsü Wei"; in Chinese, see Xu Lun; Liang, Xu Wei. Besides historical documents, Xu Wei enjoys popularity in folklore as well. For stories about Xu Wei as a character in folk tradition, see Levy, *Dirtiest Trickster*.

37. On male ventriloquism in late imperial China, see Bruneau 167–68; Widmer 124.

38. Different editions of this novel came out in late Qing, some with illustrations. For example, the stone-carving edition in 1896 has its title as *Xiuxiang Mulan qinü zhuan* (The Legend of the Extraordinary Girl Mulan with Embroidered Illustrations). The cover of the 1907 stone-carving edition titled this novel *Mulan qinü zhuan* (The Legend of the Extraordinary Girl Mulan) (*Zhong xiao yong lie qinü zhuan*, Forward, 2). In contemporary China this novel is the most popular prose version of Mulan's story among all premodern materials. In 1974 Fenghuang chubanshe in Taipei published a reprinted edition of this novel under the title of *Nüxia xiaoshuo Mulan congjun* (Fiction of Female Knights-Errand Mulan Joins the Army) with four illustrations. *Mulan qinü zhuan* was published in simplified Chinese characters in 1995 and in traditional Chinese in 1998. This novel is also available to the public free of charge on the Internet: http://www.shuku.net:8082/novels/classic/mlqnzh/mlqnzh.html; http://www.xiaoshuo.com/pages/book/0/0011087.html; http://www.millionbook.net/gd/y/yiming/mlqnz/.

39. For discussions on Mulan and other women warriors in operas, see Kaulbach 69–82; Hung 149–77; Siu Leung Li's dissertation chapter "Dressing up to Power: Woman Warriors," 111–44; Tsui-fen Jiang; Allen.

40. Mulan's name appeared in the *Tong zhi* (Zheng Qian, 1104–1162, juan 49, in *Siku Quanshu*), a comprehensive work of government institutions. This passing record

states Mulan's military service in cross-dressing briefly and mentions the ending couplet of the "Ballad." The earliest record claiming Mulan to be a historical person is said to appear in the *Xing yuan* (Collection of Family Names): "Mulan, a native of Rencheng" (cited in *Yuanhe xing zuan*, Lin Bao, fl. 9th century, vol. 10, in *Siku Quanshu*; also cited in *Gujin xingshi shu bianzheng*, Deng Mingshi, fl. 1134, 35: 496). The author He Chengtian (370–447) is dated before the sixth century, the most commonly accepted time for the formation of the "Ballad." The *Xing yuan* has long been lost, except for pieces included in other collections. It is not clear whether the person named "Mulan" in He Chengtian's work is the same character who appears in the "Ballad." Because He Chengtian's work is a collection of family names, it is possible that Mulan refers to a family name, which may or may not be related to the well-known heroine and the "Ballad." Thus, this five-word entry does not contain enough evidence either to prove that the "Ballad" took shape based on a real story of a historical heroine or to suggest that oral narratives of the "Ballad" were already circulating in the fifth century. In the Tang Dynasty, Li Rong's (ca. 9th cent.) brief record in *Du yi zhi* (Unique Strange Records) states "in ancient times there was one Mulan who took her father's place in military expedition" (279). This reference lists Mulan among the characters from the Han Dynasty. Because the anecdotes and stories recorded in *Du yi zhi* are arranged generally in chronological order, one can speculate that Li Rong considered Mulan a person living during the Han. A few centuries later, the Song scholar Cheng Dachang (1123–1195) also views Mulan as a historical figure, but one who lived around the time of the Sui or Tang dynasties (174). Cheng Dachang's writing refers to the heroine in the "Ballad" directly. He refutes the idea that Mulan's story is a legend. Cheng cites the aforementioned Tang poems by Bai Juyi and Du Mu to validate his opinion that the heroine is a historical person and her deeds are historical events instead of literary fabrication. It is important to note that Cheng's way of using literature to substantiate history presents obvious doubt to his claim of Mulan's historicity.

41. See Lu Youren's (fl. 1330–1338) *Yan bei za zhi*, vol. 3, in *Siku Quanshu*; Da Shi'an's "Record of General Filial Piety and Illustriousness of the Han Dynasty" collected in the *Wan xian zhi*, reprint of the 1731 hand-written edition (Zhu Maode and Tian Yuan vol. 9: 390).

42. In June 2002, I visited the Memorial Shrine of Mulan in Yucheng County, where I also found a cemetery of two tombs alleged to be those of Mulan and her parents. The pamphlet prepared by the Management Committee of the Shrine states that the temple was first built in the Tang Dynasty and had been rebuilt and renovated in later dynasties. At the beginning of the twentieth century, the temple was of a broad scale and quite famous. Unfortunately, most construction was destroyed by the flames of war in 1943; only a portion of the memorial hall and the two tablets survived. In recent years, the temple and the cemetery were renovated. Not only is the heroine worshiped as a goddess around the region, but her fame also has become a means for local economic development, particularly in terms of promoting tourism and attracting investment. The town distributes commemorative stamps, postcards, and souvenir badges with the image of Mulan. Yingguo town also began to celebrate the Mulan Cultural Festival in China starting in 1993.

43. For records about this region, see the *Ming yitongzhi* (Gazetteers of the Ming, Li Xian, 1408–1466 et al., 61, in *Siku Quanshu*); the *Huangzhou fu zhi* (Gazetteer of Huangzhou Prefecture, reprint of the 1500 edition, 2: 40a; 4: 30a); the *Huangpi xian*

zhi (Gazetteer or Huangpi County, reprint of the 1871 edition, 172, 215, 240); several entries in the Ming collectanea *Gujin tushu jicheng* (Chen Menglei, Jiang Tingxi et al. 1184: page 1b, 1184: 2b, 1178: 37b, 52b, 1181: 50b).

44. For example, as early as the twelfth century, Xue Jixuan (1134–1173) proposed that the Memorial Shrine in Mulan's name located in Huanggang does not necessarily have a connection with the heroine (*Lang yu ji*, vol. 12, in *Siku Quanshu*). In a nineteenth-century essay Sun Biwen discussed questioned the validity of the claims that Mulan is a local heroine of Shangqiu, Wan, Bo, and Huangpi (*Kao gu lu*, reprint of the 1888 edition, 6: 50–54).

4 / The White Tiger Mythology

1. According to Lee's essay, *History of the Three Kingdoms* was compiled in the year 1145 under the lead of the general editor Kim Pusik (1075–1151). Lee does not include any other details of the specific reference to Mulan found in this historical text. Except for excerpts, there is no English translation of *History of the Three Kingdoms*.

2. By now, more than a dozen English translations of the "Ballad" have been published. Additional information of selected translations is included in Appendix.

3. Except for the brief mentioning in Yao Darong's article, no other information about this stage performance was found.

4. I thank Floyd Cheung for introducing Tsiang's play to me.

5. Some critical references on *The Woman Warrior* are listed in Shirley Geok-lin Lim's *Approaches to Teaching Kingston's* The Woman Warrior (1991), Sau-ling Wong's *Maxine Hong Kingston's* The Woman Warrior: *A Casebook* (1999), and Sau-ling Wong and Stephen Sumida's *A Resource Guide to Asian American Literature* (2001). Some recent discussions include Sämi Ludwig's study of Kingston's allusive references to Western traditions, ideas, and images; Feng Lan's article rehistoricizing Kingston's version in relation to the Communist revolution; Gary Storhoff's essay that examines typical dysfunctions in family communications in *The Woman Warrior*; Deborah L. Madsen's book chapter, "Transcendence through Violence," contextualizing *The Woman Warrior* with women and the martial arts motif in recent American films; and Jeehyun Lim's discussion on language and body using scholarship in disability studies.

6. First published as memoirs, *The Woman Warrior* won the National Book Critics Circle Award for the best work of nonfiction published in 1976. *Time* magazine listed it as one of the ten works of nonfiction in the 1970s. Sämi Ludwig includes a list of references using autobiographical approaches to studying *The Woman Warrior* (48n5). Other studies on the genre of *The Woman Warrior* include Chin Holady; Blinde; Juhasz; Chua; Lightfoot; Shirley Lim, "Twelve Asian American Writers"; Sidonie Smith; Frye; Sau-ling Wong, "Necessity and Extravagance"; Goellnicht; Nishime; Mason; Shapiro; Grice, *Negotiating Identities*; Marino; Sabine; Tensuan; Schultermandl, "What am I"; Mejia-LaPerle.

7. It is worth noting here that Fa Mu Lan is clearly marked as Han Chinese in Kingston's retelling, although the "Ballad" may have a foreign origin.

8. The heroine's outstanding martial skills have long since become an important thread in the Chinese variations of her story, especially in the plays and novels that have emerged since the sixteenth century (as I discussed in chapter 3). Later versions

such as children's picture books and Disney Company's animated films also develop this thread (see chapters 6 and 7).

9. Kingston's avant-garde memoir has kindled heated debate over its genre since the 1970s. Scholars have referred to the ephemeral connection between memory, mythology, imagination, and reality, discussed Kingston's writing style from a variety of perspectives, and considered *The Woman Warrior* as a "postmodern autobiography" (Yalom), a Chinese American "historiography" (Robert Lee), an "ethnic autobiography" (Sato), a "textual experimentation" (Haynes), a feminist revision of autobiographical studies (Katherine Lee), a postmodernist novel that has more affinities with autobiographies (Arfaoui), and an ethnic discourse exemplifying the concept of "competence" in genre theory (Madsen, "Chinese American Writers"). Despite their disparate approaches and critical scrutiny, most critics share the common view that *The Woman Warrior* resists any single categorization, which gestures toward "a renewed postmodern, feminist aesthetic" that has changed the way people write and read autobiography (Rocío Davis 27).

10. Readings of *The Woman Warrior* as a feminist and gender discourse have produced not only a large pool of critical studies but also a variety of aspects. Critics have examined Kingston's book focusing on its invention of "the fiction of matrilineage" (Wong and Santa-Ana), Chinese American female subjectivity and cultural politics (Shu), its influence on American feminist thought in general (Grice), the female body as "a site of culture" (Crafton), foodways and motherhood/daughterhood (Raussert), and its exemplification of feminist diasporic interest (Marino). Both Sämi Ludwig and David Leiwei Li list several references that apply feminist approaches to *The Woman Warrior* (Ludwig 48n4; Li, Imagining the Nation, 49).

11. In discussing Kingston's writing as revisionary and boundary crossing, Sally Keenan concludes that Kingston's work exemplifies the best feminist critical practice from the last three decades that "has sought to break up, to dialogize, the mythological constructs that have locked both men and women into gender stereotypes" (91). If Keenan's observation, to certain degree, represents a number of feminist critics' eagerness to claim *The Woman Warrior* as a token work, some scholars think otherwise. Examining Kingston's writing within the context of Chinese American cultural politics, Yuan Shu points to the lack of critiquing on patriarchal values or institutional racism in Kingston's writing and the limitation of her effort to rewrite Chinese American female subjectivity (202, 219). More recently, contextualizing Kingston's book with contemporary American martial films, Deborah Madsen argues that the woman warrior icon Kingston creates does not dismantle the gender binarism because it is performative and transgressive only in terms of masculine, not feminine, codes ("Transcendence through Violence," 177).

12. After her study of *The Woman Warrior* as a capricious and readable "personal chronicle" that strives to keep a balance between self-actualization and social responsibility identified as necessity and extravagance, Sau-ling Wong provides a comprehensive discussion on the genre controversy and its influence on Chinese American literary studies ("Autobiography as Guided Chinatown Tour?").

13. During the past two decades, gender-related studies have flourished in the field of Chinese literature and history. Scholars in Chinese studies, such as Susan Mann, Lisa Raphals, Waiyee Li, Grace Fong, Kang-I Sun Chang, Judith Zeitlin, and Sophie

Volpp, have published considerable work on women's writing, women in history, and women in literature.

14. Frank Chin's insistence on differentiating the "real" and the "fake" in Chinese American literary representations was inaugurated in the 1980s and continues into the twenty-first century. Besides critical writing, Chin's insistence on distinguishing the "real" from the "fake" representations is also reflected in his creative writing. In his 1984 article, "The Most Popular Book in China," Chin includes a made-up memoir under the title of *Unmanly Warrior* (6–12). Chin introduces the fictional author as a "French Chinese" woman by the name of Smith Mei-jing who was born and raised in a "Frenchtown" on the edge of Canton, China. In *Unmanly Warrior*, the French heroine Joan of Arc is transformed into a "six-foot-four, 225-pound man" who resorts to female disguise in combat. This short narrative is an obvious mockery of *The Woman Warrior* and ridicules Kingston's revision of Mulan's story with his anger and repulsion clearly indicated between the lines. Commenting on the fictional author, Smith Mei-jing, Chin writes: "She is writing a work of imagination authenticated by her personal experience" ("Most Popular Book," 7). This commentary pointedly reiterates his criticism of The Woman Warrior. Similarly, a made-up book titled *The Conqueror Woman*, mentioned in his novel *Gunga Din Highway* (1994), provides another ridicule that reminds the reader of *The Woman Warrior*.

15. The theme of a person's body being a site constructed by social circumstances and challenged by boundary-crossing deeds is repeatedly explored in Kingston's writing. Another example is found in the revised story of Tang Ao, a character from the Qing novel *Jinghua yuan* (Destinies of Mirrored Flowers, Li Ruzhen, ca. 1763–ca.1830), in *China Men*. In Kingston's revision, Tang Ao's male body is transformed into a feminine object in the Land of Women after being decorated by socially defined femininity through maid grooming tactics: bound feet, pierced ears, powdered face, painted eyebrows, cheeks and lips, and swaying hips (*China Men*, 1–5).

16. As Kingston has repeatedly emphasized, her version of Mulan's story is not a Chinese legend but a Chinese American allegory. She says, "I've written down American myths. Fa Mulan and the writing on her back is an American myth. And I made it that way" (qtd. in Frank Chin, "Come All Ye," 50). The reinvented tale of Fa Mu Lan is not a Chinese legend but a story transformed by America (Kingston, "Cultural Mis-Readings," 57). Since the "White Tigers" chapter is filled with legendary elements and exciting martial confrontations, it is taken as an "inscrutable" fantasy by many readers and criticized as a prime example of "faking" Chinese tradition and a stereotypical story of the exotic Orient. Using the vocabulary and image of Orientalist discourse as her weapons, Kingston articulates her resistance to the Western construction of her ethnic identity. By resorting to Orientalism she tries to prove how "un-Oriental" she is and attempts to construct a "Chinese American discourse" to represent the history and story of Chinese Americans (Sheng-mei Ma, *Immigrant Subjectivities*, 14, 26).

17. The historical record in the *Hou hanshu* includes the full text of the two "Beifen shi" (Fan Ye, 84: 2801–03). The authorship of the poem "Hujia shiba pai" has been under debate among scholars. Conventionally it is attributed to Cai Yan. One of the "Beifen shi" is in the five-syllable meter; the other one and "Hujia shiba pai" are in "Sao" meter. For full citation of the three poems in Chinese see *Hujia shiba pai taolun ji* (Collected Essays on "Eighteen Stanzas of the Barbarian Reed Pipe") 262–69; in English translation see Frodsham 9–13; Frankel, "Cai Yan," 135–42. For studies on Cai

Yan's life and work, see *Hujia shiba pai taolun ji*; Rorex and Fong; Frankel, "Cai Yan"; Dore Levy 82–96; Sau-ling Wong, "Kingston's Handling," 32–36.

18. V looks like an inverted Chinese character "ren" 人 (meaning "human").

19. This, of course, does not mean the "double consciousness" did not exist in Chinese American literature before Kingston. One pioneer writer, Sui Sin Far (pseudonym of Edith Maude Eaton, 1865–1914), was dedicated to the pursuit of cultural reconciliation long before it became critical currency. Daughter of a Chinese mother and British father, Sui Sin Far is considered "the first Chinese woman writer in North America" (Yin 6). She is probably the first writer to use the term "Chinese-Americans" to refer to Chinese immigrants and their American-born progeny (Sui Sin Far, "Chinese Workmen," 56). Her famous statement "I give my right hand to the Occidentals and my left to the Orientals, hoping that between them they will not utterly destroy the insignificant "connecting link" shows clear awareness of the connection between two heritages (Sui Sin Far, "Leaves," 132).

20. In addition to her literary exploration of a Chinese American female identity in *The Woman Warrior*, Kingston also makes efforts to claim the unknown and unacknowledged credits for her male kin, transforming the absent into the present and the silent into the audible in American history. In her second book *China Men*, Kingston writes about the struggles of Chinese American men who participated in building up America on sugarcane plantations, mines, railroads, in Chinatown laundries and restaurants, and at other sites. Her imagination penetrates her father's silence, reflects back to her great grandfather's generation, and tries to position Chinese American men as "warriors of the Gold Mountain."

21. Scholars who have criticized Kingston's misrepresentation in *The Woman Warrior* include: Jeffrey Chan, "Jeff Chan," "Resources"; Tong; Laureen Mar (qtd. in Deborah Woo 177); Katheryn Fong; Ya-Jie Zhang; Chun; Toming Liu; Chin, "Come All Ye."

22. A number of critics have critically examined the pen war between Chin and Kingston. These include Kim, "Such Opposite Creatures"; Sau-ling Wong, "Autobiography as Guided Chinatown Tour?"; David Li, "Production," "Re-presenting"; Kingkok Cheung "Deployment."

23. When discussing the powerful charge of inauthentic that has been leveled at Asian Americans both by outsiders and insiders in 2005, Tina Chen refers to the Kingston-Chin conflict as the most well-debated instance (7, 191n6).

24. As Sucheng Chan has pointed out, due to the extremely isolated living environment in the early twentieth century, "the human beings to whom many Asian immigrant mothers were closest were their children" (*Asian Americans*, 111). In turn, in these children's rearing, their mothers play a significant role. For more discussion on this, see Chan, *Asian Americans*, 103–18.

25. David Leiwei Li's discussion on this track was first articulated in his 1992 article "The Production of Chinese American Tradition: Displacing American Orientalist Discourse" and developed further in his book chapter "Can Maxine Hong Kingston Speak? The Contingency of *The Woman Warrior*" ("Re-presenting," 44–62). In Li's criticism, the "American Orientalist discourse" appropriates the Asiatic Other—including Chinese and Chinese Americans—to consolidate the Self, and the "Chinese American discourse" is powerless and practiced by members of immigrant community ("Production," 320).

26. The 1990 U.S. Census shows that 69.2 percent of Chinese Americans were foreign-born, and 63.1 percent of the foreign-born Chinese Americans did not speak English well (cited in Ying Zeng 446n8, 446n9).

27. Sau-ling Wong has addressed the denationalization within Asian American cultural criticism in 1995.

28. In rethinking Chinese, and by extension Asian, American Studies as an academic field, some scholars have discussed its relationship with area studies in particular. Sucheta Mazumdar, for example, traces the genealogy of Asian American Studies while reviewing its interaction with Asian Studies. The four essays collected in the section, "Comparing Old and New Area Studies," in the volume *Asian Americans: Comparative and Global Perspectives* (1991) address Asian American Studies' relations with such area studies as Ethnic Studies, African American Studies, and Asian Studies (Hune et al. 1–44). Elaine Kim summarizes the necessity to construct cross-curricular connections between Asian American literary studies and other academic disciplines ("Beyond Railroads and Internment," 17). Bearing in mind the changing demographics in the Chinese American population and the input from theorists in other disciplines, Sau-ling Wong outlined three new interactive trends in 1995 in the "denationalization" of Asian American cultural criticism at a "theoretical crossroads" (1–27). David Palumbo-Liu shares a similar concern that "the ethnic canon" must "resist the essentializing and stratifying modes of reading ethnic literature that make it ripe for canonization and co-option" (*Ethnic Canon*, 17). Moreover, L. Ling-chi Wang conceptualizes "the structure of dual domination" to address the broader Chinese American experience that takes into account the interaction between Chinese Americans and their "homeland" as well as the Chinese diaspora living in various locations ("Structure," 149–69). The essays presented in the volume *Across the Pacific: Asian Americans and Globalization* (1999) expand the scope to "explore the relationships and interactions of Asian Americans in the international context of the Pacific Rim" and to examine "new meanings and practices of Asian Americans" (Hu-DeHart 11). This direction of scholarship helps to reshape Chinese and Asian American studies in response to the changing local and global context.

29. Evidences of such scholarship include Lowe, "Heterogeneity"; Sau-ling Wong, "Denationalization Reconsidered"; David Li, *Imagining the Nation*; Davis and Ludwig; Bowers; Simal and Marino; Xiaojing Zhou, "Introduction"; Lim et al.; Schultermandl, "Introduction."

30. Adapted by Deborah Rogin based on *The Woman Warrior* and *China Men* and directed by Sharon Ott, the Berkeley Repertory Theatre's production *The Woman Warrior* premiered in 1994. It was restaged at the Huntington Theatre in Boston in September and October 1994 and at the Center Theatre Group's Doolittle Theatre in Los Angeles in February 1995. The nearly three-hour, three-act saga is the biggest and most expensive production ever attempted by the Berkeley Repertory Theatre (Harmetz). Encouraged by its success, the Berkeley Repertory Theatre and the Huntington Theatre Company collaborated again in 1996 to present *Journey to the West*, adapted and directed by Mary Zimmerman, based on Anthony C. Yu's translation of the Chinese novel *Xi youji* (Harbeck 354).

5 / One Heroine, Many Characters

1. According to its end credits, Disney Company's Mulan is based on a story by San Souci. San Souci made these remarks in his interview with Linasia, in which he talks about his experience of writing the picture book and working for the Disney Studio. The reader can find a link to this interview on his personal website ("Robert D. San Souci homepage").

2. In terms of visual representation, although the Chinese folk "Ballad" lacks details to describe the cross-dressed character Mulan, Chinese artists have imagined this heroine in inserted figures, illustrated books, and stage plays for a long time, as I discussed in chapter 3. The reader also should be aware that materials of this kind might have existed in earlier times and in such diverse formats as popular drawings, wood-block prints, and vernacular stage performances. But these resources rarely would be preserved in written documents, and therefore most of them are no longer available now.

3. The cultural influence of these picture books has reached beyond the English-speaking world. For example, *The Legend of Mu Lan: A Heroine of Ancient China* was published in Spanish, French, Vietnamese, and Khmer; *The Ballad of Mulan* has been translated into Spanish, Vietnamese, and Hmong. These translations collectively contribute to Mulan's becoming a global character.

4. The bibliography of this book includes a list of retellings of Mulan's story in children's books and animated films in English and Chinese.

5. First published in 1995 and aimed at readers of all ages, Lee's book had a reprint edition in April 2006. Hardy-Gould's *Mulan* was published by Oxford University Press in both the United States and the United Kingdom.

6. Since the 1990s, a large number of picture books adapting or related to Disney's film have been published. For example, consider Cathy East Dubowski's *Disney's Mulan* (1998); *How to Draw Disney's Mulan* (1998); *The Legend of Mulan: A Folding Book of the Ancient Poem That Inspired the Disney Animated Film* (1998); Jeff Kurtti's *The Art of Mulan* (1998); Lisa Ann Marsoli's *Mulan: Classic Storybook* (1998); Russell Schroeder and Kathleen W. Zoehfeld's *Mulan: Special Collector's Edition* (1998); Sheryl Kahn, Ann Braybrooks, Vanessa Elder, and Rita Walsh-Balducci's *Disney's Family Story Collection: 75 Fables for Living, Loving, and Learning* (1998); Sarha E. Heller and Alfred Giuliani's *Disney's Adventure Stories* (2001). By and large, the stories and images of these books are limited within the scope of the film *Mulan*. Many of them are part of the commercial package for the Disney Studio's film, together with dolls, toys, and other children's products with the same theme.

7. A similar case occurred in Canada. The Canadian government officially adopted the multicultural policy in 1971 and enlisted children's books as important measures to implement the policy and to achieve the goals of multiculturalism. See Carpenter 53–73.

8. Some of Children's Books Press's bilingual Asian American picture books include Blia Xiong and Cathy Spagnoli's *Nine in One, Grr Grr!* (English-Hmong), Lina Mao Wall's *Judge Rabbit and the Tree Village* (English-Khmer), Truong Tran's *Going Home, Coming Home* (English-Vietnamese), Sun Yung Shim's Cooper's *Lesson and Kimiko Sakai's Sachiko Means Happiness* (English-Korean), Anthony D. Robles's *Lakas and the Manilatown Fish* and *Lakas and the*

Makibaka Hotel (English-Tagalog), and Amy Lee-Tai's *A Place Where Sunflowers Grow* (English-Japanese).

9. Pan Asian Publications has published a number of bilingual picture books adapting renowned traditional Chinese tales, such as the stories of the Monkey King, the Lady White Snake, among others.

10. Min Zhou has discussed the younger-generation-oriented organizations among Chinese American communities in her essay "Social Capital in Chinatown."

11. I use the term Disney publications to refer to picture books related to Disney's film, *Mulan*, even though some of them are not published by the Disney Company.

12. For instance, among the group of Disney publications for children and families, Mulan's story in *Disney's Family Story Collection* (1998) dramatizes the intense fighting scene, where Mulan is portrayed as a national heroine who changes the fate of China. Such an endowment is not from the "Ballad" but from the Disney film. A similar example that presents Mulan as a nation-saver can be found in *Mulan Saves the Day*.

13. Included in the same volume is Cao Zhi's (192–232 A.D.) "Luoshen fu" (Ode to Goddess of Luo River) that is presented in a different format than that of the "Ballad." Besides the verse and illustrations, there is also translation of the "Ode" in Mandarin. This difference indicates the continuing popularity of the "Ballad" among Chinese readers. Although Chinese readers may need assistance to understand Cao Zhi's "Ode," the author assumes he can appreciate the "Ballad" without additional information.

14. According to the back flap of Jiang and Jiang's book, other titles in the same series include: *Empress of China Wu Ze Tian, China's Most Famous Mother, Chronicler of China: Historian Ban Zhao*, and *Weaver of Words: Classical Poet of China*.

15. Victoria Flanagan specifies three cross-dressing models in children's literature: female-to-male, male-to-female, and the transgender first in her article, "Cross-Dressing as Transvestism in Children's Literature" (1999) and then in more details in her book, *Into the Closet* (2008), especially the chapter "Three Models for Gender Disguise" (19–61). According to Flanagan, the female-to-male model is most commonly found in children's literature.

16. When I was invited by Lilian Feitosa to her "Spiritual Autobiography" class to give a guest lecture on *The Woman Warrior* at the University of Massachusetts at Amherst in Spring 2003, I asked the students to create an image of Mulan in their minds for the class discussion. Even though all of them had read the heroine's story of disguise, none of the twenty-plus students pictured her as a hero in men's clothes; that is, Mulan appeared to them as a female instead of a male.

17. The spatial division between different genders has long been noted by feminist scholars. See, for example, Women and Geography Study Group of the IBG 24.

6 / Of Animation and Mulan's International Fame

1. Mulan won or was nominated for a number of awards, including twelve nominations and ten awards at the twenty-sixth Annual Annie Awards, two Golden Globe nominations, two Grammy nominations, an Academy Award nomination, and the "Best Children's Movie" at the twenty-second Annual International Angel Award, and was well received in many countries ("Mulan Timeline").

2. For example, McDonald's teamed up with the film *Mulan* for its Happy Meal program in June 1998: chicken McNuggets served in cartons designed after Chinese takeout boxes and with Szechwan dipping sauce that turned out to be quite a success in a number of the franchises ("McDonald's Links Mulan film to Happy Meal Promo" 5). It is said that McDonald's also created the Oriental McRib to help promoting the film (Keaveny 8). These and other marketing strategies have helped promote the film and have introduced the heroine to a large number of consumers, children and adults alike.

3. The posters distributed in Taiwan features a "bright-eyed, plucky heroine riding her horse before an expansive Chinese landscape" and the promotional images in Hong Kong play with Chinese culture by "superimposing the calligraphy for intelligence, honor, inner grace and courage against a mountain backdrop" (Flannery B12). An important marketing strategy used to distribute *Mulan* in Taiwan is to emphasize the character Mulan as "a war hero," "a great lady who conquers the world" (Flannery B12). Here, the universality of the Disney film is again put on the frontline.

4. In his book on animation and America, Paul Wells summarizes the mode of manufacturing "fairytales" that Disney has created as a process that echoes and uses literary fairytale tradition yet significantly relocates contemporary agendas and speaks to contemporary idioms (*Animation and America*, 105).

5. For detailed information about film cast and production team, see Angela Kuo's website "The Mulan FAQ."

6. Although the dragon is a mythical beast, it has historical relevance in China. During many Chinese imperial dynasties, the dragon had been the particular symbol reserved for the emperor. Abuse of its image often incurred severe punishment.

7. Dreamworks Animation's animated feature film *Kung Fu Panda* (2008), drawing heavily on Chinese themes and presenting a martial arts adventure, is not only a blockbuster in the United States but also a hit in China.

8. The Chinese version targeting Taiwan uses the pop-stars CoCo Lee and Jackie Chan for the voices of Mulan and Li Shang. The Mandarin version for mainland Chinese market and the Cantonese version for Hong Kong audiences feature Jackie Chan together with Chinese actress Xu Qing and Hong Kong pop singer Kelly Chen. Such a casting again embodies the target-oriented policy of this entertainment corporate.

9. *Mulan*'s premiere in Taipei attracted around 3,000 people; about 2,500 attended a similar event in Hong Kong. In a couple of weeks *Mulan* received a box office value of $1.4 million in Taiwan, breaking the record set by another Hollywood blockbuster *The Lion King*. In Hong Kong, it grossed $1.9 million in three weeks (Flannery B12). It is also worth noting that the influence of Disney's *Mulan*'s in China extends beyond the screen. A picture book, titled *Hua Mulan*, was published in 1999 in Beijing. In Mandarin characters with Hanyu pinyin romanization, this volume adapts the Disney's version of Mulan's legend with the accompaniment of images from the animated film. The introduction printed on the dust jacket depicts the character Mulan as a young girl of irrepressible spirit and is therefore regarded as a brave female hero since her birth hundreds of years before (*Hua Mulan*, 1999).

10. Another reason worth mentioning here is the speculation that the widespread pirate discs of the film in China at the time may have hurt the box office income, but statistical data on this aspect are difficult to obtain.

11. Similar comments and analyses focusing on the film's successful cultural

integration of the Chinese folk story and American spirit also appear in the following reviews and articles in Chinese: Chen Taowen; Fu Fuyuan and Zhou Dewu; Hu Huaiming; Li Shuying; Zhang Wei; Bi Geng and Li Dongqing; Li Yinsu; Jia Dongliang and Li Li.

12. For example, acknowledging that Disney's attempt in adapting Mulan's story shows that "Eastern culture has attracted attention from the West," Zhang Yanbing's general comments on the film *Mulan* focus on its westernized misunderstanding (74– 77). Moreover, through a comparison and contrast between the film and the "Ballad" on three aspects—tradition versus freedom, family priority versus individual priority, and gender discrimination versus feminism—Gao Li criticizes Disney's *Mulan* as being "tinted with American culture" with a hope that "it may arouse their cultural sensitivity and enrich their knowledge of other cultures when people enjoy movies, which would ensure the effectiveness of intercultural communication" (80). Furthermore, using Edward Said's theory on Orientalism, Zhou Linyu's essay analyzes Disney's *Mulan* as a representation of the "other" that "colonizes and marginalizes the Chinese culture" (117). According to her argument, "[i]n interpreting the Other, Disney's animated feature *Mulan* replaces the traditional Chinese culture embedded in the original Chinese ballad 'Ode of Mulan' with individualism, the ideology of American mainstream culture by means of orientalization and Americanization" (117). As a result of Disney's "deconstruction," Linyu also contends that the film *Mulan* presents "an American farce staged by the stereotyped Other" (119, 120). Similarly, another "cross-cultural analysis" also criticizes Disney's film as a westernized misinterpretation that simplifies and misrepresents Chinese tradition as "Eastern beauty, the Great Wall, the Imperial Palace Chinese dragon, Panda bear . . . and calligraphy;" the Disneyfied character Mulan has become "an ambassador to propagate Western culture and ideas" (Ni Mei 56). Such misunderstanding is harmful for the transmission of Chinese culture and will damage "the national independence and the culture uniqueness" (Wang Qian 36).

13. Among Chinese scholars, besides the scope of praising or criticizing Disney's film, there are discussions on *Mulan* from a feminist perspective (Zhang Yanbing; Xia Xiaoyan) and from the standpoint of the need to protect traditional cultural heritage in terms of copyrighting (Chen Yi; Qu Changrong and Dai Peng).

14. In this sense, the Mulan doll packaged together with Snow White, Cinderella, and other girly girls in the Disney Princess Collection in the Christmas shopping isle is not really out of place.

15. In his discussion on children's films in relation to history, ideology, and pedagogy, Ian Wojcik-Andrews states that child protagonists' entrance to an alternative world can be willingly or unwillingly (10). In the film *Mulan*, it is a self-chosen path for the character to leave for the alternative world, although the starter of her journey is bound to be the ending point as well.

16. It is said that Disney's production of *Mulan* was initiated at the suggestion of children's literature author Robert San Souci. The 1998 film lists his credit by stating that the screenplay is based on a story by San Souci.

17. I borrow the term "prefeminist" from Deborah Ross whose article discusses female imagination in Disney's animation world.

18. In the folk story, Zhu Yingtai took up men's clothes for education; in the Tang fiction, Xie Xiao'e traveled in male camouflage to take revenge for her family; and in

the Qing *tanci* script (storytelling to the accompaniment of stringed instruments), Meng Lijun resorted to a scholar's outfit to escape from a forced marriage. For these stories, see, respectively, *Liang Shanbo and Zhu Yingtai* by Zhao Qingge and *The Student Lovers* by Kristina Lindell, both adapted from a well-known Chinese folk story; Li Gongzuo's (fl. ca. 763–859) *Xie Xiao'e zhuan* (Story of Xie Xiao'e); and Chen Duansheng's (1751–ca. 1796) *Zai sheng yuan* (Predestined Relations in Revival).

19. Although Kingston's book includes an informed viewer, Fa Mu Lan's husband, the heroine's biological sex remains a secret to her troops until her mission is complete.

20. The difference between male and female cross-dressing already has been noted: "[if] men dressed as women often parody gender, women dressed as men, on the other hand, tend to perform gender" (Solomon 146). Disney's *Mulan* does not bend this rule.

21. Although it is difficult to collect specific data, it is worth noting that the growing number of Chinese girls adopted by American (mostly Caucasian) families might have contributed to Disney's decision to produce this film in the late 1990s. Such a production would appeal to those families and would also be welcome in communities that were minimizing racial difference through notions of multiculturalism.

22. It was believed that the internationally known Chinese star Ziyi Zhang would appear in a Hollywood movie that revolves around Mulan ("Zhang Ziyi to Star in Chinese Take on Mulan Tale" R4). A news report on *People's Daily* states that a Chinese fifty-two-episode animation series, *Hua Mulan*, was going through the production stage in Huangpi, Hubei Province on December 20, 2006. The CEO of the producer, Jiang Tong Animation Co. Ltd. states that, as distinguished from Disney's American perspective, "the homemade animation tires to re-create a legendary grow-up story of a heroine against the Chinese background . . . [and] aims to set up a courageous and patriotic image for the Chinese youth" ("Mulan chuanqi chonglao 'zhongguo yin'" Section 11). In other performance genres, the heroine's story continues to thrive as well. In the winter of 1998, for example, the Hebei acrobatic troupe staged a show, "Mulan chuanqi" (Legend of Mulan), in the Disneyworld in Paris and won praise from French and international audiences. In early 1999, the National Peking Opera Theatre of China performed *Hua Mulan* in San Francisco, Los Angeles, and Washington, D.C. On December 28, 2006, the national symphony orchestra *Mulan ci* (Ballad of Mulan) was staged in Zhengzhou in Henan Province and became the spotlight of the New Year Concert. Moreover, on September 18, 2005, Chinese artists staged the symphony opera *Mulan shipian* (Poem of Mulan) at Lincoln Center for Performing Arts in New York City with great success. And on December 22, 2006, a collaborative performance of this opera by Chinese and German musicians made a splash in the Great Hall of the People in Beijing. The Director Gao Mukun says: "we reinterpret and praise Hua Mulan from a contemporary perspective, using Hua Mulan's patriotism, family duty, friendship, and love as the base, symphony as the soul, and 'Chinese opera' as the art form. [In this way,] an old story like that of Hua Mulan shows unprecedented modern thoughts and meaning" (qtd. in Wu Yuehui, Section 13).

7 / Epilogue

1. It is believed that more than ten thousand books about the life of Joan of Arc have been published (Feinberg 31).

2. James Liu has provided a brief comparison between Chinese and Western

knights in the conclusion of his book (195–208). His insight is inspirational, but his discussion of the "interesting parallels and striking contrasts, with regard to both historical chivalry and chivalric literature" does not address in particular heroic women, except for brief remarks on swordswomen's feminine charms (James Liu 195, 205).

   3. For an overview of Joan of Arc in history, see Raknem 3–22.

BIBLIOGRAPHY

A Ying (pseudo. Qian Xingcun 1900–1977), ed. *Wan Qing xiqu xiaoshuo mu.* Beijing: Zhonghua shuju, 1959.

Allan, Sarah. *The Shape of the Turtle: Myth, Art, and Cosmos in Early China.* Albany: State University of New York Press, 1991.

Allen, Joseph R. "Dressing and Undressing the Chinese Woman Warrior." *Positions* 4.2 (1996): 343–79.

Arfaoui, Sihem. "Feeding the Memory with Culinary Resistance: *The Woman Warrior: Memoirs of a Girlhood among Ghosts, The Joy Luck Club* and *The Kitchen God's Wife.*" *Interactions* 15.2 (2006): 37–48.

Astell, Ann W. *Joan of Arc and Sacrificial Authorship.* Notre Dame, IN: University of Notre Dame Press, 2003.

Ayres, Brenda. "The Poisonous Apple in Snow White: Disney's Kingdom of Gender." *The Emperor's Old Groove: Decolonizing Disney's Magic Kingdom,* edited by Brenda Ayres, 39–50. New York: Peter Lang, 2003.

Bacchilega, Cristina. "Feminine Voices Inscribing Sarraute's *Childhood* and Kingston's *The Woman Warrior.*" *Textual Practice* 6.1 (1992): 101–18.

Bader, Barbara. "How the Little House Gave Ground: The Beginnings of Multiculturalism in a New, Black Children's Literature." *The Horn Book* 78.6 (2002): 657–73.

———. "Multiculturalism in the Mainstream." *The Horn Book* 79.3 (2003): 265–91.

———. "Multiculturalism Takes Root." *The Horn Book* 79.2 (2003): 143–62.

Banerjee, Mita. "The Asian American in a Turtleneck: Fusing the Aesthetic and the Didactic in Maxing Hong Kingston's *Tripmaster Monkey.*" In *Literary Gestures,* edited by Davis and Lee, 55–69.

Bao, Weihong. "From Pearl White to White Rose Woo: Tracing the Vernacular Body of Nüxia in Chinese Silent Cinema, 1927–1931." *Camera Obscura: A Journal of Feminism, Culture, and Media Studies* 60.3 (2005): 193–231.

Barchers, Suzanne I. *Wise Women: Folk and Fairy Tales from Around the World.* Englewood, CO: Libraries Unlimited, 1990.

Barnes, Ruth, and Joanne B. Eicher, eds. *Dress and Gender: Making and Meaning in Cultural Contexts.* Providence, RI: Berg, 1992.

Barry, Linda. *One Hundred Demons.* Seattle, WA: Sasquatch Books, 2002.

Barthel, Margaret. "Kritische Betrachtungen zu dem Lied-Gedicht Mulan." *Mitteilungen des Instituts für Orientforschung* 8 (1961): 435–65.

Bean, Kellie. "Stripping Beauty: Disney's 'Feminist' Seduction." In *The Emperor's Old Groove: Decolonizing Disney's Magic Kingdom*, edited by Brenda Ayres, 53–64. New York: Peter Lang, 2003.

Bell, Elizabeth. "Somatexts at the Disney Shop: Constructing the Pentimentos of Women's Animated Bodies." In *From Mouse to Mermaid: The Politics of Film, Gender, and Culture*, edited by Elizabeth Bell, Lynda Haas, and Laura Sells, 107–24. Bloomington: Indiana University Press, 1995.

Bhabha, Homi. *The Location of Culture.* London: Routledge, 1994.

Bi Geng and Li Dongqing. "Hua Mulan: Disney yanyi de dongfang chuanqi." *Journal of Zhongzhou University* 2 (2000): 35–36.

Blinde, Patricia Lin. "The Icicle in the Desert: Perspective and Form in the Works of Two Chinese-American Women Writers." *MELUS* 6.3 (1979): 51–71.

Bonetti, Kay. "An Interview with Maxine Hong Kingston." In *Conversation*, edited by Skenazy and Martin, 33–46. Jackson: University of Mississippi Press, 1998.

Bowers, Maggie Ann. "For East, Look North: Cross-Border Comparisons and the Future of North American Asian American Studies." In *Transnational, National, and Personal Voices*, edited by Simal and Marino, 107–17. Münster: Lit Verlag, 2004.

Brada-Williams, Noelle, and Karen Chow, eds. *Crossing Oceans: Reconfiguring American Literary Studies in the Pacific Rim.* Hong Kong: Hong Kong University Press, 2004.

Brandauer, Frederick P. "Women in the *Ching-hua yuan*: Emancipation toward a Confucian Ideal." *Journal of Asian Studies* 36.4 (1977): 647–60.

Bray, Francesca. "Textile Production and Gender Roles in China, 1000–1700." *Chinese Science* 12 (1995): 115–37.

Braybrooks, Ann. *Disney's Mulan.* Philadelphia: Running Press, 1998.

"Bridging East & West: Pan Asian Publications homepage." Pan Asian Publications (USA) Inc., 2009. Web. 6 Oct. 2009. http://www.panap.com/default. asp.

Brown, Corie, and Laura Shapiro. "Woman Warrior." *Newsweek* 131.23 (8 June 1998): 64.

Brownmiller, Susan. "Susan Brownmiller Talks with Maxine Hong Kingston, Author of *The Woman Warrior*." In *Maxine Hong Kingston's* The Woman

Warrior, edited by Sau-ling Wong, 173–79. New York: Oxford University Press, 1999.

Bruneau, Marie Florine. "Learned and Literary Women in Late Imperial China and Early Modern Europe." *Late Imperial China* 13.1 (1992): 156–72.

Butler, Judith. *Bodies that Matter: On the Discursive Limits of "Sex."* New York: Routledge, 1993.

———. *Gender Trouble: Feminism and the Subversion of Identity.* New York: Routledge, 1990.

Byrne, Eleanor, and Martin McQuillan. *Deconstructing Disney.* London: Pluto Press, 1999.

Canemaker, John. *Paper Dreams: The Arts and Artists of Disney Storyboards.* New York: Hyperion, 1999.

Cao Zhengwen. *Nüxing wenxue yu wenxue nüxing.* Shanghai: Shanghai shudian, 1991.

———. *Zhongguo xia wenhua shi.* 1994. Reprint, Shanghai: Shanghai wenyi chubanshe, 1997.

Carabi, Angeles. "Special Eyes: The Chinese-American World of Maxine Hong Kingston." *Belles Lettres* (Winter 1989): 10–11.

Carlitz, Katherine. "Desire, Danger, and the Body: Stories of Women's Virtue in Late Ming China." In *Engendering China*, edited by Gilmartin, Hershatter, Rofel, and White, 101–24. Cambridge, MA: Harvard University Press, 1994.

Carpenter, Carole H. "Enlisting Children's Literature in the Goals of Multiculturalism." *Mosaic* 29.3 (1996): 53–73.

Cass, Victoria. *Dangerous Women: Warriors, Grannies, and Geisha of the Ming.* Lanham, MD: Rowman & Littlefield, 1999.

Chae, Youngsuk. *Politicizing Asian American Literature: Towards a Critical Multiculturalism.* New York: Routledge, 2008.

Chan, Jeffrey Paul. "Jeff Chan, Chairman of San Francisco State Asian American Studies, Attacks Review." *San Francisco Journal* 4 (May 1977): 6.

———, et al. "Resources for Chinese American Literary Traditions." *The Chinese American Experience: Papers from the Second National Conference on Chinese American Studies (1980)*, 241–44. San Francisco, CA: Chinese Historical Society of America, 1984.

Chan, Jeffrey Paul, Frank Chin, Lawson Fusao Inada, and Shawn Wong, eds. *The Big Aiiieeeee! An Anthology of Chinese American and Japanese American Literature.* New York: Meridian, 1991.

Chan, Joseph M. "Disneyfying and Globalizing the Chinese Legend Mulan: A Study of Transculturaion." In *Search of Boundaries: Communication, Nation-States and Cultural Identities*, edited by Joseph M. Chan and Bryce T. McIntyre, 225–48. Westport, CT: Ablex Publishing, 2002.

Chan, Sucheng. *Asian Americans: An Interpretive History.* New York: Twayne Publishers, 1991.

———. "Race, Ethnic Culture, and Gender in the Construction of Identities among Second-Generation Chinese Americans, 1880s to 1930s." In *Claiming America: Constructing Chinese American Identities during the Exclusion Era*, edited by K. Scott Wong and Sucheng Chan, 127–64. Philadelphia, PA: Temple University Press, 1998.

Chang, Kang-I Sun, and Haun Saussy, eds. *Women Writers of Traditional China: An Anthology of Poetry and Criticism*. Standford, CA: Standford University Press, 1999.

Che Baoren. "*Mulan shi* suo xie zhenshi shiji chukao." *Xi'an jiaoyu xueyuan xuebao* 43.2 (2000): 29–33.

Chen Duansheng (1751–ca. 1796). *Zai sheng yuan*. Zhengzhou: Zhongzhou shuhuashe, 1982.

Chen, Fan Pen. "Female Warriors, Magic and the Supernatural in Traditional Chinese Novels." In *The Annual Review of Women in World Religions*, edited by Arvind Sharma and Katherine K. Young, 2: 91–109. Albany: State University of New York Press, 1992.

Chen Guohua. "Hua Mulan wutai yishu de yanbian" (The Transformation of Hua Mulan Stage Arts). *Henan Social Sciences* 13.6 (2005): 39–43.

Chen Menglei (1651–1741), Jiang Tingxi (1669–1732), et al., comp. *Gujin tushu jicheng*. 1726. Reprint. Beijing: Zhonghua shuju, 1934. *Harvard University Digital Resources for Chinese Studies*. Web. 25 May 2007. http://hcl.harvard.edu/research/guides/chinese/part3.html.

Chen Quansheng, Tang Yongli, and Huang Miaozi. *Gu shi wen jinghui: Luo shen fu, Mulan shi*. Beijing: Zhongguo lianhuanhua chubanshe, 1989.

Chen Quifen. *Hua Mulan*. Taipei: Dongfang chubanshe, 1965.

Chen Shan. *Zhongguo wuxia shi*. 1992. Reprint, Shanghai: Sanlian shudian, 1995.

Chen Sufen. *Hua Mulan*. Hong Kong: Xiaoshu miao jiaoyu chubanshe, 2001.

Chen Taowen. "Wenhua zhuanhuan: zhongguo Hua Mulan chuanshuo de Disney hua yu quanqiuhua." *Chuanboxue lunwen xuancui*, 12–27. Nanjing: Shifan daxue chubanshe, 2000.

Chen, Tina. *Double Agency: Acts of Impersonation in Asian American Literature and Culture*. Stanford, CA: Stanford University Press, 2005.

Chen Xiao. "Zai chuantong de suipian shang pianpianqiwu: Tang Tingting dui jingdian de gaixie." In *Querying the Genealogy*, edited by Jennie Wang, 231–39. Shanghai: Shanghai yiwen chubanshe, 2006.

Chen Yi. "Huigui de ganga." *People's Daily* (May 11, 2007): Section 14.

Chen Youbing. *Lianghan nanbeichao Yuefu jianshang*. Taipei: Wunan tushu chuban youxiangongsi, 1996. 47–48.

Chen Yujiao (1544–1611). *Qilin ji*. Shanghai: Guben xiqu congkan biankan weiyuanhui, 1955.

Cheng Dachang (1123–1195). *Yanfan lu*. In *Xuejin taoyuan*. Comp. Zhang Haipeng (1755–1816). Taipei: Xinwenfeng chubanshe, 1980.

Cheng, Vincent J. *Inauthentic: The Anxiety over Culture and Identity*. New Brunswick, NJ: Rutgers University Press, 2004.

Cheung, Floyd. "Staging Race, Fostering Coalition: H. T. Tsiang's *China Marches On* (1938)." Presented at MLA Annual Convention, Washington, D.C., December 2000.

Cheung, King-kok. *Articulate Silences: Hisaye Yamamoto, Maxine Hong Kingston, Joy Kogawa*. Ithaca, NY: Cornell University Press, 1993.

———. "The Deployment of Chinese Classics by Frank Chin and Maxine Hong Kingston." In *Querying the Genealogy*, edited by Jennie Wang, 217–30.

———. "'Don't Tell': Imposed Silences in *The Color Purple* and *The Woman Warrior*." *PMLA* 103.2 (1988): 162–74.

———, ed. *An Interethnic Companion to Asian American Literature*. Cambridge: Cambridge University Press, 1997.

———. "Pedagogies of Resonance: Teaching African American and Asian American Literature and Culture in Asia." In *Crossing Oceans*, edited by Brada-Williams and Chow, 13–28.

———. "The Woman Warrior versus The Chinaman Pacific: Must a Chinese American Critic Choose between Feminism and Heroism?" In *Maxine Hong Kingston's* The Woman Warrior, edited by Sau-ling Wong, 113–33.

Cheung, King-kok, and Stan Yogi. *Asian American Literature: An Annotated Bibliography*. New York: MLA, 1988.

"Children's Book Press homepage." Children's Book Press, 2008. Web. 6 Oct. 2009. http://www.childrensbookpress.org/about-us.

Chin, Charlie. *China's Bravest Girl: The Legend of Hua Mu Lan*. Illustrated by Tomie Arai. Emeryville, CA: Children's Book Press, 1993.

Chin, Frank. "Come All Ye Asian American Writers of the Real and the Fake." In *Big Aiiieeeee!*, edited by Chan, Chin, Inada, and Wong, 1–92.

———. "The Most Popular Book in China." *Quilt* 4 (1984): 6–12.

———. "On Amy Tan, David Hwang, Maxine Hong Kingston, An Essay." *Konch* 1.2 (1990): 25–28.

———. "Teaching the Heroic Tradition to Combat Cultural Imperialism." *Hwa Kang Journal of TEFL* 7 (2001): 22–30.

———. "This Is Not An Autobiography." *Genre* 18 (Summer 1985): 109–30.

Chin, Frank, and friends. "Uncle Frank's Fakebook of Fairy Tales for Asian American Moms and Dads." *Amerasia Journal* 18.2 (1992): 69–87.

Chin, Frank, Jeffery Paul Chan, Lawson Fusao Inada, and Shawn Hsu Wong, eds. *Aiiieeeee!: An Anthology of Asian American Writers*. Washington, D.C.: Howard University Press, 1974; reprint, New York: Meridian, 1997.

Chin Holaday, Woon-Ping. "From Ezra Pound to Maxine Hong Kingston: Expressions of Chinese Thought in American Literature." *MELUS* 5.2 (1978): 15–24.

Chow, Claire S. *Leaving Deep Waters: The Lives of Asian American Women at the Crossroads of Two Cultures*. New York: Dutton, 1998.

Chow, Karen. "'Stories to Pass On': Pedagogically Dialoging Maxine Hong Kingston and Toni Morrison." In *Crossing Oceans*, edited by Brada-Williams and Chow, 99–108.

Chow, Rey. "A Phantom Discipline." *PMLA* 116.5 (2001): 1386–95.

———. *Women and Chinese Modernity: The Politics of Reading between West and East*. Minneapolis: University of Minnesota Press, 1991.

Chu, Patricia P. "The Invisible World That Emigrants Built: Cultural Self-Inscription and the Antiromantic Plots of *The Woman Warrior*." *Diaspora* 2 (1992): 95–115.

———. "*The Woman Warrior: Memoirs of a Girlhood among Ghosts* by Maxine Hong Kingston." 2001. In *A Resource Guide*, edited by Wong and Sumida, 86–96.

Chu Renhu (fl. 1675–1695). *Suitang yanyi*. Taipei: Shijie shuju, 1962.

Chua, Chen Lok. "Two Chinese Versions of the American Dream: The Golden Mountain in Lin Yutang and Maxine Hong Kingston." *MELUS* 8.3 (1981): 61–70.

Chuh, Kandice. *Imagine Otherwise: On Asian Americanist Critique*. Durham, NC: Duke University Press, 2003.

Chun, Gloria H. "'Go West . . . to China': Chinese American Identity in the 1930s." In *Claiming America: Constructing Chinese American Identities during the Exclusion Era*, eds. Scott Wong and Sucheng Chan, 165–90. Philadelphia, PA: Temple University Press, 1998.

———. "The High Note of the Barbarian Reed Pipe: Maxine Hong Kingston." *The Journal of Ethnic Studies* 19.3 (1991): 85–94.

Clark, Beverly Lyon. "American Children's Literature: Background and Bibliography." *American Studies International* 30.1 (1992): 4–40.

———. *Kiddie Lit: The Cultural Construction of Children's Literature in America*. Baltimore, MD: Johns Hopkins University Press, 2003.

Clark, Beverly Lyon, and Margaret R. Higonnet, eds. *Girls, Boys, Books, Toys: Gender in Children's Literature and Culture*. Baltimore, MD: Johns Hopkins University Press, 1999.

Cook, Barry, and Tony Bancroft, dirs. *Mulan*. Walt Disney Company, 1998. DVD.

Cook, Rufus. "Cross-Cultural Wordplay in Maxine Hong Kingston's *China Men* and *The Woman Warrior*." *MELUS* 22.4 (1997): 133–46.

Corliss, Richard. "Mulan." *Time*, 22 June 1998: 69.

Crafton, Lisa Plummer. "'We Are Going to Carve Revenge on Your Back': Language, Culture, and the Female Body in Kingston's *The Woman Warrior*." In *Women as Sites of Culture: Women's Roles in Cultural Formation from the Renaissance to the Twentieth Century*, edited by Susan Shifrin, 51–63. Burlington, VT: Ashgate Publishing, 2002.

Crow, Charles L. *Maxine Hong Kingston*. Boise, ID: Boise State University, 2004. Print.

Cui Fengyuan. *Zhongguo gudian duanpian xiayi xiaoshuo yanjiu*. Taipei: Lianjing chuban shiye gongsi, 1986.

Currier, Susan. "A Chinese-American Woman Warrior Comes of Age: Maxine Hong Kingston's *The Woman Warrior: Memoirs of a Girlhood among Ghosts* (1976)." In *Women in Literature: Reading through the Lens of Gender,* edited Jerilyn Fisher and Ellen S. Silber, 300–302. Westport, CT: Greenwood, 2003.

Dasenbrock, Reed Way. "Intelligibility and Meaningfulness in Multicultural Literature in English." *PMLA* 102.1 (1987): 10–19.

Davis, Robert Murray. "Frank Chin: An Interview with Robert Murray Davis." *Amerasia Journal* 14.2 (1988): 81–95.

———. "Frank Chin: Iconoclastic Icon." *Redneck Review of Literature* 23 (Fall 1992): 75–78.

Davis, Rocío G. *Begin Here: Reading Asian North American Autobiographies of Childhood.* Honolulu: University of Hawaii Press, 2007.

Davis, Rocío G., and Sämi Ludwig, eds. *Asian American Literature in the International Context: Readings on Fiction, Poetry, and Performance.* Münster: Lit Verlag, 2002.

Davis, Rocío G., and Sue-Im Lee, eds. *Literary Gestures: The Aesthetic in Asian American Writing.* Philadelphia, PA: Temple University Press, 2006.

de Beauvoir, Simone. *The Second Sex.* Trans. E. M. Parshley. New York: Vintage, 1973.

de Jesús, Melinda L. "'Two's Company, Three's a Crowd?': Reading Interracial Romance in Contemporary Asian American Young Adult Fiction." *Lit: Literature Interpretation Theory* 12.3 (2001): 313–34.

de Manuel, Dolores, and Rocío G. Davis. "Editor's Introduction: Critical Perspectives on Asian American Children's Literature." *The Lion and the Unicorn* 30.2 (April 2006): v–xv.

———, eds. "Special Issue: Asian American Children's Literature." *The Lion and the Unicorn* 30.2 (April 2006).

Dearborn, Mary V. *Pocahontas's Daughters: Gender and Ethnicity in American Culture.* Oxford: Oxford University Press, 1986.

Demetrakopoulos, Stephanie. "The Metaphysics of Matrilinearism in Women's Autobiography: Studies of Mead's *Blackberry Winter,* Hellman's *Pentimentno,* Angelou's *I Know Why the Caged Bird Sings,* and Kingston's *The Woman Warrior.*" In *Women's Autobiography: Essays in Criticism,* edited by Estelle C. Jelinek, 180–205. Bloomington: Indiana University Press, 1980.

Deng Mingshi (fl. 1134). *Gujin xiangshi shu bianzheng.* Beijing: Zhonghua shuju, 1985.

Disney's Mulan: Grolier Book Club Edition. Danbury, CT: Disney Enterprises, Inc., 1998.

Dong, Lan. "Maxine Hong Kingston." In *Encyclopedia of Multiethnic American Literature,* edited by Emmanuel S. Nelson, 1251–56. Westport, CT: Greenwood Press, 2005.

———. "Writing Chinese America into Words and Images: Storytelling and Retelling of *The Song of Mu Lan.*" *The Lion and the Unicorn* 30.2 (2006): 218–33.

Dong Qianli. *Hua Mulan.* Hong Kong: Yazhou chubanshe, 1959.

Doughty, Amie A. *Folktales Retold: A Critical Overview of Stories Updated for Children*. Jefferson, NC: McFarland, 2006.

Du, Fangqin, and Susan Mann. "Competing Claims on Womanly Virtue in Late Imperial China." In *Women and Confucian Cultures*, edited by Kò, Haboush, and Piggott, 219–47.

Dubowski, Cathy East. *Disney's Mulan*. New York: Disney Press, 1998.

Eakin, Paul John. *Fictions in Autobiography: Studies in the Art of Self-Invention*. Princeton, NJ: Princeton University Press, 1985.

Ebrey, Patricia. "Women, Marriage, and the Family in Chinese History." In *Heritage of China: Contemporary Perspectives on Chinese Civilization*, edited by Paul S. Ropp, 197–223. Berkeley, CA: University of California Press, 1990.

Edwards, E. D. *Chinese Prose Literature of the T'ang Period, A. D. 618–906*. London: Probsthain, 1937–1938; reprint, New York: AMS Press, 1974.

Edwards, Louise P. *Men and Women in Qing China: Gender in* The Red Chamber Dream. Leiden and New York: E. J. Brill, 1994.

Eicher, Joanne B., and Mary Ellen Roach-Higgins. "Definition and Classification of Dress: Implications for Analysis of Gender Roles." In *Dress and Gender*, edited by Barnes and Eicher, 8–28.

Elleman, Barbara. "The Picture-Book Story in Twentieth-Century America." In *Children's Literature Remembered: Issues, Trends, and Favorite Books*, edited by Linda Pavonetti, 27–38. Westport, CT: Libraries Unlimited, 2004.

Elvin, Mark. "Female Virtue and the State in China." *Past and Present* 104 (August 1984): 111–52.

Evangelista, Susan. "Chinese-America's Woman Warrior: Maxine Hong Kingston." *Philippine Studies* 31 (1983): 243–52.

Fan, Lei, trans. "The Legend of Mulan." 1998. In *Disney's Mulan*, edited by Schroeder and Zoehfeld, 12–13.

Fang Xuanling (578–648) et al. *Jinshu*. Beijing: Zhonghua shuju, 1974.

Fan Ye (398–445). *Hou Hanshu*. Beijing: Zhonghua shuju, 1971.

Faurot, Jeannette L. "Four Cries of a Gibbon: A Tsa-chü Cycle by the Ming Dramatist Hsü Wei (1521–1593)," Ph.D. diss., University of California at Berkeley, 1972.

Feinberg, Leslie. *Transgender Warriors: Making History from Joan of Arc to Dennis Rodman*. Boston, MA: Beacon Press, 1996.

Feng, Peter X., ed. *Screening Asian Americans*. New Brunswick, NJ: Rutgers University Press, 2002.

Ferraro, Thomas J. *Ethnic Passages: Literary Immigrants in Twentieth-Century America*. Chicago, IL: University of Chicago Press, 1993.

Flanagan, Victoria. "Cross-Dressing as Transvestism in Children's Literature: An Analysis of a 'Gender-Performative' Model." *Papers: Explorations into Children's Literature* 9.3 (1999): 5–14.

———. *Into the Closet: Cross-Dressing and the Gendered Body in Children's Literature and Film*. New York: Routledge, 2008.

———. "Reframing Masculinity: Female-to-Male Cross-Dressing". In *Ways of Being Male: Representing Masculinities in Children's Literature and Film*, edited by John Stephens, 78–95. New York: Routledge, 2002.

Flannery, Russell. "Disney Markets New Animated Film to Tastes of Taiwan and Hong Kong." *Wall Street Journal* 31 July 1998, Eastern ed.: B12.

Fong, Bobby. "Maxine Hong Kingston's Autobiographical Strategy in *The Woman Warrior*." *Biography: An Interdisciplinary Quarterly* 12.2 (1989): 116–26.

Fong, Grace. *Herself an Author: Gender, Agency, and Writing in Late Imperial China*. Honolulu: University of Hawaii Press, 2008.

Fong, Katheryn. "An Open Letter/Review: To Maxine Hong Kingston." *Bulletin for Concerned Asian Scholars* (October-December 1977): 67.

Fontes, Ron, and Justine Korman. *Mushu's Story*. New York: Disney Press, 1998. Dugaw, Dianne. *Warrior Women and Popular Balladry 1650–1850*. Cambridge: Cambridge University Press, 1989.

Fox, Dana L., and Kathy G. Short, eds. *Stories Matter: The Complexity of Cultural Authenticity in Children's Literature*. Urbana, IL: National Council of Teachers of English, 2003.

Frankel, Hans H. "Cai Yan and the Poems Attributed to Her." *Chinese Literary Essays and Reviews* 5.2 (1985): 133–56.

———. *The Flowering Plum and the Palace Lady: Interpretations of Chinese Poetry*. New Haven, CT: Yale University Press, 1976.

Frodsham, J. D. *An Anthology of Chinese Verse: Han Wei Chin and the Northern and Southern Dynasties*. Oxford: Clarendon Press, 1967.

"Front Street Books homepage." Boyds Mills Press, 2009. Web. 6 Oct. 2009. http://frontstreetbooks.com.

Frye, Joanne S. "*The Woman Warrior*: Claiming Narrative Power, Recreating Female Selfhood." In *Faith of A (Woman) Writer*, edited by Alice Kessler-Harris and William McBrien, 293–301. Westport, CT: Greenwood, 1988.

Fu Fuyuan and Zhou Dewu. "Hua Mulan zoujin Disney." *People's Daily* 18 Jun. 2006: Section 6.

Fung, Eileen Chia-Ching. "'To Eat the Flesh of His Dead Mother': Hunger, Masculinity, and Nationalism in Frank Chin's *Donald Duk*." *Literature, Interpretation, Theory* 10.3 (1999): 255–74.

Gan Bao (fl. 317-332). *Sou shenji*. Changsha: Yuelu shushe, 2006.

Garber, Marjorie. *Vested Interests: Cross-Dressing and Cultural Anxiety*. New York: Routledge, 1992.

Gao Hong. *Kua wenhua de zhongguo xushi: yi Sai Zhenzhu, Lin Yutang, Tang Tingting wei zhongxin de taolun* (Cross-Cultural Chinese Narratives: Discussion Centering on Pearl Buck, Lin Yutang, Maxine Hong Kingston). Shanghai: Shanghai sanlian shudian, 2005.

Gao Li. "Shixi *Mulan ci* yu meiguo dianying *Mulan* zhong de zhongmei wenhua chayi." *Journal of Huaihua University* 25.3 (2006): 80–82.

Gao, Yan. *The Art of Parody: Maxine Hong Kingston's Use of Chinese Source*. New York: Peter Lang, 1996.

Ghymn, Esther Mikyung. *Images of Asian American Women by Asian American Women Writers*. New York: Peter Lang, 1995.

Gil, Isabel Capeloa. "'Arms and the Woman I Sing . . .': *The Woman Warrior* Reloading the Can(n)on?" In *Memory, Haunting, Discourse*, eds. Maria Holmgren Troy and Elisabeth Wennö, 229–42. Karlstad, Sweden: Karlstads Universitet, 2005.

Gilligan, Carol. *In a Different Voice*. Cambridge, MA: Harvard University Press, 1982.

Giroux, Henry A. "Are Disney Movies Good for Your Kids?" In *Kinderculture: The Corporate Construction of Childhood*, edited by Shirley R. Steinberg and Joe L Kincheloe, 53–67. Boulder, CO: Westview Press, 1997.

Goellnicht, Donald C. "Father Land and/or Mother Tongue: The Divided Female Subject in Kogawa's *Obasan* and Hong Kingston's *The Woman Warrior*." In *Redefining Autobiography in Twentieth-Century Women's Fiction*, edited by Janice Morgan and Colette T. Hall, 119–34. New York: Garland, 1991.

Goldin, Paul Rakita. "The View of Women in Early Confucianism." In *Sage and the Second Sex*, edited by Chenyang Li, 133–61.

Gong, Ted. "Approaching Cultural Change through Literature: From Chinese to Chinese American." *Amerasia Journal* 7.1 (1980): 73–86.

Goshert, John. "'Frank Chin Is Not A Part of This Class!' Thinking at the Limits of Asian American Literature." *Jouvert* 4.3 (2000): n. pag. Web. 6 Oct. 2009. http://english.chass.ncsu.edu/jouvert/v4i3/gosher.htm.

Grice, Helena. *Maxine Hong Kingston*. Manchester, England: Manchester University Press, 2006.

———. *Negotiating Identities: An Introduction to Asian American Women's Writing*. Manchester : Manchester University Press, 2002.

Griffiths, Jennifer. "Uncanny Spaces: Trauma, Cultural Memory, and the Female Body in Gayl Jones's *Corregidora* and Maxine Hong Kingston's *The Woman Warrior*." *Studies in the Novel* 38.3 (2006): 353–70.

Guisso, Richard W., and Stanley Johannesen, eds. *Women in China: Current Directions in Historical Scholarship*. Youngstown, NY: Philo Press, 1981.

Guo Maoqian (fl. 1264–1269), comp. *Yuefu shiji*. In *Guoxue jiben congshu*. Taipei: Shangwu yinshuguan, 1968.

Haas, Mary E. "Introduction." *Social Education* 58.2 (1994): 65–66.

Halberstam, Judith. *Female Masculinity*. Durham, NC: Duke University Press, 1998.

Hallett, Martin, and Barbara Karasek, eds. *Folk and Fairy Tales*. 4th ed. Buffalo, NY: Broadview Press, 2009.

Harbeck, James. "Performance Review: *Journey to the West*." *Theatre Journal* 49.3 (1997): 354–56.

Harmetz, Aljean. "Theater: It's Tough to Get Ghosts to Be Human on Stage." *New York Times*, 5 Jun. 1994. Web. 6 Oct. 2009. http://www.nytimes.com/1994/06/05/theater/theater-it-s-tough-to-get-ghosts-to-be-human-on-stage.html?pagewanted=all.

Harper, Graeme. "Enfranchising the Child: Picture Books, Primacy, and Discourse." *Style* 35.3 (2001): 393–409.

Haynes, Rosetta R. "Intersections of Race, Gender, Sexuality, and Experimentation in the Autobiographical Writings of Cherríe Moraga and Maxine Hong Kingston." In *Women of Color: Defining the Issues, Hearing the Voices*, edited by Diane Long Hoeveler and Janet K. Boles, 133–45. Westport, CT: Greenwood Press, 2001.

He Chengfeng. "Lue lun *Mulan shi* de beiju yishi" (On the Tragic Ideology of Ode to Mulan). *Journal of Tongren Teachers College* 7.3 (2005): 25–26, 37.

He Yuping. "The Research about the Poem of Mulan." *Journal of Luoyang University* 19.1 (2004): 20 21.

He, Zhongshun. "What Does the American *Mulan* Look Like?" *Chinese Sociology and Anthropology* 32.2 (1999–2000): 23–24.

Hearne, Betsy. "Disney Revisited, Or, Jimmy Cricket, It's Musty Down Here!" In *Folk and Fairy Tales*, edited by Hallett and Karasek, 386–93.

Heller, Sarah E. *Disney's Adventure Stories*. New York: Disney Press, 2001.

Hinkins, Jillian. "'Biting the Hand that Feeds': Consumerism, Ideology and Recent Animated Film for Children." *Papers: Explorations into Children's Literature* 17.1 (2007): 43–50.

Hirabayashi, Lane Ryo, and Marilyn C. Alquizola. "Asian American Studies: Reevaluating for the 1990s." In *The State of Asian America*, edited by Karin Anguilar-San Juan, 351–72. Boston, MA: South End Press, 1994.

Ho, Wendy. "Mother/Daughter Writing and the Politics of Race and Sex in Maxine Hong Kingston's *The Woman Warrior*." In *Asian Americans*, edited by Hune, Kim, Fugita, and Ling, 225–38.

Hobsbawm, Eric, and Terence Ranger, eds. *The Invention of Tradition*. Cambridge: Cambridge University Press, 1984.

Hong Shenwo. "*Mulan shi* de lingyizhong jiedu." *Liming zhiye daxue xuebao* 29.4 (2000): 3–5.

Hotchkiss, Valerie R. *Clothes Makes the Man: Female Cross Dressing in Medieval Europe*. New York: Garland, 1996.

How to Draw Disney's Mulan. Laguna Hills, CA: Walter Foster Publishing, 1998.

Hsia, Chih-Tsing. *The Classic Chinese Novel: A Critical Introduction*. New York: Columbia University Press, 1968.

Hsiung, Ann-Marie. "A Feminist Re-Vision of Xu Wei's *Ci Mulan* and *Nü zhuangyuan*." In *China In a Polycentric World: Essays in Chinese Comparative Literature*, edited by Yingjin Zhang, 73–89. Stanford, CA: Stanford University Press, 1998.

Hsu, Vivian. "Maxine Hong Kingston as Psycho-Autobiographer and Ethnographer." *International Journal of Women's Studies* 6 (1983): 429–42.

Hu Huaiming. "Fengfu de xiangxiangli chengjiu guimo pangda de meiguo dongman diguo." *Shichang bao* 16 Aug. 2006: Section 8.

Hujia shiba pai taolunji. Beijing: Zhonghua shuju, 1959.

Hu Shi. *Baihua wenxueshi.* 1960. Reprint, Shanghai: Shanghai guji chubanshe, 1999.

Hu, Shiguang, trans. "The Song of Mulan." *Chinese Literature* 1 (Spring 1994): 180–82.

Hu Yinglin (1551–1602). *Shisou.* Beijing: Zhonghua shuju, 1958, 1962.

Hu-DeHart, Evelyn, ed. *Across the Pacific: Asian Americans and Globalization.* Philadelphia, PA: Temple University Press, 1999.

Hua Mulan. Gaoxiong, Taiwan: Dazhong shuju, 1978.

Hua Mulan. Taipei: Fuyou chubanshe, 1986.

Hua Mulan. Tainan, Taiwan: Ertong jiaoyu jiuhui, 1988.

Hua Mulan. Beijing: renmin youdian chubanshe, 1999.

Hua Mulan. Tainan, Taiwan: Shiyi wenhua shiye gufen youxian gongsi, 2002.

"Hua Mulan II: li you budai, xi buru jiu." Diezhongdie [pseudo.], 2 Mar. 2005. Web. 6 Oct. 2009. http://www.filmsea.com.cn/movie_review/200503020008.htm.

Hua Mulan, Yue Fei. Hong Kong: Yimei tushu gongci, 1979.

Huang Canzhang and Li Shaoyi, comp. *Hua Mulan kao.* Beijing: Zhongguo guangbo dianshi chubanshe, 1992.

Huang, Yunte. *Transpacific Displacement: Ethnography, Translation, and Intertextual Travel in 20ᵗʰ Century American Literature.* Berkeley: University of California Press, 2002.

Huangpi xian zhi. 1871; reprint, Taipei: Chengwen chubanshe, 1975.

Huangzhou fu zhi. 1500; Reprint, Shanghai: Shanghai guji shudian, 1982.

Huc, M. *The Chinese Empire.* 2 vols. London: Longman, Brown, Green, and Longmans, 1855.

Hucker, Charles O. *A Dictionary of Official Titles in Imperial China.* Stanford, CA: Stanford University Press, 1985.

Huitu Hua Mulan zhengbei guci. Shanghai: Shanghai jingzhang tushuju, ca. 1910–1919.

Hune, Shirley, Hyung-chan Kim, Stephen S. Fugita, and Amy Ling, eds. *Asian Americans: Comparative and Global Perspectives.* Pullman: Washington State University Press, 1991.

Hung, Chang-tai. "Female Symbols of Resistance in Chinese Wartime Spoke Drama." *Modern China* 15.2 (1989): 149–77.

Hunt, Linda. "'I Could Not Figure out What Was My Village': Gender vs. Ethnicity in Maxine Hong Kingston's *The Woman Warrior.*" *MELUS* 12.3 (1985): 5–12.

Hunt, Peter, ed. *Understanding Children's Literature.* 2nd ed. London: Routledge, 2005.

Huntley, E. D. *Maxine Hong Kingston: A Critical Companion.* Westport, CT: Greenwood Press, 2001.

Hurley, Joseph. "China's Legends Run through Her Tales." *New York Newsday* 4 May 1989: 85, 88.

Hwang, David Henry. "Evolving a Multicultural Tradition." *MELUS* 16.3 (1989–1990): 16–19.

———. *FOB and Other Plays*. New York: Plays in Progress, 1979; reprint, New York: Plume, 1990.

Idema, Wilt L. "Female Talent and Female Virtue: Xu Wei's *Nü Zhuangyuan* and Meng Chengshun's *Zhenwen ji.*" In *Ming Qing xiqu guoji yantaohui lunwenji*, edited by Wei Hua and Ailing Wang, 549–71. Taipei: Zhongyang yanjiuyuan. 1997. 549–71.

Ingoglia, Gina. *Disney's Mulan: A Little Golden Book*. New York: Golden Book Publishing Company, 1998.

Jackson, Beverley. *Splendid Slippers: A Thousand Years of an Erotic Tradition*. Berkeley, CA: Ten Speed Press, 1997.

Janette, Michele. "The Angle We're Jointed at: A Conversation with Maxine Hong Kingston." *Transition* 71 (1996): 142–57.

Jen, T'ai. "The Mu-Lan Rhyme." *United College Journal* 1 (1962): 1–6.

Jenkins, Ruth Y. "Authorizing Female Voice and Experience: Ghosts and Spirits in Kingston's *The Woman Warrior* and Allende's *The House of the Spirits.*" *MELUS* 19.3 (1994): 61–73.

Jew, Kimberly M. "Dismantling the Realist Character in Velina Hasu Houston's *Tea* and David Henry Hwang's *FOB.*" In *Literary Gestures*, edited by Davis and Lee, 187–202.

Jia Dongliang and Li Li. "Cong dianying *Mulan* kan zhongxi wenhua de ronghe yu chongtu." *Journal of Bohai University (Philosophy and Social Sciences)* 27.6 (2005): 120–22.

Jiang, Tsui-fen. "Gender Reversal: Women in Chinese Drama under Mongol Rule (1234–1368)." Ph.D. diss., University of Washington, 1991.

Jiang, Wei, and Cheng An Jiang. *The Legend of Mu Lan A Heroine of Ancient China*. Monterey, CA: Victory Press, 1992.

Jiang Weilu. "Tan zenyang yanjiu *Mulan shi.*" In *Yuefu shi yanjiu lunwen ji*, edited by Wang Yunxi. Vol. 2: 131–42. Hong Kong: Zhongguo yuwenshe, 1970.

Jiao Hong (1540–1620). *Jiaoshi bi cheng*. Shanghai: Shanghai guji, 1986.

Johnson, Kim K. P., Susan J. Torntore, and Joanne B. Eicher, eds. *Fashion Foundations: Early Writings on Fashion and Dress*. Oxford: Berg, 2003.

Johnson, Taran C. "Transculturaion as a Resistance Strategy in Bilingual Children's Literature." *Chasqui* 28.1 (1999): 42–53.

Jones, Dudley, and Tony Watkins, eds. *A Necessary Fantasy? The Heroic Figure in Children's Popular Culture*. New York: Garland Publishing, 2000.

Juhasz, Suzanne. "Towards a Theory of Form in Feminist Autobiography: Kate Millett's *Flying* and *Sita*; Maxine Hong Kingston's *The Woman Warrior.*" In *Women's Autobiography: Essays in Criticism*, edited by Estelle C. Jelinek, 221–73. Bloomington: Indiana University Press, 1980.

Kaulbach, Barbara M. "The Woman Warrior in Chinese Opera: An Image of Reality or Fiction?" *Fu Jen Studies* 15 (1982): 69–82.

Keaveny, Tom. "Media Choice: Mulan." *Marketing* 25.1 (November 5, 1998): 8.

Keenan, Sally. "Crossing Boundaries: The Revisionary Writing of Maxine Hong Kingston." *Hitting Critical Mass* 6.2 (2000): 75–94.

Keightley, David N. "At the Beginning: the Status of Women in Neolithic and Shang China." *Nan Nü: Men, Women and Gender in Early and Imperial China* 1.1 (1999): 1–63.

Kennedy, Colleen, and Deborah Morse. "A Dialogue with(in) Tradition: Two Perspectives on *The Woman Warrior*." In *Approaches to Teaching* The Woman Warrior, edited by Lim, 121–30.

Kim, Elaine H. *Asian American Literature: An Introduction to the Writings and Their Social Context*. Philadelphia, PA: Temple University Press, 1982.

———. "Beyond Railroads and Internment: Comments on the Past, Present, and Future of Asian American Studies." In *Privileging Positions: The Sites of Asian American Studies*. edited by Gary Y. Okihiro, Marilyn Alquizola, Dorothy Fujita Rony, and K. Scott Wong, 11–19. Pullman: Washington State University Press, 1995.

———. Foreword to *Reading the Literatures of Asian America*, edited by Lim and Ling, xi–xvii.

———. Preface to *Charlie Chan Is Dead: An Anthology of Contemporary Asian American Fiction*, edited by Jessica Hagedorn, vii–xiv. New York: Penguin, 1993.

———. "'Such Opposite Creatures': Men and Women in Asian American Literature." *Michigan Quarterly Review* 29 (1990): 68–92.

Kingston, Maxine Hong. *China Men*. New York: Knopf, 1980; reprint, New York: Vintage, 1989.

———. "Cultural Mis-Readings by American Reviewers." In *Asian and Western Writers in Dialogue: New Cultural Identities*, edited by Guy Amirthanayagam, 55–65. London: The Macmillan Press, 1982.

———. *The Fifth Book of Peace*. New York: Knopf, 2003.

———. Interview by Bill Moyers. *A World of Ideas: Stories of Maxine Hong Kingston*. PBS, 1990. VHS.

———. "Personal Statement." In *Approaches to Teaching* The Woman Warrior, edited by Lim, 23–25.

———. *Through the Black Curtain*. Berkeley: The Bancroft Library, University of California at Berkeley, 1987.

———. *Tripmaster Monkey: His Fake Book*. New York: Vintage, 1989.

———. *The Woman Warrior: Memoirs of a Girlhood Among Ghosts*. New York: Knopf, 1976; reprint, New York: Vintage, 1989.

Knowles, Liz, and Martha Smith. *Understanding Diversity through Novels and Picture Books*. Westport, CT: Libraries Unlimited, 2007.

Ko, Dorothy. *Cinderella's Sisters: A Revisionist History of Footbinding*. Berkeley: University of California Press, 2005.

———. *Every Step a Lotus: Shoes for Boundfeet*. Berkeley: University of California Press, 2001.

———. *Teacher of the Inner Chambers: Women and Culture in Seventeenth-Century China*. Stanford, CA: Stanford University Press, 1994.

———. "The Written Word and the Bound Foot: A History of the Courtesan's Aura." In *Writing Women*, edited by Widmer and Chang, 74–100.

Ko, Dorothy, JaHyun Kim Haboush, and Joan R. Piggott, eds. *Women and Confucian Cultures in Premodern China, Korea, and Japan*. Berkeley: University of California Press, 2003.

Kong, Belinda. "The Asian-American Hyphen Goes Gothic: Ghosts and Doubles in Maxine Hong Kingston and lê thi diem thúy." In *Asian Gothic: Essays on Literature, Film and Anime*, edited bya Andrew Hock Soon Ng, 123–39. Jefferson, NC: McFarland, 2008.

Krulik, Nancy E., and Atelier Philippe Harchy. *Mulan Saves the Day*. New York. Disney Press, 1998.

Kruse, Ginny Moore, and Kathleen T. Horning. *Multicultural Literature for Children and Young Adults: A Selected Listing of Books, 1980–1990 by and about People of Color*. 3rd ed. Madison: Cooperative Children's Book Center, University of Wisconsin-Madison, Wisconsin Department of Public Instruction, 1991.

———. *Multicultural Literature for Children and Young Adults: Volume 2, 1991–1996: A Selected Listing of Books by and about People of Color*. 3rd ed. Madison: Cooperative Children's Book Center, the Friends of the CCBC, Inc., and University of Wisconsin-Madison, Wisconsin Department of Public Instruction, 1997.

Kuhn, Annette. *Women's Pictures: Feminism and Cinema*. London: Verson, 1994. Print.

Kuo, Angela. "The Mulan FAQ." 6 October 2009. Web. 6 October 2009. http://www.geocities.com/Hollywood/5082/mulanfaq.html.

Kurtti, Jeff. *The Art of Mulan A Welcome Book Adapted from the Disney Animated Film*. New York: Hyperion, 1998.

Labi, Nadya, Jeanne McDowell, and Alice Park. "Girl Power." *Time*. Time, 29 June 1998. Web. 6 October 2009. http://www.time.com/time/magazine/article/0,9171,988643,00.html.

Lai, Sufen Sophia. "From Cross-Dressing Daughter to Lady Knight-Errant: the Origin and Evolution of Chinese Women Warriors." In *Presence and Presentation*, edited by Mou, 77–107.

Lan, Feng. "The Female Individual and the Empire: A Historicist Approach to Mulan and Kingston's *Woman Warrior*." *Comparative Literature* 55.3 (2003): 229–45.

Langer, Beryl. "The Business of Branded Enchantment: Ambivalence and Disjuncture in the Global Children's Culture." *Journal of Consumer Culture* 4.2 (2004): 251–77.

Lau, D. C., trans. *Mencius*. Harmondsworth: Penguin, 1970.

Lau, Joseph S. M. "Kingston as Exorcist." In *Modern Chinese Women Writers: Critical Appraisals*, ed. Michael S. Duke, 44–52. New York: An East Gate Book, 1989.

Leddy, Thomas. "Aesthetics and Children's Picture-Books." *Journal of Aesthetic Education* 36.4 (2002): 43–54.

Lee, Ang, dir. *Crouching Tiger, Hidden Dragon*. 2000. New York: Columbia TriStar Home Entertainment, 2001. DVD.

Lee, Hai-soon. "Representation of Females in Twelfth-Century Korean Historiography." In *Women and Confucian Cultures*, edited by Ko, Haboush, and Piggott, 75–96.

Lee, Jeanne M. *The Song of Mu Lan*. Arden, NC: Front Street, 1995.

Lee, Katherine Hyunmi. "The Poetics of Liminality and Misidentification: Winnifred Eaton's *Me* and Maxine Hong Kingston's *The Woman Warrior*." *Studies in the Literary Imagination* 37.1 (2004): 17–33.

Lee, Ken-fang. "Cultural Translation and the Exorcist: A Reading of Kingston's and Tan's Ghost Stories." *MELUS* 29.2 (2004): 105–27.

Lee, Lily Xiao Hong. *The Virtue of Yin: Studies on Chinese Women*. Canberra, Australia: Wild Pheony, 1994.

Lee, Min. "Hong Kong Director Takes on Mulan with Real Actors." Associated Press, 25 November 2009. 14 December 2009. http://www.ap.org/.

Lee, Robert G. "*The Woman Warrior* as an Inversion in Asian American Historiography." In *Approaches to Teaching* The Woman Warrior, edited by Lim, 52–63.

The Legend of Mulan. Newark, NJ: Springboard Home Entertainment, 1997. DVD.

The Legend of Mulan: A Folding Book of the Ancient Poem That Inspired the Disney Animated Film. New York: Hyperion, 1998.

LeJeune, Elisabetta. "Mu-Lan, the Chinese Woman Warrior." Web. 6 October 2009. http://www.selu.edu/Academics/Faculty/elejeune/mulan.htm.

Leonard, John. "In Defiance of 2 Worlds." *New York Times* (17 Sep 1976): C21. Reprinted in *Critical Essays on Maxine Hong Kingston*, edited by Laura Skandera-Trombley, 77. New York: G. K. Hall & Co., 1998.

Leung, K. C. *Hsu Wei as Drama Critic: An Annotated Translation of the* Nan-Tz'u Hsü-Lu. Eugene: Asian Studies Program, University of Oregon, 1986.

Levdon, Joe. "Mulan II." *Variety* 398.1 (February 21, 2005): 22.

Levy, Dore J. *Chinese Narrative Poetry: The Late Han through T'ang Dynasties*. Durham, NC : Duke University Press, 1988.

Levy, Howard S. *China's Dirtiest Trickster: Folklore about Hsü Wen-ch'ang (1521–1593)*. Arlington, VA: Warm-soft Village, 1974.

———. *Chinese Footbinding: The History of a Curious Erotic Custom*. New York: W. Rawls, 1966.

Li, Chenyang. "The Confucian Concept of *Jen* and the Feminist Ethics of Care: A Comparative Study." *Hypatia: A Journal of Feminist Philosophy* 9.1 (1994):

70–89. Reprinted in *The Sage and the Second Sex*, edited by Chenyang Li, 23–42.

———, ed. *The Sage and the Second Sex: Confucianism, Ethics, and Gender.* Chicago: Open Court, 2000.

Li Chunsheng. "'Mulan shi kao." *Dalu zazhi* 31.12 (1965): 369–71.

Li, David Leiwei. *Imagining the Nation: Asian American Literature and Cultural Consent.* Stanford, CA: Stanford University Press, 1998.

———. "The Naming of a Chinese American 'I': Cross-Cultural Sign/ifications in *The Woman Warrior.*" *Criticism* 30.4 (1988): 497–515.

———. "The Production of Chinese American Tradition: Displacing American Orientalist Discourse." In *Reading the Literatures of Asian America*, edited by Lim and Ling, 319–31.

———. "Re-presenting *The Woman Warrior*: An Essay of Interpretive History." In *Critical Essays on Maxine Hong Kingston*, edited by Laura Skandera-Trombley, 182–203. New York: G. K. Hall & Co., 1998.

Li Fang (925–996) et al., comp. *Wenyuan yinghua.* Beijing: zhonghua shuju, 1982.

———. *Taiping guangji.* 1961; Beijing: Zhonghua shuju, 1986.

Li, Fei. "Plan for *Mulan*'s Marketing Strategy." *Chinese Sociology and Anthropology* 32.2 (1999–2000): 15–19.

Li Hongzhang (1823–1901), Huang Pengnian (1823–1891) et al. *Jifu tongzhi.* Shanghai: shangwu, 1934.

Li Jingxin. "Liangshou Mulanshi bijiao pingxi" (Comparative Analysis of Two Mulan Poems). *Journal of Qiongzhou University* 11.1 (2004): 48–50.

Li Rong. *Duyi zhi.* In *Baihai.* Comp. Shang Rui (fl. 1591–1602). Taipei: Xinxing shuju, 1968.

Li Shuying. "Hua Mulan zuoziji de chuanqi nüzi: wenhua jiedu Mulan shi yu Disney Hua Mulan." *Journal of Huaibei Coal Industry Teachers' College (Philosophy and Social Sciences)* 27.4 (2006): 134–35.

Li, Siu Leung. "Gender, Cross-Dressing and Chinese Theatre," Ph.D. diss., University of Massachusetts, Amherst, 1995.

Li, Waiyee. *Enchantment and Disenchantment: Love and Illusion in Chinese Literature.* Princeton: Princeton University Press, 1993.

Li Xian (1408–1466) and Wan An (d. 1489), et al., comps. *Da ming yitongzhi.* Taipei: Wenhai chubanshe, 1965.

Li Xiang. *Hua Mulan.* Illustrated by Zhang He. Taipei: Fengche tushu chuban gongsi, 1998.

Li, Xiaolin. "Chinese Women Soldiers: A History of 5,000 Years." *Social Education* 58.2 (1994): 67–71.

Li Yanshou (fl. 7th cent.). *Beishi.* Beijing: Zhonghua shuju, 1974.

Li Yinsu. "Dangdai donghuapian yishu de wenhua chanshi: *Xiaoqian, Hua Mulan he Baolian deng* bijiao fenxi." *Film Art* 3 (2001): 87–90.

Li Zhonghe. "Shuo 'Mulan shi' de xianglue nongdan chuli." *Journal of Shangluo Teachers College* 15.4 (2001): 80–81.

Liang, I-Ch'eng. "Hsü Wei (1521–1593): His Life and Literary Works," Ph.D. diss., Ohio State University, 1973.

———. *Xu Wei de wenxue yu yishu.* Taipei: Yee Wen Publishing Co. 1976.

Lightfoot, Marjorie J. "Hunting the Dragon in Kingston's *The Woman Warrior.*" *MELUS* 13.3/4 (1986): 55–66.

Lim, Jeehyun. "Cutting the Tongue: Language and the Body in Kingston's *The Woman Warrior.*" *MELUS* 31.3 (2006): 49–65.

Lim, Shirley Geok-lin, ed. *Approaches to Teaching Kingston's* The Woman Warrior. New York: MLA, 1991.

———. "Assaying the Gold: Or, Contesting the Ground of Asian American Literature." *New Literary History* 24.1 (1993): 147–69.

———. "Immigration and Diaspora." In *Interethnic Companion*, edited by Kingkok Cheung, 289–311.

———. "Twelve Asian American Writers: In Search of Self-Definition." *MELUS* 13.1/2 (1986): 57–77.

Lim, Shirley Geok-lin, and Amy Ling, eds. *Reading the Literatures of Asian America.* Philadelphia, PA: Temple University Press, 1992.

Lim, Shirley Geok-lin, John Blair Gamber, Stephen Hong Sohn, and Gina Valentino, eds. *Transnational Asian American Literature: Sites and Transits.* Philadelphia, PA: Temple University Press, 2006.

Lim, Water S. H. "Under Eastern Eyes: Ghosts and Cultural Hunting in Maxine Hong Kingston's *The Woman Warrior* and *China Men.*" In *Crossing Oceans*, edited by Brada-Williams and Chow, 155–63.

Lin Jian. "Huayi zuojia zai meiguo wentan de diwei ji guilei." *Fudan Journal: Social Sciences Edition* 5 (2003): 11–17.

Lin, Shuling, Donghe Chen, Tianzi Zhang. *Hua Mulan.* Tainan, Taiwan: Jin qiao chubanshe, 1984.

Ling, Amy. *Between Worlds: Women Writers of Chinese Ancestry.* New York: Pergamon, 1990.

———. "Chinese American Women Writers: The Tradition Behind Maxine Hong Kingston." In *Redefining American Literary History*, edited by Lavonne A. Ruoff and Jerry W. Ward, 219–36. New York: MLA, 1990.

Liu Dechang (fl. 1665) and Ye Yun (fl. 1665), comp. *Shangqiu xianzhi.* Taipei: Chengwen chubanshe, 1969.

Liu, James J. Y. *The Chinese Knight-Errant.* London: Routledge and Kegan Paul, 1967.

Liu Shaoming. "Cong Tang Tingting dao Tan Enmei: meihua xiaoshuo xin qidian." *Sinorama* (April 1992): 74–75.

Liu, Toming Jun. "The Problematics of Kingston's 'Cultural Translation': A Chinese Diasporic View of *The Woman Warrior.*" *Journal of American Studies of Turkey* 4 (1996): 15–30.

Liu Xiang (ca. 79–ca. 8 B.C.). *Lienü zhuan jiao zhu.* Ed. Liang Duan (ca. 1793–1825). Taipei: Zhonghua shuju, 1983.

Liu Xu (887–946) et al. *Jiu tangshu*. Beijing: Zhonghua shuju, 1975.

Lü Kun (1536–1618). *Gui fan*. Shanghai: Shanghai guji chubanshe, 1994.

Lu Xun. *Zhongguo xiaoshuo shilue*. 1923. Reprint. Hong Kong: xinyi chubanshe, 1985. Print.

Luo Genze. *Yuefu wenxueshi*. Taipei: Wenshizhe chubanshe, 1981.

Loh, Virginia S. "Asian American Children's Literature: A Qualitative Study of Cultural Authenticity," Ph.D. diss., San Diego State University, 2008.

Louie, Kam. *Theorizing Chinese Masculinity: Society and Gender in China*. Cambridge: Cambridge University Press, 2002.

Low, C. C., and Associates. *Liang Hongyu*. Singapore: Canfonian Pte. Ltd., 1991.

———. *Mulan Joined the Army*. Singapore: Canfonian Pte Ltd., 1995.

Lowe, Lisa. "Heterogeneity, Hybridity, Multiplicity: Marking Asian American Differences." *Diaspora* 1.1 (1991): 24–44.

———. *Immigrant Acts: On Asian American Cultural Politics*. Durham, NC: Duke University Press, 1996.

———. "The International within the National: American Studies and Asian American Critique." *Cultural Critique* 40 (Fall 1998): 29–47.

———. "Work, Immigration, Gender: New Subjects of Cultural Politics." In *The Politics of Culture in the Shadow of Capital*, edited by Lisa Lowe and David Lloyd, 354–74. Durham, NC: Duke University Press, 1997.

Lu, James. "Enacting Asian American Transformations: An Inter-Ethnic Perspective." *MELUS* 23.4 (1998): 85–99.

Ludwig, Sämi. "Celebrating Outselves in the Other, Or: Who Controls the Conceptual Allusions in Kingston?" In *Asian American Literature*, edited by Davis and Ludwig, 37–55.

———. *Concrete Language: Intercultural Communication in Maxine Hong Kingston's* The Woman Warrior *and Ishmael Reed's* Mumbo Jumbo. Frankfurt: Peter Lang, 1996.

Lull, James. *Media, Communication, Culture*. New York: Columbia University Press, 2000.

Lyons, Mike. "Times Are Changing for Disney Heroines." *Cinefantastique* 30 (1998): 7.

Ma Guohan (1794–1857), comp. *Yuhan shanfang jiyishu*. Taipei: Wenhai chubanshe, 1974.

Ma, Qian. *Women in Traditional Chinese Theater: A Heroine's Play*. Lanham, MD: University Press of America, Inc., 2005.

Ma Shaobo. *Mulan congjun*. 2nd ed. Shanghai: Shangza chubanshe, 1953.

Ma, Sheng-Mei. *The Deathly Embrace: Orientalism and Asian American Identity*. Minneapolis: University of Minnesota Press, 2000.

———. *Immigrant Subjectivities in Asian American and Asian Diaspora Literatures*. Albany: State University New York Press, 1998.

MacCann, Donnarae. "Multicultural Books and Interdisciplinary Inquiries." *The Lion and the Unicorn* 16.1 (1992): 43–56.

Madsen, Deborah L. "Chinese American Writers of the Real and the Fake: Authenticity and the Twin Traditions of Life Writing." *Canadian Review of American Studies* 36.3 (2006): 257–71.

———. *Maxine Hong Kingston*. Detroit, MI: Gale Group, 2000.

———. "Transcendence through Violence: Women and the Martial Arts Motif in Recent American Fiction and Film." In *Literature and the Visual Media*, edited by David Seed, 163–80. Cambridge: D. S. Brewer, 2005.

Maio, Kathi. "Disney's Dolls." *New Internationalist* 308 (December 1998): 12–14.

Mann, Susan. "Learned Women in the Eighteenth Century." In *Engendering China*, edited by Gilmartin, Christina K., Gail Hershatter, Lisa Rofel, and Tyrene White, 27–46. Cambridge, MA: Harvard University Press, 1994.

———. *Precious Records: Women in China's Long Eighteenth Century.* Stanford, CA: Stanford University Press, 1997.

———. "Presidential Address: Myths of Asian Womanhood." *Journal of Asian Studies* 59.4 (2000): 835–62.

Mann, Susan, and Yu-Yin Cheng, eds. *Under Confucian Eyes: Writing on Gender in Chinese History.* Berkeley: University of California Press, 2001.

Marino, Elisabetta. "On Being Diasporic: An Interview with Shirley Geok-lin Lim." In *Transnational, National, and Personal Voices*, edited by Simal and Marino, 241–55.

Marsoli, Lisa Ann. *Mulan: Classic Storybook.* Illustrated by Judith Holmes Clarke, Brent Ford, Denise Shimabukuro, Scott Tilley, Lori Tyminski, and Atelier Philippe. New York: Disney Enterprises, Inc. 1998.

Marsoli, Lisa Ann, and Judith Clark. *Disney's Mulan.* Burbank, CA: Mouseworks, 1998.

Martin, W.A.P. (1827–1916), trans. "Mulan, the Maiden Chief." *The Chinese Their Education, Philosophy, and Letters.* New York, NY: Harper & Brothers, 1881. 316–19.

Mason, Janet. "Against Assimilation: The Roots of Memoir." *Room of One's Own* 23.1 (2000): 88–96.

Mazumdar, Sucheta. "Asian American Studies and Asian Studies: Rethinking Roots." In *Asian Americans*, edited by Hune, Kim, Fugita, and Ling, 29–44.

McCallum, Robyn. "Masculinity as Social Semiotic: Identity Politics and Gender in Disney Animated Films." In *Ways of Being Male: Representing Masculinities in Children's Literature and Film*, edited by John Stephens, 116–32. New York: Routledge, 2002.

"McDonald's Links Mulan Film to Happy Meal Promo." *Brandweek* 39.25 (June 22, 1998): 5.

McNamara, Karen Hill. "From Fairies to Famine: How Cultural Identity is Constructed through Irish and Irish American Children's Literature." *The Children's Folklore Review* 26 (2003–04): 77–90.

Mejia-LaPerle, Carol. "The Ghostly Rhetoric of Autobiography: Maxine Hong

Kingston's *The Woman Warrior* as American Gothic Narrative." In *Asian Gothic: Essays on Literature, Film and Anime*, edited by Andrew Hock Soon Ng, 108–21. Jefferson, NC: McFarland, 2008.

Melchior, Bonnie. "A Marginal 'I': The Autobiographical Self Deconstructed in Maxine Hong Kingston's *The Woman Warrior*." *Biography: An Interdisciplinary Quarterly* 17.3 (1994): 281–95.

Mendoza, Jean, and Debbie Reese. "Examining Multicultural Picture Books for the Early Childhood Classroom: Possibilities and Pitfalls." *Early Childhood Research and Practice* 3.2 (2001): n. pag. 6 October 2009. http://ecrp.uiuc.edu/v3n2/mendoza.html.

Moebius, William. "Introduction to Picturebook Codes." *Word and Image* 2.2 (1986): 141–58. Print.

Moreno Gallardo, Carmen. "*The Woman Warrior* and *The Joy Luck Club*: A Search for an Ethnic and Female Identity." In *Evolving Origins, Transplanting Cultures: Literary Legacies of the New Americans*, edited by L. Alonso Gallo and Antonia Dominguez Miguela, 129–36. Huelva, Spain: Universidad de Huelva, 2002.

Mou, Sherry J., ed. *Presence and Presentation: Women in the Chinese Literati Tradition*. New York: St. Martin's Press, 1999.

Mu Zhang'a (1782–1856) et al., comps. *Da Qing yitongzhi* (also known as the *Jiaqing chongxiu yitongzhi*). Completed 1842. Reprint. Shanghai: Shangwu yinshuguan, 1934; Taipei: Shangwu yinshuguan, 1966.

Mulan. Produced by Madacy Entertainment Group. Troy, MI: Anchor Bay Entertainment, 1999. DVD.

"Mulan, the Actual Legend of Chinese Heritage: A Press Release." Victory Press, 2008. 6 October 2009. http://heroinesinhistory.com/press.html.

"Mulan chuanqi chonglao 'zhongguo yin'." *People's Daily* 21 December 2006: Section 11.

Mulan qinü zhuan (in Mandarin). Beijing: Huaxia chubanshe, 1995.

Mulan qinü zhuan (in classic Chinese). Xi'an: Sanqin chubanshe, 1998.

"Mulan Timeline." Geocities, 4 Dec. 1998. Web. 6 Oct. 2009. http://www.geocities.com/Hollywood/5082/time.html.

Needham, Tara. "Projections of America: Negotiating Boundaries of State and Self." *Journal of Modern Literature* 30.4 (2007): 156–61.

"New Formations, New Questions: Asian American Studies." Special issue of *Positions: East Asia Cultures Critique* 5.2 (1997).

Nguyen, Mimi. "Role Models: Mulan." *San Jose Mercury News* 5 July 1998. 6 October 2009. http://www.theory.org.uk/ctr-rol2.htm.

Nguyen, Viet Thanh. "The Remasculinization of Chinese America: Race, Violence, and the Novel." *American Literary History* 12.1/2 (2000): 130–57.

Ni Mei. "Yingpian *Hua Mulan* erdu bian/jiema kuawenhua fenxi." *Sichuan Drama* 4 (2006): 55–56, 47.

Nienhauser, William H., trans. "The Ballad of Mulan." In *Sunflower Splendor*:

Three Thousand Years of Chinese Poetry, edited by Wu-chi Liu and Irving Yucheng Lo, 77–80. Bloomington: Indiana University Press, 1975.

Nikolajeva, Maria. *Children's Literature Comes of Age: Toward a New Aesthetic.* New York: Garland, 1996.

Nikolajeva, Maria, and Carole Scott. *How Picturebooks Work.* New York: Routledge, 2006.

Nishime, LeiLani. "Engendering Genre: Gender and Nationalism in *China Men* and *The Woman Warrior.*" *MELUS* 20.1 (1995): 65–82.

Nodelman, Perry. "Decoding the Images: How Picture Books Work." In *Understanding Children's Literature*, edited by Peter Hunt, 128–39.

———. "The Eye and the I: Identification and First-Person Narratives in Picture Books." *Children's Literature* 19 (1991): 1–30.

———. "The Other: Orientalism, Colonialism, and Children's Literature." *Children's Literature Association Quarterly* 17.1 (Spring 1992): 29–35.

———. "The Relationships of Pictures and Words." In *Crosscurrents of Children's Literature: An Anthology of Texts and Criticism*, eds. J. D. Stahl, Tina L. Hanlon, and Elizabeth Lennox Keyser, 715–29. New York: Oxford University Press, 2007.

———. *Words about Pictures: The Narrative Art of Children's Picture Books.* Athens: University of Georgia Press, 1988.

Ono, Kazuko. *Chinese Women in a Century of Revolution, 1850–1950.* Stanford, CA: Stanford University Press, 1989.

Ordonez, Elizabeth. "Narrative Texts by Ethnic Women: Rereading the Past, Reshaping the Future." *MELUS* 9.3 (1982): 19–28.

Ouyang Xiu (1007–1072) and Song Qi (998–1061). *Xin tangshu.* Beijing: Zhonghua shuju, 1975.

Ouyang Yuqian. *Mulan Congjun.* Shanghai: Shanghai xuesheng shuju, 1939.

"Palimpsest." *Oxford English Dictionary Online.* Oxford University Press, 2009. 10 November 2009.

Palumbo-Liu, David. *Asian/American: Historical Crossings of a Racial Frontier.* Stanford, CA: Stanford University Press, 1999.

———. *The Ethnic Canon: Histories, Institutions, and Interventions.* Minneapolis: University of Minnesota Press, 1995.

Painter, Clare. "Children's Pictures Book Narratives: Reading Sequences of Images." In *Advances in Language and Education*, edited by Anne McCabe, Mick O'Donnell, and Rachel Whittaker, 40–59. London: Continuum, 2007.

Peng Pai, et al. *Zhongguo lidai nü jie.* Taizhong: xueren wenhua shiye youxian gongsi, 1980.

Perry, Elizabeth J., and Nara Dillon. "'Little Brothers' in the Cultural Revolution: The Worker Rebels of Shanghai." In *Chinese Femininities/Chinese Masculinities: A Reader*, edited by Susan Brownell and Jeffrey N. Wasserstrom, 269–86. Berkeley: University of California Press, 2002.

Petit, Angela. "'Words So Strong': Maxine Hong Kingston's 'No Name Woman'

Introduces Students to the Power of Words." *Journal of Adolescent and Adult Literacy* 46.6 (2003): 482–90.

Qian Cai (fl. 1729) et al. *Shuoyue quanzhuan*. Shanghai: Shanghai guji chubanshe, 1980.

Qin Liangyu shiliao jicheng. Chengdu: Sichuan daxue chubanshe, 1987.

Qinhuaimoke (pseudo. fl. 1606–1607). *Yangjiafu shidai zhongyong yanyi zhuan*. Shanghai: Shanghai guji chubanshe, 1980.

Qu Changrong and Dai Peng. "Chuantong wenhua gai ruhe baohu chanquan." *People's Daily* 15 December 2006: Section 11.

Quan Tang shi. Beijing: Zhonghua shuju, 1960.

Que Zhen. "Xu Wei *Ci Mulan* zai chuangzuo de sikao" (The Thinking of Recreation of Xu Wei's Drama *Female Mulan*). *Journal of Zhuzhou Institute of Technology* 17.6 (2003): 41–43.

Rabinowitz, Paula. "Eccentric Memories: A Conversation with Maxine Hong Kingston." *Michigan Quarterly Review* 26.1 (1987): 177–87.

Rabine, Leslie W. "No Lost Paradise: Social Gender and Symbolic Gender in the Writings of Maxine Hong Kingston." *Signs* 12.3 (1987): 471–92.

Radhakrishnan, R. "Is the Ethnic 'Authentic' in the Diaspora?" In *The State of Asian America: Activism and Resistance in the 1990s*, edited by Karin Aguilar-San Juan, 219–34. Boston, MA: South End Press, 1994.

Raknem, Ingvald. *Joan of Arc in History, Legend, and Literature*. Oslo, Norway: Universitetsforlaget, 1971.

Raphals, Lisa. *Sharing the Light: Representations of Women and Virtue in Early China*. Albany: State University of New York Press, 1998.

Raussert, Wilfred. "Minority Discourses, Foodways, and Aspects of Gender: Contemporary Writings by Asian-American Women." *Journal x* 7.2 (2003): 183–204.

Ren Shoushi (fl. 1825) and Liu Kai (fl. 1825) et al., comps. *Bozhou zhi*. Taipei: Chengwen chubanshe, 1985.

"Robert D. San Souci homepage." Robert D. San Souci, 1 October 2009. Web. 6 October 2009. http://www.rsansouci.com.

Robertson, Maureen. "Voicing the Feminine: Constructions of the Gendered Subject in Lyric Poetry by Women of Medieval and Late Imperial China." *Late Imperial China* 13.1 (1992): 63–110.

Ropp, Paul S. "Love, Literacy, and Laments: Themes of Women Writers in Late Imperial China." *Women's History Review* 2.1 (1993): 107–41.

Rorex, Robert A., and Wen Fong. *The Story of Lady Wen-Chi: A Fourteenth-Century Handscroll in the Metropolitan Museum of Art*. New York: The Metropolitan Museum of Art, 1974.

Rosemont, Henry, Jr. "Classical Confucian and Contemporary Feminist Perspectives on the Self: Some Parallels and Their Implications." In *Culture and Self: Philosophical and Religious, East and West,* edited by Douglas Allen, 63–82. Boulder, CO: Westview Press, 1997.

Rosen, Stanley. "Guest Editor's Introduction." *Chinese Sociology and Anthropology* 32.2 (1999–2000): 5–10.

Ross, Deborah. "Escape from Wonderland: Disney and the Female Imagination." *Marvels & Tales: Journal of Fairy-Tale Studies* 18.1 (2004): 53–66.

Rubenstein, Roberta. *Boundaries of the Self: Gender, Culture, Fiction.* Urbana: University of Illinois Press, 1987.

Sabine, Maureen. *Maxine Hong Kingston's Broken Book of Life: An Intertextual Study of* The Woman Warrior *and* China Men. Honolulu: University of Hawaii Press, 2004.

Sackheim, Eric. *The Silent Zero, in Search of Sound: An Anthology of Chinese Poems from the Beginning through the Sixth Century.* New York: Grossman, 1968.

San Souci, Robert D. *Fa Mulan: The Story of A Woman Warrior.* Illustrated by Jean and Mou-Sien Tseng. New York: Hyperion Books for Children, 1998.

Sato, Kumiko. "Differences that the Ethnic Autobiography Makes: Strategy of Maxine Hong Kingston's *The Woman Warrior.*" *Studies in American Literature* 36 (2000): 73–90.

Sawyer, Ralph D. *The Tao of Spycraft: Intelligence Theory and Practice in Traditional China.* Boulder, CO.: Westview Press, 1998.

Schroeder, Russell, and Kathleen Zoehfeld. *Disney's Mulan.* New York: Disney Press, 1998.

Schueller, Malini. "Questioning Race and Gender Definitions: Dialogic Subversions in *The Woman Warrior.*" *Criticism* 31.4 (1989): 421–37.

Schultermandl, Silvia. "Introduction: Against the (Main)stream: New Perspectives on Asian American and British Asian Identity Politics." *Interactions* 15.2 (2006): 1–12.

———. "'What am I, anyhow?' Ethnic Consciousness, Matrilineage and the Borderlands-within in Maxine Hong Kingston's and Rebecca Walker's Autobiographies." In *Close Encounters of an Other Kind: New Perspectives on Race, Ethnicity and American Studies,* edited by Roy Goldblatt, Jopi Nyman, and John A. Stotesbury, 3–17. Joensuu, Finland: Faculty of Humanities, University of Joensuu, 2005.

———. "Writing Against the Grain: The Cross-Over Genres of Maxine Hong Kingston's *The Woman Warrior, China Men,* and *The Fifth Book of Peace.*" *Interactions* 16.2 (2007): 111–22.

Seshachari, Neila C. "Reinventing Peace: Conversations with Tripmaster Maxine Hong Kingston." In *Conversations with Maxine Hong Kingston,* edited by Skenazy and Martin, 192–214.

The Secret of Mulan. Fort Mill, SC: United American Video Entertainment, 1997. DVD.

Shao, Peng. "Analysis of *Mulan*'s Selling Points and Marketing Operations." *Chinese Sociology and Anthropology* 32.2 (1999–2000): 11–14.

Shapiro, Elliott H. "Authentic Watermelon: Maxine Hong Kingston's American Novel." *MELUS* 26.1 (2001): 5–28.

Shen Deqian (1673–1769). *Gu shi yuan*. Reprint, Beijing: Zhonghua shuju, 1977.

Shen Yue (441–513). *Songshu*. Reprint. Beijing: Zhonghua shuju, 1974.

Shi Nai'an (ca. 1290-ca. 1365). *Shuihu zhuan*. Reprint. Beijing: Renmin wenxue chubanshe, 1990.

Shu, Yuan. "Cultural Politics and Chinese-American Female Subjectivity: Rethinking Kingston's 'Woman Warrior.'" *MELUS* 26.2 (2001): 199–223.

Silko, Leslie Marmon. *Storyteller*. New York: Arcade Publishing, 1981.

Siku Quanshu. Harvard University Digital Resources for Chinese Studies. 25 May 2007. http://hcl.harvard.edu/research/guides/chinese/part3.html.

Silverman, Kaja. "Fragments of a Fashionable Discourse." In *Studies in Entertainment: Critical Approaches to Mass Culture*, edited by Tanio Modleski, 139–52. Bloomington: Indiana University Press, 1986.

Simal, Begona, and Elisabetta Marino, eds. *Transnational, National, and Personal Voices: New Perspectives on Asian American and Asian Diasporic Women Writers*. Münster: Lit Verlag, 2004.

Simmons, Diane. *Maxine Hong Kingston*. New York: Twayne Publishers, 1999.

———. "Maxine Hong Kingston's Woman Warrior and Shaman: Fighting Women in the New World." *FEMSPEC* 2.1 (2000): 49–65.

Simpson, Alyson. "What Happens When a Book Gets Judged by Its Cover? The Importance of a Critical Understanding of Images in Children's Picture Books." *Bookbird: A Journal of International Children's Literature* 42.3 (2004): 28–36.

Skenazy, Paul, and Tera Martin, eds. *Conversations with Maxine Hong Kingston*. Jackson: University of Mississippi Press, 1998.

Smith, Katharine Capshaw. "Introduction: The Landscape of Ethnic American Children's Literature." *MELUS* 27.2 (2002): 3–8.

Smith, Katharine Capshaw, and Margaret R. Higonnet. "Bilingual Books for Children: An Interview with Nicolás Kanellos, Director of Piñata Press." *MELUS* 27.2 (2002): 217–24.

———, eds. "Special Issue: Multi-Ethnic Children's Literature." *MELUS* 27.2 (2002).

Smith, Sidonie. *A Poetics of Women's Autobiography: Marginality and the Fictions of Self-Representation*. Bloomington: Indiana University Press, 1987.

Solomon, Alisa. "It's Never too Late to Switch: Crossing toward Power. In *Crossing the Stage: Controversies on Cross-Dressing*, edited by Lesley Ferris, 144–54. London: Routledge, 1993.

Solovitch, Sara. "Finding a Voice." *The Mercury News* 30 June 1991. Web. 6 October 2009. http://www.sarasolo.com/mn2.html.

Song Xiangfeng (1779–1860). *Guoting lu*. Beijing: Zhonghua shuju, 1986.

Southerland, Lynne, and Darrell Rooney, dir. *Mulan II*. Walt Disney Company, 2005. DVD.

Spruiell, William C. "Intermodal Congruence in Children's Picture Books: A Pilot Study." *LACUS Forum* 31 (2007): 317–24.

Srikanth, Rajini. "Presidential Meditations." *AAAS Newsletter* 25.2 (2008): 1–2.

Stacey, Judith. "A Feminist View of Research on Chinese Women." *Signs* 2.2 (1976): 485–97.

Stanton, W., trans. "Muk Lan's Parting: A Ballad." *The China Review: Notes and Queries on the Far East* 17 (1888–1889): 171–72.

Steiner, Stanley F. "Who Belongs Here? Portraying American Identity in Children's Picture Books." *MultiCultural Review* 7.2 (1998): 20–27.

Stephens, John. "Gender, Genre and Children's Literature." *Signal* 79 (1996): 17–30.

Stephens, John, and Sung-Ae Lee. "Diasporan Subjectivity and Cultural Space in Korean American Picture Books." *Journal of Asian American Studies* 9.1 (2006): 1–25.

Sterritt, David. "A Girl, A Dragon, and A Good Disguise: Disney Formula at Its Best." *Christian Science Monitor* 26 June 1998: B3.

Stewart, Michelle Pagni. "Emering Literacy of (An)Other Kind: Speakerly Chidren's Picture Books." *Children's Literature Association Quarterly* 28.1 (2003): 42–51.

Storhoff, Gary. "'Even Now China Wraps Double Binds around My Feet': Family Communication in *The Woman Warrior* and *Dim Sum*." In *Reading the Family Dance: Family Systems Therapy and Literary Study*, edited by John V. Knapp and Kenneth Womack, 71–92. London: Associated University Presses, 2003.

Sui Sin Far (pseudo. Edith Maude Eaton). "Chinese Workmen in America." *The Independent* 3 Jul. 1913: 56.

———. "Leaves from the Mental Portfolio of an Eurasian." *The Independent* 21 January 1909: 125–32.

Sumida, Stephen H. "Centers without Margins: Responses to Centrism in Asian American Literature." *American Literature* 66.4 (1994): 803–15.

Sun Biwen. *Kao gu lu*. 1888. Reprint, Beijing: Beijing chubanshe, 1997.

Taihetang zhuren and Yibai zhuren [pseudo.]. *Dongxi liangjin yanyi*. Written during the Ming Dynasty (1368–1644). Changchun: Shidai wenyi chubanshe, 1987.

Tang, Jun. "A Cross-Cultural Perspective on Production and Reception of Disney's *Mulan* through Its Chinese Subtitles." *European Journal of English Studies* 12.2 (2008): 149–62.

Tang, Weimin. "Zone of Negotiation: Storytelling, Intersubjecitivity and Transcultural Metamorphosis—Reading the Ethnic Texts *The Woman Warrior* and *The Bonesetter's Daughter*." In *Oral and Written Narratives and Cultural Identity: Interdisciplinary Approaches*, edited by Francisco Cota Fagundes and Irene Maria F. Blayer, 153–71. New York: Peter Lang, 2007.

Tao Zongyi (fl. 1360–1368). *Chuogeng lu*. In *Sibu congkan xubian*. Taipei: Shangwu yinshuguan, 1976.

———. *Shuo fu*. Taipei: Shangwu, 1972.

Tensuan, Theresa M. "Talking-Story: Reading *The Woman Warrior* and Rearticulating American Identity." In *Transnational, National, and Personal Voices*, edited by Simal and Marino, 25–41.

Thacker, Deborah Cogan, and Jean Webb. *Introducing Children's Literature: From Romanticism to Postmodernism*. London: Routledge, 2002.

T'ien, Ju-K'ang. *Male Anxiety and Female Illustriousness: A Comparative Study of Chinese Ethical Values in Ming-Ch'ing Times*. Leiden: E. J. Bill, 1988.

Tong, Benjamin R. "Critic of Admirer Sees Dumb Racist." *San Francisco Journal* 11 (May 1977): 6.

Tosi, Laura. "Did They Live Happily Ever After? Rewriting Fairy Tales for a Contemporary Audience." In *Folk and Fairy Tales*, edited by Hallett and Karasek, 367–86.

"Tribute to Mulan." *New Straits Times* 30 Jan. 2007: Local 7.

Trinh, Minh-ha T. *Woman, Native, Other: Writing Postcoloniality and Feminism*. Bloomington: Indiana University Press, 1989.

Trites, Roberta Seelinger. "Introduction: Multiculturalism in Children's Literature." *Children's Literature Association Quarterly* 28.2 (2003): 66–67.

Tsiang, H. T. *China Marches On: A Play in Three Acts*. New York: published by the author, 1938.

Tu Wei-ming. "The Confucian Tradition in Chinese History." In *Heritage of China: Contemporary Perspectives on Chinese Civilization*, edited by Paul S. Ropp, 112–37. Berkeley: University of California Press, 1990.

———. "Probing the 'Three Bonds' and 'Five Relationship.'" In *Confucianism and the Family*, edited by Walter H. Slote and George A. De Vos, 121–36. Albany: State University of New York Press, 1998.

Tuotuo (1313–1355) et al. *Songshi*. Beijing: Zhonghua shuju, 1977.

Ty, Eleanor. "Beyond Autoethnography: Recent Developments in Chinese North American Narratives." In *Querying the Genealogy*, edited by Jennie Wang, 336–46.

———. "Rethinking the Hyphen: Asian North American and European Ethnic Texts as Global Narratives." *Canadian Review of American Studies* 32.3 (2002): 239–52.

Ty, Eleanor, and Donald C. Goellnicht, eds. *Beyond the Hyphen: Asian North American Identities*. Bloomington: Indiana University Press, 2004.

"U.S. Sunny Publishing homepage." U.S. Sunny Publishing Inc. Web. 6 October 2009. http://ussunnypublishing.com/.

Volpp, Sophie. "The Male Queen: Boy Actors and Literati Libertines," Ph.D. diss., Harvard University, 1995.

Waley, Arthur, trans. "The Ballad of Mulan." In *Chinese Poems*, 113–15. London: George Allen and Unwin Ltd., 1946. Reprinted in *The Columbia Anthology of Traditional Chinese Literature*, edited by Victor H. Mair, 474–76. New York: Columbia University Press, 1994.

Waltner, Ann. "Widows and Remarriage in Ming and Early Qing China." In *Women in China*, edited by Guisso and Johannesen, 129–46.

Wang, Chi-Chen. *Traditional Chinese Tales*. New York: Columbia University Press, 1944.

Wang, C. H. "Towards Defining a Chinese Heroism." *Journal of the American Oriental Society* 95.1 (1975): 25–35.

Wang, Georgette, and Emilie Yueh-yu Yeh. "Globalization and Hybridization in Cultural Products: The Case of *Mulan* and *Crouching Tiger, Hidden Dragon*." *International Journal of Cultural Studies* 8.2 (2005): 175–93.

Wang, Jennie. *The Iron Curtain of Language: Maxine Hong Kingston and American Orientalism*. Shanghai: Fudan University Press, 2007.

———, ed. *Querying the Genealogy: Comparative and Transnational Studies in Chinese American Literature*. Shanghai: Shanghai yiwen chubanshe, 2006.

Wang, Jian. *Hua Mulan: China's Sweetest Magnolia*. Singapore: Asiapac Comic Series, 1996.

Wang, Jianping. "Between Memory and History: Maxine Hong Kingston's *China Men* and *The Woman Warrior*." In *Crossing Oceans*, edited by Brada-Williams and Chow, 133–38.

Wang, L. Ling-chi. "Roots and Changing Identity of the Chinese in the United States." *DAEDALUS: Journal of the American Academy of Arts and Sciences* 120.2 (1991): 181–206.

———. "The Structure of Dual Domination: Toward a Paradigm for the Study of the Chinese Diaspora in the United States." *Amerasia Journal* 12.1–2 (1995): 149–69.

Wang Lei. "Xushi celue yu jiazhi quxiang: cong meiguo *Hua Mulan* yu zhongguo *Baolian deng* de bijiao tanqi." *Art Observation* 6 (2004): 17.

Wang Li. *Zhongguo gudai haoxia yishi*. Hefei: Anhui renmin chubanshe, 1996.

Wang Qian. "Disney jingtou xia de Hua Mulan jiedu." *Journal of Zhengzhou Institute of Aeronautical Industry Management* (Social Science Edition) 25.3 (2006): 34–36.

Wang, Robin R., ed. *Images of Women in Chinese Thought and Culture: Writings from the Pre-Qin Period through the Song Dynasty*. Indianapolis, IN: Hackett Publishing Company, 2003.

Wang Rongpei, trans. "The Mulan Ballad." In *Chinese-English Three Hundred Poems from the Han, Wei, and Six Dynasties*, 540–45. Changsha: Hunan renmin chubanshe, 1998.

Wang Rubi. *Yuefu sanlun*. Xi'an: Shaanxi renmin chubanshe, 1984.

Wang, Veronica. "Reality and Fantasy: The Chinese-American Woman's Quest for Identity." *MELUS* 12.3 (1985): 23–31.

Wang Yinglin (1223–1296), comp. *Yuhai*. Taipei: Huawen shuju, 1967.

Wang Yunxi. *Yuefushi luncong*. Shanghai: Zhonghua shuju, 1962.

Wang Zhiyong. *Hua Mulan*. Tainan: Longmen tushu gufen youxian gongsi, 1988.

Wang Zhong. *Yuefu shiji*. Taipei: Xuesheng shuju, 1968.

Watson, Burton, trans. *Basic Writings of Mo Tzu, Hsün Tzu, and Han Fei Tzu.* New York: Columbia University Press, 1967.

Wei Tai (ca. 11th or 12th cent.). *Linhan yinju shihua.* In *Wenyuange siku quanshu.* Taipei: Shangwu yinshuguan, 1983.

Wei Zheng (580–643) and Zhangsun Wuji (d. 659). *Suishu.* Beijing: Zhonghua shuju, 1973.

Wells, Paul. *Animation and America.* New Brunswick, NJ: Rutgers University Press, 2002.

———. "'I Wanna Be like You-oo-oo': Disnified Politics and Identity from Mermaid to Mulan." In *American Film and Politics from Reagan to Bush Jr.,* edited by Philip John and Paul Wells, 139–54. Manchester: Manchester University Press, 2002.

———, *Understanding Animation.* London: Routledge, 1998.

Wheelwright, Julie. *Amazons and Military Maids: Women Who Dressed as Men in the Pursuit of Life, Liberty and Happiness.* London: Pandora, 1989.

Widmer, Ellen. "Xiaoqing's Literary Legacy and the Place of the Woman Writer in Late Imperial China." *Late Imperial China* 13.1 (1992): 111–55.

Widmer, Ellen, and King-I Sun Chang, eds. *Writing Women in Late Imperial China.* Stanford, CA: Stanford University Press, 1997.

Winslow, David J. "Children's Picture Books and the Popularization of Folklore." *Keystone Folklore Quarterly* 14 (1969): 142–57.

Wojcik-Andrews, Ian. *Children's Films: History, Ideology, Pedagogy, Theory.* New York: Garland Publishing, 2000.

Wolf, Margery, and Roxanne Witke, eds. *Women in Chinese Society.* Stanford, CA: Stanford University Press, 1975.

Women and Geography Study Group of the IBG. *Geography and Gender: An Introduction to Feminist Geography.* London: Hutchinson, 1984.

Wong, Sau-Ling Cynthia. "Autobiography as Guided Chinatown Tour? Maxine Hong Kingston's *The Woman Warrior* and the Chinese-American Autobiographical Controversy." In *Multicultural Autobiography: American Lives,* edited by James Payne, 248–79. Knoxville: University of Tennessee Press, 1992.

———. "Denationalization Reconsidered: Asian American Cultural Criticism at a Theoretical Crossroads." *Amerasia Journal* 21.1 & 2 (1995): 1–27.

———. "Ethnicizing Gender: An Exploration of Sexuality as Sign in Chinese Immigrant Literature." In *Reading the Literatures of Asian America,* edited by Lim and Ling, 111–29.

———. "Kingston's Handling of Traditional Chinese Sources." In *Approaches to Teaching* The Woman Warrior, edited by Lim, 26–36.

———, ed. *Maxine Hong Kingston's* The Woman Warrior: A Casebook. New York: Oxford University Press, 1999.

———. "Necessity and Extravagance in Maxine Hong Kingston's *The Woman Warrior*: Art and the Ethnic Experience." *MELUS* 15.1 (1988): 3–26.

———. *Reading Asian American Literature: From Necessity to Extravagance.* Princeton, NJ: Princeton University Press, 1993.

Wong, Sau-Ling Cynthia, and Jeffrey Santa-Ana. "Gender and Sexuality in Asian American Literature." *Signs: Journal of Women in Culture and Society* 25.1 (1999): 1–91.

Wong, Sau-Ling Cynthia, and Stephen H. Sumida, eds. *A Resource Guide to Asian American Literature.* New York: MLA, 2001.

Woo, Celestine. "Toward a Poetics of Asian American Fantasy: Laurence Yep' Construction of a Bicultural Mythology." *The Lion and the Unicorn* 30.2 (2006): 250–64.

Woo, Deborah. "Maxine Hong Kingston: the Ethnic Writer and the Burden of Dual Authenticity." *Amerasia Journal* 16.1 (1990): 173–200.

Woo, Terry. "Confucianism and Feminism." In *Feminism and World Religions,* edited by Arvind Sharma and Katherine K. Young, 110–47. Albany: State University of New York Press, 1998.

Wu, Pei-Yi. "Yang Miaozhen: A Woman Warrior in Thirteenth-Century China." *Nan Nü: Men, Women and Gender in Early and Imperial China* 4.2 (2002): 137–69.

Wu Renchen (ca. 1628–1689). *Shiguo chunqiu.* Taipei: Guoguang shuju, 1962.

Wu, William F. "The Ginseng Potion." In *Warrior Enchantresses,* edited by Kathleen M. Massie-Ferch and Martin H. Greenberg, 119–43. New York: Daw Books, 1996.

Wu Youru (d. ca. 1893). *Wu Youru huabao.* Shanghai: Biyuan huishe, ca. 1909.

Wu Yuehui. "*Mulan shipian:* zhongxi hebi hechu sange diyi." *People's Daily,* 19 Jan. 2007, Overseas ed.: Section 13.

Wyile, Andrea Schwenke, and Teya Rosenberg, eds. *Considering Children's Literature: A Reader.* Buffalo, NY: Broadview Press, 2008.

Xia Xiaoyan. "Chenggong huazhuang de dandouzhe: ping Hua Mulan ji donghua dianying *Hua Mulan.*" *Forum for Chinese Literature of the World* 3 (2000): 42–46.

Xiang, Jing. "Light and Relaxing: Watching *Mulan.*" *Chinese Sociology and Anthropology* 32.2 (1999–2000): 28–29.

Xiao Difei. "Cong Du Fu, Bai Juyi, Yuan Zhen shi kan Mulan shi de shidai." In *Yuefu shi yanjiu lunwenji.* 2: 143–50. Beijing: Zhongguo yuwenshe, 1970.

Xiao Li. "Yixingyun de wanmei jiehe." *Nanhua daxue xuebao shehui kexue ban* 1.2 (2000): 71–72.

Xiong Damu (fl. ca. 1522–ca. 1619). *Yangjia jiang zhuan.* Changsha: Yuelu shushe, 1980.

Xu Lun. *Xu Wenchang.* Shanghai: Shanghai renmin chubanshe, 1962.

Xu Shuofang. "Ping Luo Genze xiansheng guanyu Mulan shi de kaoju wenzhang." In *Yuefu shi yanjiu lunwenji.* 2: 151–56. Beijing: Zhongguo yuwenshe, 1970.

Xu Wei (1521–1593). *Xu Wei ji.* Beijing: Zhonghua shuju, 1983.

———. *Mulan nü.* Shanghai: Shangwu yinshuguan, 1958.

Xu Zhongshu. "*Mulan ge* zai kao." *Dongfang zazhi* 22.14 (1925): 72–89.

Yalom, Marilyn. "*The Woman Warrior* as Postmodern Autobiography." In *Approaches to Teaching* The Woman Warrior, edited by Lim, 108–15.

Yang Shen (1488–1559). *Sheng'an waiji.* Reprint, Taipei: *Xuesheng shuju*, 1971.

Yang, T. L., trans. *General Yue Fei.* Hong Kong: Joint Publishing Co. Ltd, 1995.

Yao Darong. "Mulan congjun shi di biaowei." *Dongfang zazhi* 22.2 (1925): 80–97.

———. "Mulan congjun shi di pushu." *Dongfang zazhi* 22.23 (1925): 66–75.

Yao Ying (1785–1853). *Kangyou jixing.* In *Biji xiaoshuo daguan xubian.* Taipei: Xinxing shuju, 1973.

Yao Zhenzong (fl. 1897), comp. *Suishu jingjizhi kaozheng.* In *Ershiwushi bubian.* 1934. Reprint, Taipei: Kaiming shudian, 1969.

Yep, Laurence. "Paying with Shadows." *The Lion and the Unicorn* 30.2 (2006): 157–67.

Yi Junzuo. *Zhongguo baimeitu.* Taipei: Daming Wangshi chuban youxiangon gsi, 1972.

Yin, Xiao-huang. *Chinese American Literature since the 1850s.* Urbana: University of Illinois Press, 2000.

Yu Guanying. *Hanwei liuchao shi luncong.* 1952. Reprint, Shanghai: Tangli chubanshe, 1953.

Yu, Henry. "The 'Oriental Problem' in America, 1920–1960: Linking the Identities of Chinese American and Japanese American Intellectuals." In *Claiming America: Constructing Chinese American Identities during the Exclusion Era*, edited by K. Scott Wong and Sucheng Chan, 191–214. Philadelphia, PA: Temple University Press, 1998.

Yu, Su-lin. "Orientalist Fantasy and Desire in Maxine Hong Kingston's *The Woman Warrior.*" In *Transnational, National, and Personal Voices*, edited by Simal and Marino, 67–86.

Yu Zhengxie (1775–1840). *Gui si cun gao.* 1848. Reprint, Taipei: Yiwen yinshuguan, 1966.

Yuan, Yuan. "The Semiotics of China Narratives in the Con/Texts of Kingston and Tan." *Critique* 40.3 (1999): 292–303.

Zamora, Lois Parkinson. "Finding a Voice, Telling a Story: Constructing Communal Identity in Contemporary American Women's Writing." In *American Mythologies: Essays on Contemporary Literature*, edited by William Blazek and Michael K. Glenday, 267–94. Liverpool: Liverpool University Press, 2005.

Zeitlin, Judith. *Historian of the Strange: Pu Songling and the Chinese Classical Tale.* Stanford, CA: Stanford University Press, 1993.

Zeng, Ying. "The Diverse Nature of San Diego's Chinese American Communities." In *The Chinese in America: A History from Gold Mountain to the New Millennium*, edited by Susie Lan Cassel, 434–48. Walnut Creek, CA: Alta Mira Press, 2002.

Zhang Jing. "Cong *Meng* deng jishou minge kan zhongguo gudai funü de xingge guangcai." *Xinzhou shifan xueyuan xuebao* 16.4 (2000): 47–51.

Zhang Qiao (fl. 1232), annotated. *Gu wen yuan*. Collected by Qian Xizuo (1801–1844). In *Guoxue jiben congshu*. Taipei: Shangwu yinshuguan, 1968.

Zhang, Renjie. "Ode to Mulan: Seeing the Animated Film *Mulan*." *Chinese Sociology and Anthropology* 32.2 (1999–2000): 30–32.

Zhang Rufa. "*Mulan shi* de zhuti sixiang shi shenme?" *Yuwen xuexi* 11 (1981): 14–15.

Zhang Shaoxian (fl. the nineteenth century). *Beiwei qishi gui xiao lie zhuan*. Shanghai: Shanghai guji chubanshe, 1990.

Zhang Siwei (fl 1567). *Shuanglie ji*. Changchun: Jilin renmin chubanshe, 2001.

Zhang, Song Nan. *The Ballad of Mulan*. Union City, CA: Pan Asian Publications, 1998.

Zhang Tingyu (1672–1755) et al. *Mingshi*. Beijing: Zhonghua shuju, 1974.

Zhang Wei. "Cong *Hua Mulan* kan wenhua 'jianrong.'" *Movie Review* 6 (1998): 32–33.

Zhang Weiqi. "Mulan shi shidai bianyi." *Guoxue yuebao* 2.4 (1927): 161–79.

Zhang Xiaobing and Ma Guangrong. "Mulan shiji bian." *Huaxia wenhua* 1.2 (2000): 38–39.

Zhang, Ya-Jie. "A Chinese Woman's Response to Maxine Hong Kingston's *The Woman Warrior*." *MELUS* 13.3/4 (1986): 103–07.

Zhang Yanbing. "Liangzhong shijiao kan *Hua Mulan*." *Social Sciences* 3 (1999): 74–77.

Zhang, Yang. "Thoughts Elicited by an Illustration." *Chinese Sociology and Anthropology* 32.2 (1999–2000): 26–27.

Zhang Zhidong (1837–1909) and Ye Erkuan (ca. 19th cent.), eds. *Bai xiao tu*. Guangzhou: no publisher indicated, ca. nineteenth century.

"Zhang Ziyi to Star in Chinese Take on Mulan Tale." *The Globe and Mail*, 6 Sep. 2006: R4.

Zhao Qingge. *Liang Shangbo yu Zhu Yingtai*. Bejing: xinshijie chubanshe, 1998.

Zhao Ye (fl. 40–80). *Wuyue chunqiu*. In *Sibu beiyao*. Taipei: Zhonghua shuju, 1965.

Zhao Yuping and Yuan Zhongmei. *Hua Mulan*. Taipei: Zongjing xiao yuan feng shuju, 1987.

Zhong Nianren, ed. *Ming ke lidai baimeitu*. Tianjin: Tianjin renmin meishu chubanshe, 2003.

Zhong xiao yong lie qinü zhuan. 1878. Reprint, Shanghai: Shanghai guji chubanshe, 1990.

Zhongguo tongsu xiaoshuo zongmu tiyao. Beijing: Zhongguo wenlian chuban gongsi, 1990.

Zhou Linyu. "Tazhehua yu zhengzhi jingxiang: dui Disney donghuapian *Mulan* wenhua shenfen de xingsi." *Comparative Literature in China* 63.2 (2006): 117–27.

Zhou, Min. "Social Capital in Chinatown: The Role of Community-Based Organizations and Families in the Adaptation of the Younger Generation." In

Contemporary Asian America: A Multidisciplinary Reader, edited by Min Zhou and James Gatewood, 315–35. New York: New York University Press, 2000.

Zhou, Xiaojing. "Introduction: Critical Theories and Methodologies in Asian American Literature Studies." In *Form and Transformation,* edited by Zhou and Najmi 3–29.

Zhou, Xiaojing, and Samina Najmi, eds. *Form and Transformation in Asian American Literature.* Seattle: University of Washington Press, 2005.

Zhou Zhongming. "Preface." *Si sheng yuan* (Four Cries of a Gibbon). Xu Wei. Shanghai: Shanghai guji chubanshe, 1984. 1–7.

Zhu Guozhen (1557–1637). *Yongchuang xiaopin.* Taipei: Guangwen shuju, 1991.

Zhu Jialiang. "Nanbei wenhua tonghua de jiejing." *Suihua shizhuan xuebao* 20.2 (2000): 22–24.

Zhu Maode and Tian Yuan, comp. *Wan xian zhi.* 1731. Reprint, Taipei: Chengwen chubanshe, 1976.

Zhu Xi (1130–1200). *Zhuzi yulei.* Beijing: Zhonghua shuju, 1986.

Zhu, Yi. "Seeing *Mulan* in the United States." *Chinese Sociology and Anthropology* 32.2 (1999–2000): 20–22.

Zhu Yingyuan. "On Cultural Spirit of Mulan Poem." *Social Sciences Journal of Colleges of Shanxi* 15.1 (2003): 57–59.

Zhuang Chaogen. *Mulan congjun.* Tainan, Taiwan: Shiyi wenhua shiye gufen youxian gongsi, 1994.

Zipes, Jack. *Fairy Tales and the Art of Subversion: The Classical Genre for Children and the Process of Civilization.* 2nd ed. London: Routledge, 2006.

———. "Once Upon a Time beyond Disney: Contemporary Fairy Tale Films for Children." In *In Front of Children: Screen Entertainment and Young Audiences,* edited by Cary Bazalgette and David Buckingham, 109–26. London: British Film Institute 1995.

Zoehfield, Kathleen Weidner. *Disney's Mulan.* New York: Disney Press, 1998.

Zou Zhilin. *Nüxia zhuan.* In *Xu shuo fu,* 1047–57. 1646. Reprint, Taipei: Xinxing shuju, 1972.

Index

women holding up half of the sky, 159
Wong, Sau-ling, 118, 120, 212n12, 215n27, 215n28
Woo, Deborah, 118
worship, 92, 203n12, 210n42. *See also* goddess
Wu, William, 3
Wu Youru, 22, 24, 27, 41, 43, 60, 64, 74, 206n14
Wuyu chuunqiu, 39

Xia Quan, 35
Xianbei, 53, 131
Xie Xiao'e, 46, 219n18
Xin Tangshu, 19, 20
Xu Wei, 59, 66–80, 81, 107, 207n23, 208n27, 208n31, 208n32, 209n36
Xun Guan, 17–18, 23, 30, 31, 32

Yang An'er, 34, 35
Yang Miaozhen, 34–36, 48, 204n25
Yang Weizhen, 66

Yao Darong, 211n3
Yeh, Emilie Yueh-yu, 166
Yi, Gang, 123, 124, 129, 142, 144, 153–57
Yijing, 11
young adults, 126, 127
youth, 32, 85, 133, 164
Yucheng County, 88, 210n42
Yue Fei, 104–05
yuefu, 55, 56, 57, 65, 209n34
Yuefu shiji, 2, 56, 87. *See also* Guo Maoqian
yüeh-fu. *See* yuefu
Yuenü, 39, 151–52

Zhang, Song Nan, 123, 128, 129–40, 145
Zhang Xianzhong, 28
Zhang, Ya-jie, 122
Zhijiang, 52, 205n2. See also *Gujin yuelu*
Zhong xiao yong lie qinü zhuan, 44, 83, 84–85, 90
Zhu Xi, 11
Zipes, Jack, 124, 164, 174
Zou Zhilin, 38, 86, 87, 204n27

ABOUT THE AUTHOR

Lan Dong is Assistant Professor of English at the University of Illinois at Springfield.